A Garland Series

Foundations of the Novel

Representative Early Eighteenth-Century Fiction

A collection of 100 rare titles
reprinted in photo-facsimile in 71 volumes

Foundations of the Novel

compiled and edited by

Michael F. Shugrue
Secretary for English for the M.L.A.

with New Introductions for each volume by

Michael Shugrue, *City College of C.U.N.Y.*
Malcolm J. Bosse, *City College of C.U.N.Y.*
William Graves, *N.Y. Institute of Technology*
Josephine Grieder, *Rutgers University, Newark*

La Saxe Galante

or, the Amorous Adventures and Intrigues of Frederick-Augustus II

by

Karl Ludwig,
Freiherr von Pöllnitz

with a new introduction
for the Garland Edition by

Josephine Grieder

Garland Publishing, Inc., New York & London

1972

The new introduction for the

Garland *Foundations of the Novel* Edition

Bibliographical note:

This facsimile has been made from a copy in the Beinecke Library of Yale University (BR92 109l)

Library of Congress Cataloging in Publication Data

Pöllnitz, Karl Ludwig, Freiherr von, 1692-1775.
La Saxe galante.

(Foundations of the novel)
Reprint of the 1734 ed.
1. Friedrich August I, der Starke, Elector of Saxony and King of Poland, 1670-1733. I. Title. II. Series.
DD801.S396P72 1972 943.8'02 [B] 78-170589
ISBN 0-8240-0571-6

Printed in the United States of America

Introduction

The title page of the work here reprinted is worth citing in full for the forthrightness with which it describes the kind of entertainment it promises to the curious reader: La Saxe Galante: or, the Amorous Adventures and Intrigues of Frederick-Augustus II. Late King of Poland, Elector of Saxony, etc. Containing, Several Transactions of his Life, not mentioned in any other History. Together with Diverting Remarks on the Ladies of the several Countries thro' which he travell'd. *And the author, Charles-Louis, Baron de Pöllnitz (to use the French version of his name by which the English knew him), delivers precisely what he anonymously promises: a fairly accurate historical account of Frederick II, considerably embellished by dramatic scenes of love and discovery and a modest pretense at explaining the psychology of those involved.*

Though the name of Pöllnitz may be unfamiliar to the modern reader, it was definitely not so to the eighteenth-century audience, for his Memoirs, *written in French in 1734 and subsequently translated into English and German, made him a celebrated man. The first paragraph of the "Preface, By the Translator," Stephen Whatley, to the 1737 English edition vaguely indicates the reasons for his celebrity: "The Author of these* Memoirs, *who is a Person of an honourable Family in*

Prussia, *and confess'd by all that know him to be a Gentleman of extraordinary Talents, is one that may truly be said to have seen the World; he having not only travell'd twice thro' the principal Parts of* Europe, *but by his Acquaintance with People of the first Rank, and a diligent Inquiry and nice Inspection into Men and Things, attained to that Knowledge of Both, which is of such Service and Entertainment to Mankind in the general, and so particularly necessary for All who attend to what is doing in high Life."*[1]

What may more candidly be said is that Pöllnitz was an astonishingly successful adventurer who, thanks to excellent family connections and a ready wit, managed to escape innumerable times from financial, political, and amorous imbroglios and at last died tranquilly at the age of eighty-three at the court of Frederick II of Prussia.[2] *Born in 1692 of distinguished stock – his grandfather was Master of the Horse, Minister of State, Chamberlain, etc. at the court of Frederic-William, elector of Brandenburgh, and his grandmother the daughter of Maurice of Orange – he had an excellent education at the Académie des Princes, at the same time growing up in the whirl of court intrigues upon which his thrice-married mother (and he) depended for income. He volunteered for the army in 1708; but after the wars, and indeed, until he found asylum at Frederick the Great's court, his life was a perpetual scramble for pensions and preferments to pay off debts incurred by gambling and debauch. No step was too hazardous to undertake if profit might be forthcoming:*

financial speculation (he was ruined by the failure of John Law's monetary system in France); political involvement (he participated in the unsuccessful coup organized by the Duchesse de Maine and the Spanish ambassador and avoided imprisonment only by pretending to be a servant); religious conversion (he alternated between Catholicism and Protestantism some half dozen times, according to which party might promise him a rich marriage, an annuity, or advancement). And the traveling he did was prodigious, for in search of favors, he visited all the principal courts of Europe to solicit his titled friends' assistance.

It is not unexpected, thus, that in the 1730s he should have thought of literature as a way to turn a quick profit. His own experiences furnished him both with an insight into real historical intrigues and a fund of adventures; well-educated, he was accustomed to the kind of wit and entertainment that his social acquaintances expected. The history of his first production is worth recounting, for it illuminates his chameleon-like character.

In 1721, pressed for money as usual and about to make a trip to England, Pöllnitz wrote a manuscript called Cunigonde, Princesse des Cherusques. *This was a thinly disguised account of the imprisonment at Ahlden of Dorothea, the errant wife of George I, the details of which had been shrouded in secrecy from the British public. Pöllnitz, acquainted with the affair, intended to use the manuscript to blackmail the king or his ministers. But Townshend would have none of it, and when Pöllnitz approached the opposition – chiefly the Duchess of Marlborough – he was coldly rejected by them as well. He tucked the manuscript away until 1732, when most parties were safely past caring. Then, with a little judicious revising to whitewash Dorothea's amours and to flatter the Hanoverian line, he issued it as the* Histoire Secrette de la Duchesse de Hanovre, Epouse de Georges Premier, Roi de la Grande Bretagne. *Though it was not translated into English, it was published in London, and no doubt afforded amusement to bi-lingual British readers. The work here reprinted followed it two years later.*

La Saxe Galante *is not, alas, quite as exciting as the previous biographical account might suggest. It is, in fact, a fairly straightforward relation of the life of Frederick-Augustus: his voluntary exile from his brother's court in Saxony; his ascent to the throne upon the latter's death; his participation in various military campaigns; the political intrigues which placed him on the throne of Poland; and his final tranquil retirement. But Frederick was equally well known for his numerous liaisons and resultant bastards; and it is this aspect which Pöllnitz chooses to describe in most detail, occasionally creating dramatic or humorous tableaux which it is possible he might have heard retailed at the various courts he frequented.*[3]

The portrait of Frederick is notable for its insistence on the king's admirable qualities, and nowhere does Pöllnitz ever make a moral judgment on his behavior, irregular though it might have been in a bourgeois. "His excellent Aspect, Strength, Address, Splendor and Politeness caused an universal Admiration" (p. 7), the author recounts. He is generous, prudent, and valiant – in fact, he possesses all the virtues of the fairy-tale prince. But "his Heart was never design'd for Constancy" (p. 94), "[it was] never to be free from Passion" (p. 110), and his amorous penchant leads him to gratify his desires by any means possible. Frederick "was chiefly pleased with married Women, and those who discovered a nice Capacity for intriguing" (p. 180), and the husband is frequently an unwilling – and often divorced – participant. Nor does he hesitate to buy a daughter's favors from her mother. But the flesh eventually grows weary, and Frederick finally retires to live with his children in Poland, where he is impervious to female wiles because "paternal Love had smother'd in him all unlawful Affection" (pp. 306-307).

The king's mistresses are generally distinguished less by their personalities than by their situations or the circumstances under which they are wooed. Thus, Frederick steals away the young Marchioness of Manzera from both her suspicious mother and her husband. In Venice he keeps an assignation with a widow and passes three delightful days and nights with her. He arranges an affair with a woman living in a convent; he takes as mistress a converted Turk; he seduces the daughter of a French wine merchant. Incognito, he woos the actress Duparc and installs her at Dresden.

Two mistresses are better characterized. The beautiful Aurora, Countess of Koningsmark, has come with her two sisters to Frederick's court to seek redress of a law suit, and the king, much struck, launches his attack. Aided by one of her sisters, he prevails over her modesty, and they "at last promised a constant Love to each other" (p. 131). Her virtue is so evident that even the Electress his wife does not reproach him, for, as she says, "I am pleased . . . with having a Rival, since she is a Person of great Merit" (p. 144). Frederick praises her too: "In you, my dearest Countess, I adore not only the most perfect Beauty; but also that virtuous Soul, that exalted Mind, that benevolent Heart" (p. 146). Eventually he deserts her, but, notes Pöllnitz, "she was the only one of all his mistresses, for whom he seemed to have always retained a great Esteem" (p. 112).

The other mistress is Madame Hoyhm, later Mme Cosel, a much less admirable figure than the modest and retiring Countess. Though beautiful, "her Character was not equal to the other Accomplishments she had just Reason to boast of. She was lively and pleasant in her Repartees, but discover'd little solid Sense, and less Sincerity" (p. 210). "Sometimes her Behaviour was charming, and at other times as unpleasant; she would condescend to act the meanest part for Riches and Honour" (p. 211). Nevertheless, she knows just how to manage the king, and under the guise of his benevolence, acquires both personal power and ministerial animosity. At last the machinations of the ministers replace her with a new face, and the intriguing Mme Cosel is cast aside.

What may be considered the fictional elements in

Pöllnitz' work are his use of interpolated dialogue – particularly in scenes between the king and his mistresses, past, present, and future – and his presentation of various dramatic or humorous tableaux. Thus, the husband of the Marchioness of Manzera, on discovering her infidelity, stabs her waiting woman, forces her to take poison, and dies in effusive repentance. Frederick catches his amorous Venetian widow in flagrante *with a Dominican monk, whose discomposure is laughable. The king solves the riddle of the dreadful apparition which is frightening the King of the Romans to death, revealing it to be a Jesuit. By his companions' amusing casuistry, the husband of the Countess d'Esterle is persuaded to give over his resentment at the king's poaching and apply for a position in the royal service.*

Though certainly a more solid work factually, La Saxe Galante *belongs to the scandal-chronicle tradition in early eighteenth-century English literature, and it is to be presumed that the contemporary reader was entertained by the lively change of scenes, the elevated personages involved, and the touching sentiments occasionally articulated. The work displays Pöllnitz' facility in fictionalizing historical events while at the same time preserving the dignity of all involved. But his talent had by no means been used to the full; and for a far superior work, in terms of content, style, and variety, the reader is advised to investigate* Les Amusemens de Spa.

Josephine Grieder

INTRODUCTION

NOTES

[1] The Memoirs of Charles-Lewis, Baron de Pöllnitz *(London: Brown, 1737), I, vii.*

[2] *The most complete modern biography appears to be that by Edith E. Cuthell,* A Vagabond Courtier, from the Memoirs and Letters of Baron Charles Louis von Pöllnitz, *in two volumes (London: Stanley Paul, 1913).*

[3] *A remark from the "Author's Preface" to his* Memoirs *may serve to explain why* La Saxe Galante *qualifies as fiction: "The far greatest part of what the World reads is Trifles, and a History will make its fortune not by the instructive Facts that are in it, but by the Romantic Turn the Author gives it" (I, xv).*

La SAXE GALANTE:

OR, THE

Amorous ADVENTURES

AND

INTRIGUES

OF

FREDERICK-AUGUSTUS II.

Late KING of *POLAND*,
ELECTOR of *SAXONY*, &c.

Containing,
Several Transactions of his LIFE, not mentioned in any other HISTORY.

Together with
Diverting Remarks on the Ladies of the several Countries thro' which he travell'd.

Translated from the French,
By a Gentleman of OXFORD.

Printed; and Sold by the Booksellers of
London and *Westminster*.

La SAXE GALANTE.

CHAP. I.

Of the Splendor of the Saxon Court in the Reign of the Elector John-George IV. *Of his Mistress, Marriage, Disputes with his Brother, Attempt to stab his Electress, how his Brother hinder'd him, reprov'd the Elector's Mistress, and of* Frederick-Augustus's *Departure from Saxony on that Account.*

NO part of Germany could ever boast of more Gallantry and Splendor, than the Electorate of Saxony, whose Magnificence was more particularly conspicuous in the Reigns of *John-George* IV. Elector, and *Frederick-Augustus*, chosen King of Poland. This latter was a polite, graceful, and amorous Prince, and though ſeveral of his Paſſions were innate, yet did he by the continual ardency of his Love, ſeem to be but lately enamour'd. No Court was ever adorn'd with ſuch beautiful Ladies, and no leſs accompliſh'd Gentlemen; Nature ſeem'd to have delighted in placing the moſt exquiſite of her Beauties in a reſort of Perſons of the greateſt diſtinction. The Princes of the Electorate exceeded all others, and the Charms of the Princeſſes were not to be equall'd.

John-George IV. was very young when he ſucceeded his Father. His natural qualifications would have render'd him amiable, had he not given himſelf over to the conduct of an imperious, haughty, revengeful, and always incenſed Miſtreſs, who, ſacrificing all to her own Ambition and Intereſt, eſteem'd nothing ſacred. Such was Mademoiſelle *Neitſch*, whoſe Command over this Prince was ſo abſolute, that ſome Perſons have accus'd her of having made uſe of ſupernatural means in the attainment of it.

Prince *Frederick-Auguſtus* was extreamly perplex'd to ſee the Regard his Brother had for ſo unworthy a Miſtreſs. He pleas'd himſelf with the hopes of diverting his Fancy from her, by perſuading him to marry a Princeſs; and though ſuch a perſuaſion was diſadvantageous to himſelf, yet did his generous

rous disposition not suffer him to neglect it: thus he postpon'd his personal Advantages to the Welfare of the Common-wealth, and the Honour of his Family.

The great influence Mademoiselle *Neitsch* had over the Elector's Mind did not impower her to undertake a dissuasion from consenting to what was propos'd; and the Advice of his Ministers induced him to make choice of *Eleonor* of Saxe-Eisenach, Widow of the Marquis of Brandenburgh-Anspach; a Princess, whose excellent Accomplishments gain'd a great Veneration, and beautiful Person the Admiration of all that saw her. Her Husband was the only Person insensible of her Merits: though by her Agreeableness, obliging Carriage, and an uncommon Patience, she endeavour'd to obtain his Favour, yet could she not untie that fatal knot, which ally'd him to Mademoiselle *Neitsch*; she would have been happy, had this arrogant Mistress been contented with attracting a Heart that was her own, and not occasion'd the Abuse of the Person she had already injur'd.

Frederick-Augustus was sensibly touch'd with the Perplexities of the Electress; for, had she not been his Sister-in-Law, common Generosity would have induc'd him to lament her. He frequently comforted her, and made as frequent intercessions with the

Elector in her favour; but those endeavours prov'd ineffectual: for his Advice was rejected, and he forbid interposing in his Brother's Quarrels with the Electress. Was it
'your fate to lead a conjugal Life, said the
'Elector) I should not interrupt your me-
'thod of governing your Spouse; why may
'not I insist upon an equal Privilege? How
'can I prevail upon myself (reply'd the
'Prince) to be a Spectator of such Injus-
'tice? my Concern for your Interest is so
'peculiar, that I cannot but represent to
'you the Injury your Reputation suffers by
'your inhuman usage of an amiable Prin-
'cess, to please a Mistress so little worthy
'of you. I presume not to prescribe you
'Rules, and should be heartily sorry to find
'that I had in the least deviated from the
'Respect I owe you; but think myself ca-
'pable of telling you, that you have a
'Lady, whose Birth, Beauties and Virtues
'ought at least to gain your Respect.' The Elector, being incens'd with these Reproaches, and Mademoiselle *Neitsch* having by several Insinuations persuaded him to believe, that the Prince and Electress were unlawfully acquainted, he look'd upon his Brother with Eyes inflam'd; 'Alas! (said
'he in a threatening Tone) I perceive your
'vile Affection for my unworthy Wife, but
'shall soon be capable of ridding myself of

'you

'you both.' He then left his Brother precipitately, and directed his Course to the Electress's Apartment, giving himself over to the great Rage, that had taken possession of his Heart, he approach'd the Lady's Bed, and had certainly stabb'd her, If his Brother, acquainted with the Violence of his Passion, and suspecting his Design, had not pursued and disarmed him. 'By no 'means, dear Brother, (cry'd he) when 'he depriv'd him of his Sword) it shall 'not be reported that an Elector of Saxony 'was the Murderer of his Wife;' and when the Elector attempted to draw nearer to the Princess, threatening to strangle her, the Prince seiz'd him with that extraordinary force, which he only was famous for, and carry'd him to his Chamber. The Elector, being highly exasperated, spoke whatever Words his Anger supply'd him with; but the Prince, not ignorant of his furious Temper, and assured, that the sentiments of his Heart differ'd a little from the Words, his Rage induced him to utter, suffer'd him to give vent to all his Fury, and did not leave him till his Passion was cool'd.

As soon as he had left the Elector, he went to Mademoiselle *Neitsch*; and found in her Apartment the Countess of *Rochlitz*, her Mother and her unworthy Confident. 'I am very glad, Ladies, (said he with an

" Air, that ſhew'd a Contempt of them) to
' find you together, for I deſign to treat
' with you about ſome Things, relating to
' you all. The Elector has juſt now been
' venting the effects of thoſe vile Maxims
' you have infected him with. The Reſpect,
' that is naturally due to him from me, per-
' mits me not to take any Revenge; I have
' beſides ſo good an Opinion of my Bro-
' ther, that I am perſuaded he will one day
' be acquainted with the Snares you have
' laid for him, and puniſh you for having ſo
' highly abuſed the Confidence he has re-
' pos'd in you. In the mean while I ſhall
' prevent the perpetration of a piece of
' Injuſtice, and, if poſſible, deprive you
' of the means of ſlandering the Virtue
' of the Electreſs. In order thereto I
' am reſolved to retire from hence. But
' you may be aſſured, that whilſt I let
' you have the free uſe of your Speech up-
' on that ſubject, I ſhall have a watchful
' eye upon your pernicious ſchemes, and be
' capable of preventing the execution of
' them; you are now acquainted with my
' intention of making you reſponſible for
' the Fate of the Electreſs. I command
' you to let her quietly enjoy the Honours,
' ſhe is here entitled to; and if my Brother
' ſhould ſo far injure himſelf, as to abuſe
' her in my abſence you ſhall be applied to
' for

'for Satisfaction. You know me, (added
'he in a threatening manner) and you
'may be assured that my Promises shall be
'performed.' He did not wait for any Answer from them, but went home to give Orders for his Departure.

The Elector hearing of his Resolve of quitting Dresden, was heartily sorry for it. His Anger ceased, and Passion gave way in his Heart to the Affection he had for his Brother. He intreated him not to depart, but the Prince desired him so earnestly not to be displeased with his removing from thence for some time, that the Elector could no longer refuse his Consent. He even gave him all the Retinue, requisite to make him appear in foreign Courts with a Grandeur becoming the Brother and Heir apparent of one of the most potent Electors of the Empire.

Europe at that time enjoy'd so profound a Tranquility, that all Countries were open to satisfy his Curiosity. He undertook to view the most celebrated States and Provinces. His excellent Aspect, Strength, Address, Splendor and Politeness caused an universal Admiration. Being persuaded that Grandeur is sometimes obnoxious to Pleasure, never conducive towards it, he determined to travel incognito, and took upon him every-where the Title of Count of Misnia, which was a shelter from tedious Ceremonies, and sufficient to procure him a handsome Reception. Whilst he retained this Name he met with several Adventures, of which those shall be mentioned here that will seem most agreeable to the Publick. After having travelled thro' all the Courts of Germany, he went to Holland, from thence to England, and at last to France. He had in all these several Countries various Amours: but as these were only the Attendants of transient Flames, in which the Heart had a less share than that intriguing Spirit, which never suffered him to be idle, I think it most proper to pass by them silently.

CHAP

CHAP. II.

Of Prince Frederick-Augustus's *Voyage to Spain, his Adventure at a Bull-Feast at Madrid, Reception at the Spanish Court, Amour with the Marchioness of Manzera, ill Success in this Amour, the Marquis of* Manzera's *Order to assault the Prince, executed; the Marquis's Barbarity to his Spouse, her Murder, and the Prince's Departure from Spain.*

THAT same courtly Mind induced him to undertake a Voyage to Spain. The Descriptions he heard of the Beauty of the Spaniards and of their courtly Behaviour occasioned his Visit to that Country, as a Place deserving his Presence. He arrived at Madrid the Evening before a great Bull-Feast, which King *Charles* II. gave to entertain his new-married Spouse *Mary-Ann* of Neuburg, Princess Palatine. When he was informed that an Entertainment was preparing for the next day; 'Behold, (said he with that charming Grace, that accompanied his Discourses, when he addressed himself to the Lords his Attendants) 'an 'Opportunity of signalizing ourselves, and 'of acquiring a Reputation here; let us 'wrestle and sacrifice some Bulls to the 'Honour of our Mistresses.' The Courtiers approved of the Project, and the manner of putting it in execution was next consulted upon.

On the Day of the Entertainment the Prince and his Retinue went richly dressed to the place called Majore, one of the greatest and finest Theatres in the World. Scaffolds and Amphitheatres were erected, which contained an infinite number of persons next to the first Rank. The Balconies, of which all the Windows that border upon that place are beautify'd, were adorn'd with rich Carpets. An infinite number of Ladies was seen there, who by their Beauty and splendid appearance formed an admirable prospect.

If the Prince of Saxony was surprised to find there so many beautiful Ladies, all the Spectators were in no less Amazement to see him; for he spared no Expence or Pains to appear in a stately manner at such a Solemnity; the Richness of his Dress, and that noble Air, with which he presented himself, drew the Eyes of all the Spectators upon him. They omitted no enquiry after the Quality of the Stranger, and soon after the King and Queen made their appearance. Their Majesties took a Seat in a Balcony shining with Carpets and Squares em-

embroidered with Gold. The King's Trumpets, Fifes, Hautbois and Drummers gave the Signal; the Gentlemen appeared, the Bulls were let looſe, and the Battle begun. The Prince was for ſome moments a Spectator, but ſoon became an Actor, the Sight was new, and the manner of the Battle agreeable to his Fancy. He was ſoon as ſkilful at it, as any that were in the Career, and quitting his Balcony, mounted on Horſe-back, and preſented himſelf at the Bar, which was ſoon opened unto him; he then entered the Career, and there ſhewed his ſurprizing Dexterity and Strength. He ſtruck the hinder-part of the Neck of one of thoſe furious Animals with ſuch Force with his Hanger, that he had almoſt deprived it of its Head, and cauſed its final Fall. The Spaniards could not ſufficiently admire him, nor could they be perſuaded that a Man, not a Spaniard born, was Maſter of ſuch Strength and Dexterity.

The King was greatly aſtoniſhed, and deſirous of knowing who this Stranger was, her Majeſty ſeeming as curious, the Marquis of los Velos Gentleman of the Golden Key, was ordered to enquire after it. This Nobleman thought he could be no better informed, than by addreſſing himſelf to the unknown Perſon. He accoſted the Prince very gracefully and ſaid, 'Your extraordi-

'nary

'nary Aſpect, Sir, your Dexterity, and
'the invincible Courage you juſt now diſ-
'cover'd, have deſervedly attracted an
'univerſal Applauſe, and juſtly obtained
'the Regard of their Majeſties. By their
'Order I take the Liberty of aſking you,
'who that Perſon is, whom our Gentry
'acknowledge to be their Superior, and
'whom we cannot ceaſe admiring?' The
Prince replied modeſtly, 'That he could
'claim no Right to the Praiſes, they would
'feign honour him with: as for his Name,
'he doubted whether that was a fit place
'to diſcover it to their Majeſties; but ſince
'they ſeemed very eager after the Know-
'ledge of it, he begg'd they would pardon
'the Boldneſs of the Prince of Saxony in
'appearing before them, without having
'previouſly had the Honour of an Audi-
'ence from them.' The Marquis of los
Velos having reported his Anſwer to their
Majeſties they were extreamly ſurprized,
that a Prince of ſo eminent a Birth had
ventured to enter into mutual Combat with
the Bulls, and ſent him a Congratula-
tion thereon. The King, by reaſon of the
Ceremonies, not capable of ſeeing him that
day, acquainted him by a Meſſenger with
his being welcome to his Country and at
his Court, and that he was heartily glad to
ſee him. The Queen, leſs inclined to ſubmit.

mit to those Ceremonies, invited him to an Entertainment the same Evening, and to be introduced to her by the private Staircase.

The Prince was at the entry of the Queen's Apartment receiv'd by the Countess of *Berlips* her Majesty's Favourite, who conducted her into Germany. The Queen was standing, leaning against a Table upon a Canopy. at some distance from her Majesty stood on the Right-hand Side, the Chief Lady of the Bed-chamber, *Catherine of Macade-Arragon*, Spouse of the Duke of *Fernandine*. On the Left-hand Side were the Ladies of the Pallace; and a little more backwards were the Chamberlains. The Prince approaching the Queen, intended according to Spanish Custom, to Kneel on one Knee and to Kiss her Majesty's Hand: but She would not suffer it. He intreated to be permitted to pay that Homage to a person of her Beauty and Distinction; whereupon the Queen presented to him her Hand, to which he gave so respectful a Kiss, that That Princess, who had been extreamly pleas'd with his Dexterity and Courage, was no less with his Politeness. The Pleasure, with which she receiv'd him, the extraordinary Honours she conferr'd on him, the marks of Benevolence and Esteem she shew'd him, cannot be Verbally express'd.

Whilst

Whilst she was entertaining herself with the Prince, all the Ladies fix'd their Eyes on him, and view'd him with as much Admiration, as formerly the Followers of Statira did Alexander.

Among these Ladies that surrounded the Queen, the Prince observ'd one, that seem'd to him to exceed all her Comrades in Beauty. He could not but shew some particular regard for her, which the Lady took notice of. The Prince had the pleasure of seeing her Eyes fix'd modestly on him. The Satisfaction he was sensible of in seeing her, induc'd him to exceed the common limits of a Visit; it was of a tedious length, and had not the Queen finish'd it by saying it was late, and the king's Supper-hour approaching, the Prince would probably have staid longer.

Tho' he only address'd himself to the Queen, yet he saluted the Ladies in so graceful a manner, that they were charm'd with it; they could not be weary of admiring him. The Queen was highly pleas'd in hearing the gesture of a Prince of her Nation applauded, nor could she sufficiently praise him. 'Alas! (said she to the Countess of Berlips,) how do these Princes differ from those of our Nation!' Perhaps she meant the King her Consort, who, being of small size, tender and sickly constitution

tion and disagreeable temper, could certainly not be an amiable Object. During Supper time she diverted the King with a description of the Prince of Saxony. 'His 'Mind and Politeness, said she, equal his 'fine Aspect; you cannot but esteem him: 'my Women are all taken with him, and 'have tir'd me with commendations of him. I suspect that even the Dutchess of Fernandine (continu'd she laughing and looking at that Lady) has such Regard for him, as she has hitherto not been sensible of for her Spouse. 'Women of my Age (repli'd the Dutches 'with a grave Air that was appropria- 'ted to her) are incapable of rais- 'sing Suspicions of that kind, and I 'am fully persuaded, that your Ma- 'jesty is only pleas'd to divert yourself in 'accusing me of having been smitten with 'the Prince's Merits: neverthelefs I protest 'before your Majesty that I find him de- 'sign'd to imprison Hearts; and if our 'young Ladies will hearken to my Advice, 'they'll shun his acquaintance.' The Dutchess in speaking these Words incessantly look'd on the young Marchioness of Manzera, her Daughter, Lady of the Court, and the same Person whom the Prince had taken so particular a view of. She observ'd that the Marchioness did just lift up her Eyes and looking on her Mother precipitately chan-

ged

ed colour. The Dutchefs needed no more to confirm her Sufpicion. She thought the Prince of Saxony had left an impreffion on her Daughter's Heart, by her manner of looking at him, and becaufe fhe was the fole perfon that omitted praifing him. She refolv'd to watch her Daughter, and if poffible, to preferve her from the precipice of Love. Vain Projects! that fatal Star which fometimes determines the Heart to engage itfelf for the remaining part of Life, had fo powerful an Influence over the Marchionefs, that her Deftiny was inevitable, and the prefervation from it impoffible to the Dutchefs.

In the mean while the Prince of Saxony defperately in Love with the Marchionefs, ftrove diligently to be inform'd of her Quality, and to find fome means of acquainting her with his Tendernefs for her. By the Superiority fhe feem'd to have near the Queen in Rank he conjectur'd that fhe was one of the firft Ladies of the Court. The next morning he found himfelf not in the leaft miftaken; by the account fome young Lords, who came to pay him a Vifit, gave of her, he was inform'd of her Name, and that her fole dependance was upon a very jealous Husband, and as fevere a Mother; fo that fhe was thought to be inacceffible.

This News wou'd have mortify'd any one

except

except the Prince of Saxony, for his intrepidity in Amorous adventures, equall'd that in the middle of a Slaughter in War, the more difficult the Conquest of the Marchioness was, the more he esteem'd her worthy of himself; for some Days he could not attain at the happiness of the sight of her.

The King being indispos'd the Night after the Bull Feast, confin'd himself to his Chamber: the Queen did not leave him, and the young Marchioness being serviceable to both, remain'd in the Anti-chamber, where the Prince could not appear, not having yet visited the King.

In this interval of Time he was told, that the Marchioness had a Chamber-maid in whom she greatly confided; he knew that she was an old Maid, who had several Nieces, that were supported by the Generosity of of her Mistress. He despair'd not of gaining this person's Interest, and making use of her to procure him a good reception with the Marchioness. His only Obstacle was the almost impossibility of conferring with her; he could not be admitted into her House, nor was he master of the Spanish Language, and she whom he design'd for his Confident could apparently speak no other but that Tongue. But what can be an Impediment to Love? after having well consider'd of the execution of his Project, he re-

resolv'd

ſolv'd upon entruſting a Brother Mendicant Friar Recollect, Italian by Birth, and a bare-fac'd intrepid Intriguer. He went every Day, and procur'd ſome Salads and Flowers, which he brought to reap the effects of the Prince's Bounty. To him the ſentiments of an amorous Heart were diſcover'd, he was charged to ſpeak with Freedom in the Houſe of the Marchioneſs; and the officious Friar obey'd his Orders ſo zealouſly, that he perceiv'd Donna *Lora* (which was the Confident's Name) was a perſon of ſuch mercenary Views, that a Refuſal of the Prince's Liberality was inconſiſtent with her temper. He boaſted much of the Preſents he had receiv'd. He gives me more (ſaid he in one Day) than all the Gentry of Spain do in a Month. He deſcrib'd the graceful appearance and uncommon Strength of the Prince, of which latter he related ſuch Prodigies, that ſhe was aſtoniſh'd at and charm'd with it. Old *Lora* reported all this to the young Marchioneſs, who heard her with the utmoſt attention and pleaſure. when Donna *Lora* had no News to tell her, ſhe ſaid with a ſorrowful Countenance 'how 'now! have you nothing to relate of the 'beautiful Stranger?' That was the Denomination given the Prince by the Ladies of Madrid.

The King being recover'd, the Prince appear'd

appear'd in publick at Court by the appellation of Count of *Misnia*, and was introduc'd there by the Count of Benavente. He saw in the anti-chamber the Duke of Montalte and several Lords, that attended him. The King receiv'd the Prince in his Closet, He was standing cover'd and leaning against a Table, having a Chair of State at his right Hand. He uncover'd his Head at the second Bow the Prince made him. His Majesty was addressed in Italian, answered in Spanish; but afterwards they both made use of the Italian Tongue in their Conference. The Prince was desired to be covered, and those that were present, and all the Officers of the Court were ordered to pay him the respect due to a Prince of the Blood. He was at last intreated to go to pay his Compliments to the Queen, who impatiently waited for him. The Prince return'd Thanks to his Majesty for the great Civilities receiv'd at Court, and the Count of *Benavente* went to inform the Queen of his coming.

All the Lords that were in the King's Apartment accompanied the Prince to that of Her Majesty, who in the reception she gave him testified the same Esteem, that she had honoured him with at the first Visit. The Prince whilst his Discourse was directed to the Queen, sought for the Marchioness of

Manzera

Manzera whom he easily distinguished in the crowd, which was the only advantage he could that Day gain, a Conference with her being yet impracticable. On the Prince's departure from the Queen he went to the Palace of the Queen Mother *Mary-Ann* of Austria, Widow of King *Philip* IV. That Princess demonstrated an uncommon esteem for him. She remember'd an acquaintance with the Elector *John-George* III. at Vienna, and was pleased to see his Son at Madrid.

The Day after the Prince had been at Court, the Queen Regent, young, beautiful and loving diversions, persuaded the King to give a Ball; to which the Prince of Saxony was invited. He appeared there in a Dress that set off the Charms of his Aspect. The Queen and he opened the Ball, his Majesty being unwilling to Dance; and leading the Queen back to her place, he asked her, which Lady she was pleased to chuse for his next partner; She replyed, that she was unwilling to constrain him, and desir'd he would make choice of her that seem'd to him most Beautiful. Upon this answer he bowed very gracefully, and without hesitation applied to the Marchioness of Manzera; addressing himself respectfully to her, 'Madam, said he, the Queen has en-
' join'd me to Dance with the most Beau-
tiful Lady in this Assembly, I doubt not

of

'of her Majeſty's Intentions to recommend
'me to the Marchioneſs of Manzera. I be-
'live Sir, (*replied* the Marchioneſs) the
'Queen will not approve of your Choice,
'and I fear her Majeſty will be diſpleas'd
'to ſee you have ſo little regard to her
'Orders. Madam, (replied the Prince)
'her Majeſty has too much Diſcretion not
'to allow you to be the moſt perfect Lady
'in theſe Kingdoms, and was ſhe not to do
'you that Juſtice, it would not obſtruct my
'Opinion of your being the moſt accom-
'pliſh'd Lady in the World, and the moſt
'deſerviug of a reſpect equal to that which
'is paid the Gods.' The Marchioneſs un-
derſtood the Prince's Words very well, tho'
ſhe pretended to be ignorant of what he ſaid.
She continued to Dance towards the End of
the Room with a Grace, that tranſported
the Prihce with amaſement, and forgetting
the place where he was; 'Good God! (cri-
'ed he) couldſt thou poſſibly joyn ſuch
'Graces to ſuch Beauty! this Tranſport
changed the Marchioneſs's Colour, and was
obſerved by t' e Dutcheſs of *Fernandine* her
Mother. The old Lady was ſolicitous about
the matter, for ſhe foreſaw, that, if the
Prince made any ſtay at the Spaniſh Court,
her Daughter would be expoſed to his purſuits; But the Prince's Expreſſions rendered
the Marchioneſs's condition more deplorable.
Her

Her Husband was from that time extreamly jealous of her, and accosting her, desired plainly that she would desist dancing with the Prince. The young Marchioness knowing his perverse humour, was not at all surprized at this Order; she obeyed it, and placed herself behind the Chair of State all the Evening; but could not deny herself the pleasure of beholding the Prince in a manner that assured him, that his Expressions were not at all disagreeable to her. He was desirous of speaking to her, but she so carefully avoided his Addresses, that he could not approach her.

In the mean time, his above-mentioned Words produc'd all the desir'd Effect, and entirely convinced her of his Passion; for the Prince's Actions were so agreeable to his Words, that she had no reason to doubt of his Sincerity, she did not endeavour to love him, but to keep him ignorant of her tender Affection for him, which was no very easy Undertaking, but she not being acquainted with the difficulty of it, thought the only means of succeeding therein would be to avoid his Company. A slight Indisposition served for some time as a pretence to remain at home, and shun all those places, where she was in fear of meeting her Persecutor. Moreover, she ordered Donna *Lora* to make no farther mention of the Prince.

It

'It is an Idea which my Heart (ſaid ſhe)
' is unwilling to retain.' But Donna *Lora* being by ſeveral preſents already engaged in his Service, thought it improper to obey her Miſtreſs. She ſpoke of him inceſſantly, and the Marchioneſs was incapable of ſilencing her Servant. The Prince, informed of what paſſed at his Miſtreſs's, undertook to write to her, and charged the Brother-Recollect to deliver his Letter to Donna *Lora*. This Woman directly made great Difficulties of the matter, ſhe ſaid her Miſtreſs had given her ſtrict Orders not ſo much as to mention the Prince to her; and that ſhe dared not, without venturing her Fortune, give her a Letter. The Monk perceived the Deficiency; he offered her a fine Diamond, with which ſhe was ſo dazzled, that ſhe determined to deliver the Billet.

The ſame Evening ſhe told the Lady *Manzera* that her retired Life and long Silence could not diſcourage the Prince from adoring her, and that he had got a Monk to give her a Letter, which ſhe was charged with. At theſe Words the Marchioneſs's Colour changed. 'Will you ruin me, *Lo*-
'*ra*, (ſaid ſhe) and will you be the Cauſe
' of my forgetting the Obligations I am
' under to Lord *Manzera*? Can you not
' foreſee what perplexities and miſeries I
' ſhall be expoſ'd to, if I engage in the

' Cor-

'Correſpondence you endeavour to per-
'ſuade me to? No, I am reſolved to have
'no reaſon to blame myſelf, ſpeak no more
'(continued ſhe ſhedding ſome Tears) of
'the Prince of Saxony, my Heart is too
'full of him. -- Thus Madam, (ſaid Donna
'*Lora*) do you refuſe his Letter? ----- Yes,
'(replied ſhe) I refuſe it, return it to him
'that has undertaken the Care of it, and
'enjoin him from me, to depart from my
'Houſe and never to return hither again.'
Donna *Lora* was not a little ſurprized at
this Reſolution. 'You will cauſe the Prince's
'Death (ſaid ſhe) or elſe he will take to
'ſome Extream, of which you will ever re-
'pent. --- Let me alone, *Lora*, (replied the
'Marchioneſs) the Refuſal is almoſt intole-
'rable to me: but I do my Duty, which
'muſt be poſtponed to any private Satis-
'faction.' At theſe Words her Eyes were
covered with Tears. Donna *Lora* thought
that a lucky minute to open the Prince's
Letter. 'Madam, (ſaid ſhe proſtrate at
'her Feet) do not, I beg of you, refuſe
'me to read this Billet. The Prince will
'be perſuaded that you ſlight him; and
'how can a Gentleman of his Rank put up
'with ſuch Uſage? What is it to me?
'(cried ſhe) let him ſuffer me to enjoy my
'deſired Tranquility, that is all I demand
'of him.' Her Heart was ſo burdened
with

with Grief, that ſhe could no longer contain her Sighs. *Lora* ſtudied all her Miſtreſs's motions, and continued to preſs and propoſe to her numberleſs motives to open the Letter. The Marchioneſs ſeeing that ſhe did not ceaſe perplexing her, aroſe precipitately and retired to her Cloſet. Donna *Lora*, having promiſed to ſee the Letter accepted, was deſirous of keeping her Promiſe, and not being able to prevail upon the Marchioneſs to receive it, opened it herſelf, took off the Cover, and put the Letter between ſome Embroidery, at which the Marchioneſs uſed to employ ſome time after Dinner. This Stratagem ſucceeded. Some hours afterwards the Marchioneſs being come to finiſh a Noſegay, which ſhe had begun, found this Letter. She could not help reading it, when Donna *Lora* ſurprized her at this Employment; ſhe continued to intreat her to anſwer it, but the Marchioneſs conſtantly refuſed.

Donna *Lora* related to Brother *Stepoano* what had happened. He found Virtue and Tenderneſs in Lady *Manzera*'s Proceedings; could not help lamenting her, and would feign have perſuaded the Prince to diſengage himſelf from his Miſtreſs, or elſe to look for another Commiſſioner. At preſent he deſiſted not intreating Donna *Lora* to make ſome freſh Attempts to obtain a Line or two of her Hand. She renewed her Reasons and Intreaties; but the Marchioness displeased with her Importunities, threatned to acquaint her Husband with these Persecutions. And consequently the Friar could be of no further Service there, but returned to his Patron. The Prince was at the Window, when his Confident was coming, knew him at a distance, and could not patiently stay, but ran to meet him, and desired to know what Answer Lady *Manzera* had made? But the Friar, having brought none, begg'd he would hear him patiently.

The Narrative he heard threw him into a deep Melancholy. He fancied himself more unhappy than he really was, and imagin'd that Donna *Lora*, induced by Interest, had composed all those flattering Conferences, which she insinuated to have had with her Mistress; but that she however was but indifferently inclined to him, because he had not a Line from her. This Opinion he retained so deeply in his Heart, that his Pain began to grow extream.

Thus he passed three Days, desiring sometimes one, sometimes another thing, and at last determined to send *Stephano* again to the Marchioness, and to write a respectful and lamentable Letter that might affect her. The Friar told him, that he should

ſhould ſucceed no better in the ſecond, than he did in the firſt Negotiation. The Prince reproached him for the little Regard he ſeemed to have for his Orders, and for his Ingratitude, and oblig'd him to perform his Commands. Donna *Lora*'s Alacrity was ſoon renewed by a Preſent of an hundred Piſtoles from the Prince. She gave the ſecond Letter to the Marchioneſs, who was then ſo weak, as to peruſe it. This revived Donna *Lora*'s Eloquence, and occaſioned her to endeavour to perſuade her Miſtreſs, that Juſtice would not permit her to refuſe her Compaſſion to a Perſon, that adored her. She raiſed the Prince's Merits to the Skies. I am poſitively aſſured, (ſaid ſhe) that any Woman in the World beſides yourſelf, Madam, would think her ſelf happy in ſuch a Man's Affection. In fine, this dangerous Confident vexed, and troubled the Marchioneſs ſo much, that, notwithſtanding the Reſolution ſhe had taken not to write to him, ſhe could not prevail upon herſelf to be ſilent. The Prince having always kept the Letter, and not communicated the Contents of that, which he writ to the Marchioneſs, to any-body, the Reader will find himſelf diſappointed, if he expected to read them here. All the Intelligence that could be had from one of the Prince's Confidents, is, that the Marchioneſs anſwer'd him to this purpoſe. 'That ſhe was ſenſible of his Love: 'that ſhe would feign acknowledge her 'preſent and promiſe a future and laſting 'Affection for him; but that was all ſhe 'was capable of aſſiſting him in: that ſhe 'begg'd he would be contented therewith; 'hoped he did not expect to ſpeak to her, 'becauſe it could not be done except either 'one or the other of them was expoſed to 'the greateſt Dangers.' This Letter fed the Prince with ſo many Hopes, that he would proceed further. The Danger did not diſhearten him, nor was it a motive to induce him to deſiſt. He pleaſed himſelf with the Thoughts of eſcaping them by the means he was going to make uſe of, and had a Conference upon this Subject with Donna *Lora*, who met him for that purpoſe, under pretence of taking the Air, at the Caſa del Campo, a Royal Palace, the Gardens of which look out upon the River Mancanares. The Prince was accompanied by *Stephano*, and paſſed for the Friar's Italian Friends. He had covered his brown Cheſnut-colour'd Hair, with a Light-Wig, which perfectly diſguiſed him. Donna *Lora* had one of her Nieces with her, whom ſhe without any Difficulty left with *Stephano*, whilſt ſhe turned into a Walk with the Prince alone. When they were together, he he emptied his Pockets filled with Pieces of Gold, and gallantly begg'd her to accept of them, as Witnesses of his Acknowledgment, assuring her that that should not be all, and that, if she continued to be favourable to him, he mould promote her Fortune and that of her Nieces. He conjured her finally to procure him an Opportunity of conversing with the Marchioness. Though he said all these Things in scarce intelligible Spanish, yet Donna *Lora* understood him very well: but an Offer of Gold for her Niece rendered her more tractable. 'I wish to God (said she) I 'was the Marchioness! you should see me, 'if I was to die the moment afterwards.' The Prince thanked her for the Good-will she testified for him, and continued to intreat her, to invent some method of conferring with the Marchioness. After several Projects, they agreed, that, if her Mistress still refused to receive him, Donna *Lora* should introduce him into her Chamber. 'You are to fall down at her Feet, (said *Lora*) ask her Pardon, and I am al-'most assured she will grant it. But you 'are not to leave her (added she) till she 'promises to pardon me for the Fraud I 'shall have put upon her.' These matters being thus concluded upon, both Parties were sworn, and the Prince on Departure

conjured his Confident to haſten the Execution of it. Donna *Lora* being returned to her Miſtreſs, told her, 'That ſhe had
'been at the Caſa del Campo; that ſhe
'had there ſeen the Prince, who had di-
'rectly moved her Pity, he was ſo changed.
'But (added ſhe) I could not contain my-
'ſelf from crying, when he told me, that
'his Love for you had almoſt killed him.
'He threw himſelf at my Feet, and con-
'jured me to procure him a moment's
'Converſation with you. I found myſelf
'compelled to promiſe him to propoſe the
'matter to you; and really, Madam, your
'Conſcience muſt oblige you to ſpeak to
'him, ſince you know it will ſave his Life.
'See him and tell him, that his Hopes are
'ill-founded. —— What do you perſuade
'me to, *Lora*, (anſwered ſhe) you, that
'know the deplorable Condition of my
'Heart? and how can I alter it! — But
'Madam, (replied the dangerous Woman)
'can you prevail upon yourſelf to ſee him
'die? for, if you perſiſt in refuſing him
'Admittance, I cannot inſure for his Life.
'By the manner in which he ſpoke to me
'I have Reaſon to fear his Deſpair. What
'Harm will there be in ſuffering him to
'come and telling him that his Hopes are
'unneceſſary, and that he cannot too ſoon
'endeavour to recover? When you have
'eſcaped

'escaped his memory, I doubt whether
'you will retain him in yours. ----- God
'send I may not! (cried the Marchioness
'shedding Tears) but I fear the Reverse.
'However that you may have no Reason
'to blame me, I consent to it: Contrive
'some quarter of an Hour for me to see
'him.' Pleased with this Permission Donna *Lora* informed the Prince that he might come instantly.

He extreamly satisfied with this News, dressed himself neatly, and at the Hour appointed, being covered with a Cloak, he took Mr. *Fitztuhm* Gentleman of his Bed-Chamber, who had long since been accustomed to his nocturnal Gallantries; and was at the Garden-Door of Lord *Manzera*'s House, as he had agreed with Donna *Lora*.

His Undertaking was so rash that he dared not to consider of it. He was subject to the Discovery of a Jealous Husband and a Watchful Mother. The dire Effects of their Resentment, if he had been discovered would have been intolerable, and nothing was more probable: The Marquis of Manzera and the Dutchess of Fernandine lodged in the same House, and the Windows of their Apartments were towards the Garden. Thousand unforeseen and unfortunate Accidents might easily happen: Neverthelefs his natural Intrepidity and his Love permitted him not to look upon thefe Dangers in any other than a bold manner; he ran thither without Hefitation.

Every Thing was fo luckily prepared, that he found the Garden-Door open, and the officious *Lora* waiting for him. He ordered Mr. *Fitztuhm* to ftay for him, and followed Donna *Lora*, who conducted him through a private Stair-cafe to the Marchionefs's Apartment. I do not relate here the Satisfaction with which this enamoured Couple met, nor can I repeat their Words; for the one may be as eafily imagined, as defcribed; the other is a Myftery never revealed to any one. However they did not probably tire each other, for they remained together three Hours; and notwithftanding the Refolution the Marchionefs had taken not to fee the Prince, but to difcharge him, fhe could not keep it.

A Sicknefs that perplexed Lord *Manzera* favoured our Lovers for fome time. He kept his Chamber and fuffered not his Lady to lye there. But this very Circumftance, that feemed fo favourable to their Defigns was alfo the Caufe of their Mifery. Lord *Manzera*'s Diftemper deprived him of Reft; he got up almoft every Night and took a Walk in a Balcony that had the profpect of of the Garden. One Night an excessive Heat obliged him to open a Window that was cool, when by Moon-light he perceived a Man led by a Woman, coming from the Lady *Manzera*'s Apartments, and after having crossed the Garden going out at a Door that led him to the little Street. He saw the Woman return, and knew her to be Donna *Lora*. As her Age clear'd her of the Suspicion of having Followers, he doubted not, but the Person that he had seen was his Wife's Lover; and recollecting at the same Time the Prince's Transport at the Ball, became the more suspicious. No Man could ever be in greater Despair than was at that Time the Marquis. The Treachery of a person whom he loved as a Mistress, and the Shame of being thus deceived by a Woman gave him so great an Uneasiness, that it almost deprived him of the Use of his Reason. He was a long while determining what to do in this Affair. His first Emotion had almost caused his going to stab his Wife and Donna *Lora*: Afterwards reflecting, that by such an Action his Shame would be publish'd, and the Author of it remain unpunished, he proposed first to sacrifice him to his Fury, and afterwards to demand Reparation for the Treachery of his Spouse, for whom he thought no Torment great enough. Day-light surprized him in his Despair, with which he would not acquaint his Domesticks; but laid down and feigning to be more indispos'd, than he was before, he refus'd to see anybody, not even the Marchioness herself, who had since his Indisposition passed the Afternoons with the Dutchess of Fernandine. One of his Domesticks remained with him, who was a Servant in whom he could confide. The Marquis discovered the Sentiments of his Heart to him, and consulted with him upon the manner of revenging himself. The Death of the Prince of Saxony, or of the Marchioness's Lover, whoever he might be, was in this wicked Conference resolved upon. The Valet de Chamber undertook the Execution of it, and promised to procure three Men, who, without knowing upon whose Destruction his Design was formed, were to kill every Man, that dared to present himself at Night at the Little Garden-Door.

Whilst the Marquis entered into this Combination, the two Lovers being entirely occupied in their Amours, were far from thinking of the Evil that was preparing for them. The Marchioness went to her Husband's Chamber-Door, and a Refusal of Admittance did not at all surprize her, because she was accustomed to it: The Marquis was subject to violent Head-

Head-Aches, and when they tormented him he commonly ſhut himſelf up, and none, but one Valet de Chambre, dared to approach him. She ſuppoſed that the ſame pain perplexed him ſtill, and that he was only on that Account deſirous of Solitude. The Valet de Chambre not being able in leſs than two Days to compleat the propoſed number of Aſſaſſins, acquainted his Maſter that all Things were ready and that only the Victim was wanting to be ſacrificed. The Marquis not doubting, but that this Object of his Hatred would be preſent there that ſame Evening could not delay his Revenge. He gave the Aſſaſſins Orders to preſent themſelves in the Duſk of the Evening in the ſmall Street, where the little Garden-Door was, and there to aſſault every Man that dared to walk there. The Execution of the project anſwered the Deſign of it. The four Aſſaſſins (at the Head of which was the Valet de Chambre) did not wait a long while in the little Street, before they ſaw a Man advance towards *Manzera*'s Garden-Door, covered with a Cloak, and who was going with a Key to open the Door. They aſſaulted and gave him ſeveral Blows, before the Prince (for he was the perſon) could put himſelf in a poſture of Defence. But having pulled out the Pocket-piſtols, with which he was provided,

vided, he broke that person's Head, that seemed most forward to kill him. The Shot came to *Fitztuhm*'s Ears, who had waited at the Bottom of the Street, and hastened up. He found the Prince with Sword in Hand in Opposition to three Men, and joined to his Assistance, whereupon the Fight became obstinate: Another Assassin lost his Life, and a third was mortally wounded. The fourth took to his flight, that neither the Prince nor *Fitztuhm* could overtake him. The Prince, well satisfied with having escaped the Danger, notwithstanding the pain the Wounds gave him made all possible Haste to get to his Lodging. This Care preserved him from the Affront of being seized by the Watchmen, who at the Sound of the Shot ran to the place from whence it proceeded. These Officers of Justice lifted up the dead and wounded Bodies. The latter of which desired the Benefit of having a Confessor, to declare in the presence of the Constable and other Witnesses, that the Marquis of Manzera's persuasion first engaged him in the Assault, a little while after which Confession he expired. In the mean Time the Prince having reached his Lodgings, sent for a Surgeon to visit his Sores, which seemed not to be mortal, by the Assurance the first Surgeon gave him, that if he would

would keep his Bed three or four Days, he needed no longer keep his Room, but would be able to go out. The Prince enjoined him Secrecy in this Affair, as he did Mr. *Fitztuhm*, whom he begg'd not to mention the Adventure; seeming careful to preserve the Marchioness's Reputation, whose Fate gave him more Uneasiness than his own Wounds, for he doubted not, but that the Condition he was then in was only to be imputed to the Marquis of Manzera. He supposed her subject to the Effects of her jealous Husband's Rage, and foresaw the sad Event of this Amour. He told *Fitztuhm*, that he pardon'd the Marquis for having designed Ill upon his Life, but, if he attempted to take away that of his Spouse, he should never be forgiven; and, was he to be so unfortunate as to commit an Action of that Kind, it should be resented in a manner, that might be reported throughout Spain. Whilst he was thus disquieting himself, Confusion, Grief, and Horror had taken possession of *Manzera*'s House. The Marquis being informed that his Antagonist the Prince of Saxony had escaped his Vengeance, and that the Assault had reached the Magistrate's Ears by the Declaration the wounded person made, thought himself utterly ruined; but was resolved that a Satisfaction from his

Spouse

Spouſe, ſhould precede his perdition; purſuant to which Reſolve he took a Dagger in one Hand, and a fine Cup full of Poiſon in the other; with theſe diſmal Arms he haſten'd to his Wife's Apartment, whom he found with Donna *Lora* ſtruck with Fear and Trembling. They had heard the Piſtol-ſhot, and not ſeeing the Prince dreaded what had happened, and at the ſame Time thought their Death inevitable. The Idea of which had poſſeſſed their minds and ſo terrify'd them, that they forgot to ſhut their Chamber-Door. The Air with which the Marquis made his Entry, and the Dagger and Cup he had in his Hands ſoon ſignified to them the imminent Danger, it ſo ſtartled Donna *Lora*, that ſhe ſwooned away. 'Oh! thou Monſter of Iniquity, '(cried he) thy Death is moſt certain, but 'it ſhall be haſten'd by my Hand.' At the ſame Time he ſtabb'd her, and turned about to the Marchioneſs, caſting an incenſed Eye upon her, deſired ſhe would chuſe either Fire or Poiſon. 'Dear Sir, '(cried ſhe lifting up her Hands) have 'Compaſſion upon an unfortunate Wo'man, whoſe Actions have not been ſo 'criminal, as you imagine. Allow me at 'leaſt a ſmall ſpace of Time to recom'mend my Soul to God.' The unmerciful Huſband was not at all moved.

'Your

'Your Sentence is pronounced, (anſwered
' he in a terrible Tone) you muſt die. I
' give you your Choice of Fire, or Poi-
' ſon, which is more than you deſerve.'
The Marchioneſs not being able to prevail upon her Huſband to wait, determined to take the Poiſon, he remained there to ſee her take it, without looking any other Way, reproaching her ſeverely till he thought the Poiſon had ſufficient Effect to render all further Aſſiſtance ineffectual; then he left her alone, with Donna *Lora* lying at her Feet. As ſoon as he was gone the Marchioneſs would have called her Servants, but could not. She fell into a great Chair and would have died there unknown to any one but her barbarous Huſband, had not a little Dog, that was her Favourite, ſcratched at the Door of the Wardrobe, when a Chambermaid opening it, ſaw her Miſtreſs ſitting and Donna *Lor* lying on the Ground. She called her Companions, and inſtantly acquainted the Dutcheſs of Fernandine with the miſerable Condition of her Daughter. The diſtreſſed Mother ran to her Daughter's Aſſiſtance, and found her ſitting in a Chair. Her fine Eyes, formerly full of Fire, ſparkled no longer, ſhe was extreamly pale, ſpoke nothing, and ſighed conſtantly. Sometimes ſhe cried, *I am poiſon'd!* all her Servants

wept;

wept; the Dutchess was in Despair; she conjured her Daughter to let her know what had happen'd to her, though she was too sure of it. Donna *Lora* breathless, her Daughter dying, and Lord *Manzera* not appearing, when they call'd him, assured her sufficiently of his being the Author of this misery. She sent for the Physicians, who told her, that the Marchioness had but few Hours to live. Her Death could not be prevented, because she would not take any Remedy; and a little while afterwards she died in her Mother's Arms. Whilst this deplorable Scene was acted in the unfortunate Marchioness's Chamber, the Marquis suffered the most dreadful Torments in his. No Despair was perhaps ever so violent; he was struck with Horror and called Death to his Assistance, and in fine not being able to resist the Aggravation of his misery, he was taken with the Fever, that same Day, and other Circumstances instantly shewed his Disease to be incurable. And seeing that his Life was almost ended, he sent to the Dutchess of Fernandine and begg'd of her not to refuse him the Comfort of seeing him; she went directly to his Apartment and the Marquis desired her by Signs to sit down at his Bed-side; when in a sad and mournful Tone, he related to her all that a furious Jealousy had induced him

him to commit, testifying an inexpressible Sorrow, intolerable Checks of Conscience, a sincere Repentance for what he had done, and an earnest desire of pardon, by which he so moved the Dutchess that she could not help deploring his Condition. The Dutchess's presence had caused such an Emotion in Lord *Manzera*, having strove with might and main to speak to her, and the Remembrance of all that he had done shock'd him so, that when he had done speaking he swooned away, lost the Use of his Senses; and his last moment seemed to approach. The Dutchess unwilling to be a Spectator of such a horrid Sight, left him among his Domesticks, in whose Arms he expired soon afterwards. The Quality of the Marquis and the Share he had in the King's Friendship, occasioned the Magistrates not to proceed against him, whilst he lived; and the King, hearing of his Death, forbid any one to stain his memory; so that perhaps we should have been ignorant of all these Circumstances, had not the Dutchess of Fernandine related them to one of Donna *Lora*'s Nieces, who informed the Prince of them by his Confident *Stephano*. The Prince hearing of these unfortunate Catastrophes, was sensibly touch'd with them. He has been heard to say, even upon his Death-bed, that he had never loved

any

any Woman more tenderly than he did Lady *Manzera*, and had never been afflicted ſo, as he was for her Loſs.

In the mean while, being perfectly cured of his Wounds, he looked upon Madrid as a place too mournful for him to make any longer Stay in, ſince the Death of the Marchioneſs of *Manzera*. Wherefore he gave Orders for his Departure, and went to Court to have an Audience of Leave of their Majeſties, where he was received with all the Tokens of Eſteem and Benevolence, he could deſire. They begg'd, he would reſide ſome time longer there, but he excuſed himſelf, ſaying, matters of great Importance occaſioned his Return into Saxony. The King gave him four ſaddled Horſes, eight Mules, and a Sword enriched with Diamonds. The Queen gave him two Suits of Hangings of an admirable Taſte and uncommon Sort, a large Quantity of Indian Rarities, and beſides all this her Picture ſet in Diamonds. And in ſhort, had he not been ſtill afflicted with the Death of his dear Marchioneſs, he would have left Spain with great Satisfaction on Account of the Honours he had there received, and the obliging Behaviour of the Spaniards. He directed his Courſe through the Kingdoms of Valencia and Catalonia to Barcellona, where he ſtaid ſome Days; the Count

of

of Corzano, Governor of the place, honoured him in an extraordinary manner. This was the ſame Nobleman, that ſome Years afterwards held out a Siege of two months againſt the Duke of Vendoſme, to whom he was at laſt obliged to ſurrender the place, ſeeing himſelf forſaken by M. de Velaſco, Governor of the Principality. From Barcellona the Prince went to Perpignan, the Capital of Rouſſillon. He there obſerved with Amazement the great Fortifications Lewis XIV. had raiſed about that Town. At length paſſing through Provence and Languedoc he arrived in Italy.

CHAP. III.

Of the Prince of Saxony's Voyage to Venice, the Honours ſhewn him there, his Love of Lady Mocenigo, her Refuſal, his amorous Adventure with a Widow, her Infidelity.

AS time leſſen'd the Prince's Grief, and all imaginable diſpoſitions to Gallantry, and the Qualities requiſite to gain good Succeſs therein, were innate to him, he had ſeveral new Amours there, which at laſt made him forget the unfortunate Marchioneſs of Manzera. Venice and Rome having

having always been the moſt noted Cities in Italy both for Politicks and Gallantry, they were the places at which the Prince made the longeſt Stay. The Senate of Venice to do him Honour, mitigating of that ſevere Statute which forbids Noblemen to converſe with Strangers, permitted them to ſee him, and choſe three Noblemen to attend him, and to ſhew him the Curioſities of the Town. They permitted the Ladies to make uſe of their Diamonds and to wear colour'd Habits during the Prince's Stay at Venice. Since *Henry* III. King of France and Poland no Prince received greater Honours of the Republick. Every particular Nobleman was eager to entertain the Prince of Saxony. There was nothing to be ſeen every Day, but Balls, Treats, Concerts, and ſeveral other Diverſions; which together with the Ceremony of the Sea-Nuptials, the Celebration of which was ſoon after the Prince's Arrival there, drew together a large number of Strangers. Never was Venice ſo magnificent. The Doge performed the Ceremony of eſpouſing the Sea on one of thoſe fine days, on which the Sun is ſo hid, that neither Wind nor Heat are inconvenient. The Number of Boats was infinite, and they were filled with numberleſs maſqued People of both Sexes. The Prince was in one of the Pleaſure-

Boats

Boats with his Attendants and ſeveral young German Noblemen, all dreſſed after the Spaniſh manner. As he was extreamly well-ſhaped, this Dreſs ſet him off more advantageouſly ; and drew on him a ſhower of Sugar-plumbs, which the Ladies threw at him, as a ſign of Applauſe. He obſerved, that among all the Maſques only two neglected to do him that Honour. Theſe were two Women dreſſed in Spaniſh Cloaths, and who, by the quiet poſture in which they ſate in their Boat, ſeemed rather to have come thither for the Benefit of the Air, than to partake of the pleaſure of the Entertainment. One of them ſeemed to be very well ſhaped, her Neck was of a dazzling white Colour, and gave reaſon to think that that which was covered with the Maſque was no leſs admirable. Her Dreſs was plain, but perfectly neat, and an exquiſite Taſte appeared all over her perſon. The Prince, to whom ſhe appeared charming, not being able to know of the Watermen, who ſhe was, ordered them to purſue the Boat in which were the two Spaniſh Ladies. They landed at the place of St. Mark, where all the Maſques meet on the day of that Solemnity. The Prince ſtepp'd out of his Boat about the ſame Time, that they did out of theirs. Whilſt he endeavoured to addreſs them, though he knew

them

them not, he was himſelf accoſted by Lord *Mocenigo*; 'I beg your Highneſs's permiſſion ' (ſaid he) to preſent you my Spouſe. She ' is yeſterday returned from a Journey to ' Loretto, and has conſequently not yet ' been able to pay you her Compliments.' The Prince, who at any other Time would have been glad of an Acquaintance with a perſon of ſo great Quality as Lady *Mocenigo*, was then thinking of an Excuſe to diſpenſe with it: but Lord *Mocenigo* giving him no Time to anſwer, cried Madam, Madam! The Prince, who had all the while eyed the two Spaniſh Ladies ſaw them turn at Lord *Mocenigo*'s Cry, and come back inſtantly. When they came to the place where he was: 'Come, Madam, ' (ſaid the Nobleman to her, whom he ' had chiefly obſerved) pay your Reſpects ' to the Prince of Saxony, and aſſiſt me ' in acquitting myſelf, if poſſible, with ' him, for the Honours I was heaped with ' at Dreſden by his Father the Elector.' The Lady quitted the Arms of Lady *Corrano* who accompanied her, and having taken off her Maſque, advanced towards the Prince, who being likewiſe unmaſqued prevented and addreſſed her with that polite Air and noble Loftineſs, which ſignalizes perſons of his Rank. Lady *Mocenigo* addreſſed him in her Turn with a pleaſant and

and modeſt Air, no leſs agreeable to the Prince, than the Beauty he obſerved in her perſon. She entertained him in a very obliging manner, with an Account of the Satisfaction Venice was ſenſible of in ſeeing him within its Walls, and of what ſhe had heard of his extraordinary Qualifications. The Prince anſwered her ſo politely and with ſo much Senſe, that Lady *Mocenigo* was ſoon convinced, that his Merit exceeded all the Reports that had been ſpread of him. After the firſt Compliments ſhe preſented to him Lady *Cornaro*, one of the moſt beautiful Ladies of Venice. The Prince addreſſed her with all the Reſpect due to her eminent Birth. The two Ladies, the Prince and Lord *Mocenigo* having put on their Maſques again, they walked together. The Prince entertained them with numberleſs pleaſant Diſcourſes, and their Converſation was the moſt agreeable and better ſupported, than any other in the place. They were ſo much delighted with it, that they had almoſt been the laſt Maſques remaining in the place. Lady *Cornaro* was the firſt that took Notice of it, and ſaid it was Time to retire. Whereupon Lord *Mocenigo* addreſſing himſelf to the Prince, told him, that his Lady and he had invited ſome Friends to dine with them: that he dared not take the Liberty

to beg of him to honour the Company with his presence: But if they might be bless'd with that Favour, he should be received at their House with a Respect due to him. Lady *Mocenigo* here interrupted her Husband to tell him: that he was mistaken, in inviting the Prince to so slight a Dinner as theirs; but he replied, 'That
'he took the Liberty at all Hazards to
'offer his Dinner to the Prince: that he
'relied upon his Kindness in excusing him
'if he was not served as he ought to be;
'and that he would endeavour to supply
'the deficiency of his Dinner, by a Re-
'past, which he would presume to beg his
'Highness to accept of at his House: that
'then he would use him as Count of Mis-
'nia, but at another Time he should shew
'the Esteem he had for the Prince of Sax-
'ony.' The Prince thanked him, and offering his Service said, 'That he desired
'his Friendship both as Count of Misnia,
'and as Prince of Saxony, and assured
'him of his Esteem: that he took the
'obliging manner with which he enter-
'tained him, as a great Favour; and that
'if he knew that his presence would not
'be disagreeable to Lady *Mocenigo*, he
'would gratefully accept of the Offer he
'made him.' Lady *Mocenigo* replied, 'That
'his presence at their House could not but

'please

'please her, and when therein she so di-
'rectly opposed her Spouse, it was out of
'Fear that her Dinner would not be agree-
'able to him.' The Prince in a gallant manner answered, 'That he preferred the
'Honour of being near her to any other
'Satisfaction,' and then he handed her into her Boat, into which Lady *Cornaro* went after her; and he followed with Lord *Mocenigo* in another Boat. At the Palace of *Mocenigo* he met with the Ladies *Foscarini*, *Pesero* and *Nani* together with the Lords *Justiniani*, and *Grimani*. All these Persons were related, and had erected among themselves a Society, at which few others were admitted. They were all amazed to see the Prince of Saxony come; that free manner of inviting another Person to Dinner, which Lord *Mocenigo* had made Use of not being customary in Italy; and though they did not remain under the Constraint of their Society, yet had they not sufficiently laid aside that prejudice of their Education, to be persuaded that Strangers ought to be used with Familiarity. The Prince excused himself so politely for having entered into their Company, and begg'd with so much Grace and Condescension, that they would put him upon a Level with them, that they at last thought themselves obliged to Lord *Mocenigo* for having brought him to his House. They

laid aside the troublesome Constraint they should have been under, and perhaps no Repast at Venice could ever boast of having seen an equal Satisfaction more generally diffused. After Dinner the whole Company agreed upon diverting themselves in a Pleasure-Boat in the great Channel Murena, after that they went to the Place of St. Mark, and from thence to the Opera. They returned to Supper to Lord *Mocenigo*'s, and did not depart from thence till the next-Morning, when Day-light begun to appear.

Lord *Mocenigo*'s Presence was the only Obstacle, that hindered the Prince from declaring openly to that Gentleman's Spouse the Impression she had made upon his Heart. But he had made her Signs enough, to be understood, and she had comprehended them very well. Lady *Mocenigo* was in Respect of her Character the finest Woman in the World. She easily perceived the Prince's Sentiments, and they occasioned no little Uneasiness in her. She loved and esteemed her Husband, and since the Beginning of the six Years after their Marriage she had not in the least disagreed with him, but now feared that the Prince designed to set them at Variance; she resolved however to behave herself in a manner that might deprive him

of

of all Hope, and preſerve her future Qui-et. In purſuance of this Reſolution ſhe would not ſhun his Preſence; for her O-pinion was, that the Difficulties a newly enamoured Lover at firſt meets with, ſerve only to inflame his Paſſion the moɪe. Thus did ſhe, without flying or ſearching for him, propoſe to live in her uſual manner. The Prince utterly impatient to acquaint her with the Condition of his Heart, was at her Door when he expected to ſee her. Though the Lady *Mocenigo* was by herſelf, when he deſired to ſpeak to her, yet was he not refuſed. Their Converſation was directly very indifferent; ſhe ſpoke of what had been done and diſcourſed upon the Night before; but the Prince made her at laſt attentive to what concerned him. He made ſo gallant and ſo polite a Declaration of Love, that any one beſides Lady *Mocenigo* would have been taken with it. She quietly heard him, and ſuf-fering him to expreſs at his Eaſe whatever his native paſſion inſpired him with, did not anſwer till he had quite done ſpeaking: 'I have with Attention heard all the fine 'Things you have been pleaſed to di-'vert me with (ſaid ſhe with a gay and 'charming Air) and do not conceal 'from you that the excellent Turn you 'have given it, and eaſy manner in which

'you expreſſed yourſelf in our Language,
'have extreamly pleaſed me. I am be-
'ſides all this very much obliged to you
'for the Expreſſion you have made of the
'Sentiments of your Heart concerning
'me. But as I neither can nor will anſwer
'them, I beg you would change your
'Love into Eſteem; and then you may
'be aſſured of my Gratitude.' Dear Madam! (cried the Prince) 'you deſerve
'quite different Sentiments and —— I
'beg, Sir, (replied ſhe) you would not
'interrupt me; I have permitted you to
'ſpeak whatever you pleaſed, ſuffer me to
'ſpeak in my Turn. Hitherto God be
'thanked my Virtue has not been ſtained.
'Several Men have declared a paſſion for
'me, but their Diſcourſes have neither
'affected, nor troubled my Mind; being
'perſuaded that Virtue is not ſolely con-
'ſiſtent with Auſterity, I have not an-
'ſwered their Sentiments, and then they
'ceaſed to be Lovers. As I am reſolved
'to act in the ſame manner with you, I
'hope you will follow the Example of
'others; and that will be the moſt ac-
'ceptable mark of your Eſteem, you can
'ſhew me. I dare even ſay, that is the
'only Thing you can do; for what can
'you after all pretend to? I am not free;
'and if I was I know too well, that my
'For-

'Fortune would not be sufficient to pro-
'cure me a Sovereignty; and I am more
'sensible that it would be inconsistent with
'my Virtue to be your Mistress. Judge
'then, Sir, since I am married to the most
'worthy Gentleman of the present Age,
'whom I love, whom I esteem, and who
'has for me a very tender Affection, whe-
'ther I can, without running precipitately
'into Ruin, be sensible of any other
'Flame. No, Sir, nothing shall induce
'me to neglect my Duty to my Spouse
'and myself. If I can, I will deserve your
'Esteem, which I cannot do without pre-
'serving my Virtue. I believe you are
'too subtil a Lover, to be capable of lov-
'ing a person, whom you cannot esteem.
'What Advantage shall I reap then by
'answering your Sentiments? I shall be
'guilty of a great Crime to the best of
'Husbands, forfeit your Esteem, and that
'of Consequence a little while after your
'Love; and then I shall pass the remain-
'ing part of Life covered with Shame,
'for having been so weak as to comply
'with your Desires. I tell Your Highness,
'(continued she) what another person
'would have perhaps concealed from you
'for some Years; but I shall at least enjoy
'the Satisfaction of not having perplexed
'you with deceitful Hopes. Believe me,
 '(ad-

'added ſhe laughing) loſe not your Time :
'there are numberleſs Ladies here, that far
'exceed me in Beauty, and will perhaps
'not be diſpleaſed to ſee you attach'd to
'them. You may there find a more lucky
'Deſtiny.' The Prince had given Lady
Mocenigo an extreamly impatient Audience,
and the Reſpect he had for her ſilenced
him. When ſhe had done ſpeaking he endeavoured to confute her Reaſons. He
told her all, that he thought would affect
her: and at laſt threw himſelf at her Feet.
'You give yourſelf too much Trouble,
'Sir, (ſaid ſhe lifting him up again) hi-
'therto I have taken all your Words for
'meer Gallantries, but I ſee that the mat-
'ter begins to be ſerious, and that I muſt
'ſpeak ſeriouſly to you. I beg of you,
'(continued ſhe) if you are unwilling to
'oblige me to leave you, to ceaſe men-
'tioning Love to me. Let me tell you
'once more, that you muſt addreſs your-
'ſelf ſomewhere elſe; for I neither will
'nor can I hearken to your propoſals: if
'you ſtill continue theſe Diſcourſes, you
'will give me the Trouble of retiring to
'ſome remote Village, during your Stay
'here. That will cauſe great Uneaſineſs
'in Lord *Mocenigo*; and I dare ſay that
'the Reſpect and Value he has for Your
'Highneſs, deſerve to have ſo great a
'Grief

'Grief ſpared on your Hands.' This Diſcourſe ſupported by a noble Loftineſs, had almoſt deprived the Prince of all his Gallantry. He ſaw that he had nothing left to hope for; but could not be pleaſed to give up a Coquette, who he thought was his own. He would feign continue his fine Expreſſions, but Lady *Mocenigo* pretended not to hear him, ſhe propoſed two or three Queſtions to him, which utterly fruſtrated his Meaſures. He had at the ſame Time the good Luck of ſeeing Company come in, which gave him Time to recover from his Diſorder. They offered him a party at a Game, called Milchiade, which he accepted of, but play'd ſo diſtractedly, that he knew not what he did; whilſt Lady *Mocenigo* was in the merrieſt Humour imaginable. That occaſioned his Deſpair. When their Game was finiſhed Lord *Mocenigo*, who was come in, when they play'd, would have kept the Prince to Supper, but he ſaid he had ſome Letters to write, that required Expedition, and obliged him to return home. When he ſtepped out of his Boat his firſt Waterman gave him a Billet. The Prince could not think, who it came from: he opened and read it at the Bottom of his Stair-caſe, and found it to be an Appointment to meet him at Midnight: he was invited to come ſingly, and told, that his Waterman would inform him of what he had previoufly to do to get into the Arms of a Perfon, who dared think of herfelf worthy of him. The Prince, delighted with Adventures of that Kind, and defirous of driving away the Melancholly, his ill Succefs with Lady *Mocenigo* had caufed, inftantly refolved upon undertaking, what had been propofed to him: he ventured the Honefty of his Waterman, of whofe Fidelity he had Intelligence of one of the moft eminent Bankers of Venice. Midnight was near, and feeing, that he had no Time to lofe, he wrapped himfelf up in a Cloak, furnifhed his Pocket with Piftols, and entered into his Boat, without knowing where he was row'd to. The Waterman, that had given him the Billet, left the management of the Boat to his Comrade, and placed himfelf at the Side of the Prince. 'Your Highnefs (faid the 'Man) is a handfome Prince, and well 'deferving of a beautiful Miftrefs. I am 'going to procure you one, that is a 'Lady of eminent Birth, and cannot be 'equall'd in Beauty. She is but fixteen 'Years of Age, and never lov'd a Man 'befides you.' The Prince fmiled at this Preamble; preffingly afked the Name of the Lady and how the Billet fhe fent, came to his Hands; in fhort, how he, as a Waterman

terman, came to be acquainted with her but his Curiosity was scarce at all satisfied. 'As for the Lady's Name, (answered the 'Waterman) I am forbid mentioning it, 'and nothing shall induce me to discover a 'Secret I have been entrusted with. The 'Billet was given me this Morning at the 'Church where I heard Mass; an old Wo-'man, covered with a long Cloak, came 'near and beckon'd to me, whereupon I 'followed her; she led me into a Lane, 'and there, giving me the Billet I deliver'd 'to you, told me that her Mistress loved 'you and should be glad to see you. I 'agreed with her to conduct you at Mid-'night to the Windows of the Lady's 'House; that she should be there to tye a 'Ladder of Rope, by which you should 'go up into the House; that she should 'lead you into her Mistress's Chamber; 'and that when you are got in, I should 'retire with my Boat; that at Three o' 'Clock in the Morning I should come to 'fetch you back; that you should again 'descend by this Ladder, and return into 'your Boat, and I see you home.' The Prince found this Project very well ma-naged without his Knowledge; but the Execution of it seemed a little dangerous to him. He recollected his Adventure of Madrid which so intimidated him, that he

 con-

confidered fome moments whether it would be better to hazard the Adventure, or to return home. The Waterman feeing him thus dubious, perfuaded him to fear nothing; that he would infure for any Misfortune that fhould happen to him; that he might confide in him, who was a Man of Honour and incapable of deceiving any Perfon. The Prince, ignorant of what Fear was, had almoft been enraged againft his Waterman for fufpecting him to be fubject to it. He told him that Fear did not hinder him from engaging in the Adventure; but that he apprehended the Lady not deferving of the Pains. The Waterman folemnly protefted that fhe was the moft beautiful Woman of Venice. In fhort, the Prince fatisfied with the Reafons he alledged and befides little accuftomed to long Invitations ordered him to row towards the appointed place. After feveral Turnings the Boat landed in a narrow Channel. All neceffary meafures were taken fo carefully, that the Ladder was found prepared. The Prince ftepp'd up and having entered the Window, he felt himfelf taken by the Hand, and heard fome-body fay to him, 'Fear nothing, 'Sir, you are here in Safety, follow me; 'who am going to make you happy.' Her Voice fignified her to be a Woman.

She

She conducted him through ſeveral dark Chambers, and at laſt he arriv'd at a Door, by which he enter'd into a large, light and magnificently adorn'd Apartment; they then croſſed a Chamber richly furniſh'd, and at laſt arrived at a little Cloſet, which equall'd the others in Splendor. His Guide begg'd he would not be diſpleaſed at her leaving him for a ſmall ſpace of Time to go and acquaint her Miſtreſs with his preſence. She left him; and directly afterwards he ſaw a Lady enter, whoſe Beauty, graceful Appearance, and extraordinary fine Dreſs ſtruck him with Amazement. He thought he was in an inchanted place; ' It ' is impoſſible, (ſaid he to himſelf) that ' this ſhould not be a Woman of great ' Birth: her noble Air, and the Grandeur ' that ſurrounds her, are ſufficient proofs ' of it.' He complimented her reſpectfully. The Lady took him by the Hand and led him to a Sopha deſiring him to ſit down. ' What I am now doing (ſaid ſhe looking ' modeſtly on him) plainly convinces you ' of the preſent State of my Heart, pardon ' then the profeſſion of a paſſion, whoſe ' Ardency I have for a whole Month in vain ' reſiſted; and pity an unfortunate Perſon, ' that is ready to die for Shame of what ſhe ' is doing, but could no longer have ſupported her enamoured Soul, had ſhe ſtill

' de-

'denied herſelf the pleaſure of your Conver-
'ſation.' The Prince took her Hand and kiſſed it in a Tranſport, and having thank'd her for the Eſteem ſhe had teſtified for him, he told her he ſhould reckon that the moſt delightful Night of his Life-time, and himſelf in her Embraces the happieſt of Mankind. His Thoughts at that Time exactly correſponded with his Words. The unknown Beauty, having already cauſed the Oblivion of Lady *Mocenigo*, appeared incomparably charming to him. He could not comprehend how ſhe could be hid from his Sight during the three Months he had been at Venice, and how he arrived at that pitch of Happineſs to be beloved by her. The Lady explained thoſe Myſteries to him in giving him an abridged Account of her Life. She told him, 'That her Pa-
'rents had given her away in Marriage
'very young, and againſt her Conſent to
'Lord *N*------ who being a ſuperannuated
'old Man had kept her under Conſtraint,
'and confined her for ſix Years together;
'that he at laſt died two Months ago, and
'had left her poſſeſſed of great Wealth;
'but what ſhe eſteemed far more excellent
'than the Poſſeſſion of theſe Riches, was
'an unuſual and ineſtimable Liberty, that
'the Cuſtom, that confined Widows at
'home the three firſt Months of their Wi-
'dowhood,

'dowhood, was the Occasion of her living,
'then so retiredly; that consequently she
'could not yet frequent the Assemblies.
'I go no-where (said she) but to Church,
'where I at first saw you about a Month
'ago; since that my Mind has retained
'a painful Idea of you, and as I could not
'deny myself the Pleasure of seeing you,
'determined to trouble you with a Billet,
'and therein humbly to desire that Satis-
'faction. Moreover (continued she) par-
'don the Precautions I took to introduce
'you. I pretended to conceal my Name
'from you, and even my Abode, till I
'knew how agreeable my Person would
'be to a Prince of so exquisite a Taste.
'My Happiness I find to be at present
'so great, that I presume to flatter my
'self, with having some Return from
'your Hands, and your Presence here
'will be very acceptable whenever you
'shall think proper to honour me with
'it.'

The Prince returned kind Thanks to the beautiful Widow for all the endearing Expressions she had made use of in her obliging Address; he assured her, that he was very sensible of her Passion, and his Affection for her should never cease. The Widow believed all his tender Assurances and kind Promises, for Women are naturally inclined

clined to believe what they wiſh for; and her Lover took no ſmall Advantage of her Credulity; for he refuſed to depart, when the Widow's Confident gave him Notice, that his Servants waited for him, and begged the Lady's Conſent to ſupply the vacant Place of the Deceaſed. She ſoon made ſome Objections to that Propoſal, but afterwards poſtponing Virtue and Reaſon to Love, did not refuſe her Compliance with his unjuſt Requeſt. The old Woman ſent the Servants away, and deſired they would not return again; this proved afterwards no uſeleſs Precaution; for the enamoured Pair were ſo delighted with pleaſing each other, that they remain'd together three Days. The old Woman ſupplied them with Diet, and the Prince wore the Deceaſed's Linnen. Whilſt thus they gave themſelves over to all Kinds of amorous Pleaſures, his Servants were highly ſurprized at his long Abſence. Mr. *Fitztuhm* intended to impriſon the Watermen to know which Way they carried him. The firſt of which, who had negotiated the whole Matter, begg'd he would not be in the leaſt uneaſy on the Prince's Account, who he proteſted was then in a very ſafe Place, and readily offer'd to remain impriſon'd in the Palace, and to be that ſame Evening, if the Prince did not appear, de-

deliver'd into the Magiſtrate's Hands. This was the Day after the Prince had diſappear'd, whereupon Mr. *Fitztuhm* accepted of his Offer. The Waterman as willingly conſented to execute his Propoſal, as he had offer'd it, he laughed, ſung, and drank merrily: but when he ſaw the laſt Hour of the Day approach and the Prince not yet returned he was ſo mortified that he had almoſt loſt the Uſe of his Reaſon by it. He cried out inceſſantly, *Jo ſono ingannato*, *Jo ſono tradito*, I am deceiv'd, I am betray'd! At laſt he had the good Luck to ſee the Prince come in at the ſame Time that Mr. *Fitztuhm* reſolved earneſtly to ſeize him. The Waterman was ſo tranſported with Joy at this, that not being Maſter of his Paſſion, he embraced the Prince and almoſt tired him with Demonſtrations of Joy. The Prince order'd him to be preſented with ſix Zechins, which ſoon alleviated the Trouble his Maſter's Abſence had cauſed. Since this Time the Prince paid frequent and publick Viſits to his beloved Widow, whereby all the Inhabitants of Venice were informed of his tender Affection for her. Lady *Mocenigo* was heartily glad, that he was otherwiſe engaged. She jeſted with him ſometimes upon his Inconſtancy; but the Prince told her, that he was not of ſo fickle a Diſpoſition, as

ſhe

ſhe imagined him to be; that ſhe ſhould be always the Object of his Worſhip, and that he only look'd upon the Widow as a Confident, to whom he diſcloſed the Sentiments of his Heart concerning Lady *Mocenigo*. 'I am very willing, Sir, (re-
'plied the Lady *Mocenigo*) that you ſhould
'all your Life-time love me in the man-
'ner you now do, provided that you be
'ſatisfied with only declaring your Paſſion
'to your Confident.' In the mean while the Prince continued to love the Widow, and thought her Love to be equal to his. But how impenetrable is a Woman's Heart! whilſt ſhe teſtified the moſt lively and moſt tender Affection for the Prince, ſhe deceiv'd him. He happened one Day to go to her at an unuſual Hour, and the Servants, who already eſteemed him as Maſter of the Houſe, giving no Notice to their Miſtreſs of his coming, he directly went up towards the Widow's Apartment. He met upon the Stair-caſe the ſeemingly faithful old Chamber-maid, who being forbid to admit him, begg'd he would not go to her Miſtreſs's Bed-Chamber, becauſe finding herſelf ſlightly indiſpoſed, ſhe was gone to Bed to take a little Reſt. The diſordered Look of the old Woman cauſed the Prince juſtly to ſuſpect the Widow's Fidelity, and therefore haſtened to her

Cham-

Chamber, to surprize her in an Action he feared her to be too guilty of. But his Surprize was greatly increased, when he found her in the Enjoyment of a Dominican Friar's Embraces. These two Lovers were so eager in the Fruition of their Pleasures, that the Prince was at the Bed-side before they knew of his Entrance. The Widow first saw him, and cried out loud, which together with her Endeavours to push the Fryar from her, made him fall upon the Bed, in which they were mutually engaged in this amorous Combat, and when the Lady was rising, she unfortunately intangled one of her Feet in the Fryar's Gown and fell upon him. This Accident increased their Confusion. Whilst they were rising again, the Prince reproached her severely, and the Fryar content with taking his Hat and Cloak, went out holding his Breeches in his Hand. The Prince pursued and caned him so, that he cried out, *I am a Priest, and if you strike me, you shall be excommunicated*; but the more he cried the more the Prince beat him, and the poor Saint, finding no Boat to run into, leap'd into the River, and would infallibly have been drowned, had not one of the Widow's Domesticks run out to his Assistance, and saved his Life. This noble Scene well worthy of the Italian Stage, finished the

the Prince's Correſpondence with the graceleſs Widow; and the Adventure filled her with ſo much Shame and Confuſion, that ſhe ſome Days afterwards retired into a Convent, in which ſhe paſſed the remaining part of her Life, and having gained the Reputation of a pious Woman, died there ſome Years ago.

CHAP. IV.

Of the Prince's acquaintance with Trompettina, *his Intrigue with Signora* Mathei, *and a* Nun, *his departure from Venice.*

THE Treachery of a Perſon in whom the Prince had ſo greatly confided, mortified him extremely, but the Melancholy it had occaſioned in him could not obſtruct his deſire of an acquaintance with Trompettina, a Lady of pleaſure. He commonly ſupped at her Houſe with the brighteſt young perſons at Venice. Debauchery was practiſed there in the greateſt degree, which proved prejudicial to the Health of ſeveral of them, but His remained unchangable. However, though as he ſaid himſelf, he was a Don Quixote in Gallantry, yet had he but little ſucceſs there. He received ſeveral Billets, with appointments where to meet him, and went, but found they were only

only Ladies of pleasure, whose chief design was upon his purse. During the Prince's stay at the City of Venice, his faithful Waterman was of no small assistance to him, for to him was all his master's good fortune to be duly ascribed. He one Day brought his Prince a Billet, which was really writ in an exquisite Style, the Prince was therein desired to come to the assistance of an unfortunate Woman, whose passion for him was so excessive, that she despaired of her Life; among several fine expressions in this Letter were these, 'that 'the only reason why she desired to see 'him was, to tell him, that he was adored by her, that it was the only weakness 'she, that was in expectation of him, was 'guilty of, if it might be called a weakness to adore a God.' The Romantick Style of this Billet raised the Prince's curiosity to know, who writ it, but sent word in the mean while, that he should be at the appointed place. His Waterman told him, that the person, that expected him, was the Wife of a Merchant, called *Mathei*, that she lived in Mercer's street, and that he would not find a Window open to receive him, for the Lady had agreed with the Waterman to leave her House door open, and that there his Highness should meet with an obliging recep-

tion

tion from her Hands. But they were both deceived in their expectations. For Mr. *Mathei* who was to have gone to Parma, was by some affairs detained at Venice, and consequently his House-door was found shut. The Lady was at a Window, and excused herself, for not performing her promise, in a sorrowful manner. The Prince was obliged to return home, not a little dissatisfied, with having been put to so much unnecessary trouble. Some Days past after that in which he heard nothing of Mrs *Mathei.* One morning, when he was in his Bed still, Notice was brought, that a Woman, who was unwilling to discover her Name, and had her Face covered with a Veil, desired Admittance to him; he gave orders to admit her, and desired his Servants to leave him alone with her. The unknown Lady being entered, the Prince excused himself for having received her so freely, and begged of her to sit down, and let him know in what manner he could be servicable to her. The Lady having taken a Seat, sighed and addressed him in a very low tone, ' Your Highness (said she) has been pleased to give yourself the trou-
' ble of coming to my House some Days
' ago; I could not have the honour of
' giving you a reception. and am for that
' Reason come to excuse myself, and, if
' pos-

'possible, to make you amends for that 'incivility.' By this Address the Prince perceived her to be Mrs *Mathei.* He assured her of his pleasure at, and grateful Acknowledgment of the Favour she did him, and begged she would pull of her Veil, and not refuse him the satisfaction of seeing her. But he was amazed to hear Mrs *Mathei* say that nothing in the World should oblige her to pull off her Veil; that it was not the effect of any Woman's prudence, to appear in a Man's Chamber with her Face uncovered, especially when he is in Bed; That he should see her at her House after she should be convinced of the sincerity of his Love, which she assured him required more time than one Day. The Prince did his utmost to persuade her to it, but could have no other answer. She staid two Hours with him, repeating some passages out of *Tasso*, and at last left him, after having agreed to meet him at her House the next Evening. The Prince went, and found her Face covered as it was before. She conducted him to a lower Room, adorned with excellent pieces of Painting, where a Collation was served up very nicely, Mrs *Mathei* seemed extreamly glad to see him, and sung an Ode, which she said, she had made on purpose for him; But the Prince could not prevail upon her to pull

off

off her Veil. That manner of Courting not being agreeable to his Tafte, and fufpecting, that the beautiful Lady had fome fecret caufe, perhaps little for her own advantage, to be fo obftinate in perfifting to hide herfelf became very indifferent, which fhe foon perceived, and made her tremble 'I fee (faid fhe in a languifhing Tone) that 'your Will requires Compliance with it. 'Look on me then, (continued fhe lifting 'up her Vail) and give your Sentence either for my Life or Death.' The Beauty of Mrs *Mathei* furprized the Prince fo, that he could not conceal his amazement. She on the other hand faw with inexpreffible fatisfaction the fpeedy effect of her Charms, and lofing the command over her Paffion, fell about his Neck, and called him her *Caro*, her *Angelo*; in fhort fhe finifhed the affair much fooner than fhe had propofed to do, and than the Prince hoped fhe would. He continued to vifit her during the time that her Husband remained at a proper diftance: but the difficulties he was afterwards troubled with, to get into her Company, and the Natural inconftancy of his mind induced him to break off that Correfpondence, and, forfaking Mrs *Mathei*, to enter into an intrigue with a Lady who led a Monaftick Life in the Convent of ----------- to which none, but

Noble-

Noblemen's Daughters can be admitted, who enjoy numberleſs extraordinary Liberties. The Prince found himſelf reduced to a regular method of Courtſhip. The Lady obliged him to ſhew the greateſt and moſt tender fondneſs he was capable of, before ſhe admitted him to an enjoyment of the effects of all his pains. During the courſe of theſe Intrigues he paſſed whole Days at the Church of ------ at the Door of the Parlour. This raiſed a report throughout Venice of his having embraced the Roman Catholick Religion, and the Monks mentioned his Converſion as an evidenced and miraculous Fact. The pious perſons admired the goodneſs of divine Providence in having thus guided a ſtrayed Sheep to the boſom of the Church. They had almoſt made a Declaration of the pious Nun, and the reſt of Mankind, who were not of the Vulgar Opinion, knew the whole project. The Prince freely diſregarded popular Opinion, and purſuing his own way, thought of nothing but how to ſatisfy his eager deſire of pleaſure. Thus did he paſs a year and a half at Venice, enjoying the Love, Eſteem and Reſpect of all Mankind. The exceſs of Gallantry is not reckoned Criminal there, and on account of the Prince's Youth, it

was

was overlooked in him. He at last quitted that Town to take a turn through Italy.

CHAP. V.

Of the Prince's Journey to Bologne, from thence to Florence, his reception at the Grand Duke's Court, his Challenge to the Duke of Mantua, and the Duke's answer, his Journey from Florence to Sienna, and an adventure, wherin the Prince shewed his uncommon Generosity.

BOlogne was the first Town, that was honoured with the Prince's stay after his departure from Venice. The Nobility of this place, famous for obliging strangers in a manner to accept of the civilities they are fond of shewing them, honoured the Prince of Saxony in an extraordinary manner. The Pope's Legate, Cardinal *Buoncompagno*, † gave him a grand Entertainment; but all these uncommon Civilities could not detain the Prince any long while at

This Cardinal was Uncle to Cardinal Buon Compagno Arch Bishop of Bologne, in whose Presence the Electoral Prince of Saxony, since Elector, and Crowned King of Poland, professed the Faith of the Roman Catholick Church.

at Bologne, for he ſoon ſet out from thence for Florence. Here he had the pleaſure of ſeeing *Coſmus* III. Great Duke, and of contracting an inviolable Friendſhip with the Great Prince, who had eſpouſed the Siſter of the deceaſed Electors of Cologn and Bavaria. He was charm'd with the ſight of this Princeſs, whoſe Beauty rendered her the chief Ornament of the Tuſcan Court, and whoſe polite and engaging Deportment and uncommon Modeſty occaſioned all Italy to look upon and hear of her with Admiration. Pleaſure, Grandeur and the concomitants of theſe were her chief Delight; Her Spouſe and her ſelf ſtrove to procure their ſerene Gueſt the Prince of Saxony all the Diverſions that were capable of publiſhing his Dexterity and of expoſing to publick view the Splendour of their Court. Preparations were immediately made for the moſt magnificent Balls and Comedies imaginable; but theſe Diverſions the Grand Duke thought to be too private for he was deſirous of ſome, whoſe Pomp might be more ſignal. He therefore reſolved upon a Military Entertainment, at which all Perſons of eminent Births might be admitted as Actors, and all the common People as Spectators of ſo uncommon a Sight. The Prince, whom few, if any, could equal in Exerciſes of that kind, joyfully approved of the Great Duke's project, and proposed that there should be four Troops of Horse, to represent the four Monarchies, which should be commanded by the Prince of Saxony; the Great Prince, the Dukes of Mantua and Guastalla: that there should be besides four Generals, to command; and those Gentlemen, who had best exerted their Valour, should receive a Prize, the value of which should be left to the discretion of those that were to be appointed Judges; that all the Gentlemen, as well those of Florence, as Strangers, should produce some proof of their Nobility before an Offiicer of Arms, without which they should not expect Admission. Matters being thus ordered and concluded upon, the Princes and Lords employed most of their Time in giving orders for whatever seemed requisite for them to appear with Grandeur, and in putting something into their Cyphers, the Gallantry of which might relate to the objects of their Love. The Day of this Martial Exercise at last appeared. The great Duke, the Cardinal de *Medicis* his Brother, and the great Princess accompanied by several Ladies, placed themselves in those Galleries and Scaffolds that had been appointed for them. The four Commanders appeared with their Troops at the Career, followed

by

by a large Number of Horſe and Livery-men, which formed the moſt magnificent Sight, that was ever ſeen at Florence. The Prince of Saxony was at the Head of his Men: whoſe Liveries were of a white and blue Colour, being equal to thoſe of the Great Princeſs, with which he deſigned to honour her, not having had a Miſtreſs at Florence yet. The Prince's Dexterity was ſuch, as never was ſeen nor heard of. Tho' the Great Prince was the beſt Horſeman of all Italy, yet did it ſeem dubious to which of the two the Preference was due. All the Prince's Actions were accompanied with ſo agreeable a Grace, that they could not help deciding it in his Favour; and the Ladies teſtified an inexpreſſible Joy, when he had luckily run the Race. He gained the firſt Prize, and would not have failed of any of the reſt, had he not been apprehenſive of mortifying the other Gentlemen too much. The Duke of Mantua, who thought his Dexterity not inferior to any other, impatiently ſuffered the Superiority the Prince of Saxony carried over him; he happened in his envious Rage to ſlip ſome Words, by which the Cauſe of his Uneaſineſs was perceived. Theſe were the next Day reported by ſome very indiſcreet Perſon to the Prince of Saxony, who was directly in ſearch after Revenge. Soon afterwards he reſolved to write a Billet to the Duke, in which he challenged him to a Duel, and gave him his Choice of Weapons. *Rose*, † Gentleman of the Bed-Chamber carried this Challenge instantly to the directed Person. The Duke of Mantua, who did not aim at an immortal Renown for valiant Deeds, trembled at the perusal of this Billet. He told *Rose*, 'That he could not remember any 'Action by which he thus disobliged the 'Prince; that he begg'd his Pardon, and 'that rather, than fight the Duel, no sub-'missive Excuse should be thought of, that 'he was not ready to make to His High-'ness.' *Rose* answered him, 'That he be-'lieved his Master would be satisfied, if 'His Highness would write a Declaration 'and sign it with his own Hand, therein 'to acknowledge, that His most Serene 'Highness the Prince of Saxony had chal-'lenged him to a Duel; but that not trust-'ing to his own Courage, he dared not 'undertake a Combat with so valiant a 'Prince.' The Duke of Mantua embraced *Rose*, and thanked him affectionately for having invented Means to escape the Battle. He wrote a Billet conformable to those Particulars *Rose* had proposed to him, and af-

† He was before he died Lieutenant General in the Saxon Service.

ter having ſigned, he ſealed it with his own Seal. The Prince, when he ſaw this Billet, lifting up his Shoulders, 'Is it poſ-' ſible (ſaid he) that a Prince ſhould be ' guilty of ſo much Cowardice, as to ſign ' ſuch a Declaration!' In the mean Time the Duke of Mantua had ſome Reaſon to fear, that the Prince was not yet ſatisfied, took a private Poſt, and retired to the Capital of his Eſtates. Some days after this Adventure, the Prince departed from Florence, extreamly well pleaſed with the Honours he had there received. As he had been at little Expence during his Stay at this Court, becauſe the Great Duke defray'd his Charges, he gave ſplendid Preſents to all the Officers and other Servants of that Prince. He reſided ſome days at Sienna, where an Adventure happened, in which he ſo diſcover'd his uncommon Generoſity, that he drew upon him the Veneration of all that had any Pretenſions to common Honour. The Adventure was this: When he was at Florence an Abbot, Native of Sienna had mentioned a young Lady of his Kindred, as the moſt beautiful Woman in Italy, and had promiſed that on his Journey to Sienna he ſhould be bleſs'd with the Sight of her. The Prince, as ſoon as he was arrived at this Town inſiſted upon the Performance of the Abbot's Pro-

 miſe;

miſe; whereupon the Abbot conducted him the ſame Evening to the Great Church, where ſhe was waiting for the Bleſſing. The Prince found the young Perſon to be exceeding charming and conjured the Abbot to procure him a private Conference with her. The officious Prieſt directly made Anſwer, ' That the Execution of ' his Deſire was not utterly impoſſible: ' but that it would not only coſt him ' very much pains, but alſo a very large ' Sum of Money.' The Prince replied, ' That, as for the Trouble he ſhould ' eſteem it but little; and in Regard to ' the Expence, he ſhould never grudge ' that, and, provided he could but obtain ' his End, he was ready to diſburſe what- ' ever Sum ſhould be required of him.' The Abbot furniſhed with theſe ample Ingredients without Heſitation undertook the Matter; he went to the young Woman's Mother, and found her more pliable than ever he expected. This inhuman Woman conſented to ſacrifice her Daughter for a Thouſand Piſtoles, to be paid at the Delivery of the innocent Victim. The Project being thus agreed upon, ſhe ſpoke to her Daughter, whom ſhe found very unwilling to comply with her Requeſt. The young Woman was deterred from conſenting to this propoſal, not only by the Hor-

ror

ror of being expoſed to publick Diſhonour, but alſo by an Amour between her and a young Man, who had promiſed her Marriage, and of which Match her Mother refuſed her Approbation. She threw herſelf at her Mother's Feet, and conjured her not to compel her to an Action, which would infallibly cover her with Shame and Infamy. The Mother, deaf to her Intreaties, threaten'd, that if ſhe did not obey, Impriſonment in a Convent ſhould be her Fate ever afterwards. Theſe Threats made the unfortunate Daughter tremble; but her Deſpair ſuggeſted to her ſome means of preventing a Proſtitution. She hid her Intention from her Mother, and feigning to ſubmit totally to her Will, told her the Prince of Saxony might be admitted. The Abbot, well ſatisfied with this Anſwer, introduced the Prince to his Couſin. The Mother gave him a very kind Reception, but the Daughter caſt down her Eyes and ſpoke not a Word. So cold an Entertainment did not at all ſurprize the Prince, for he imputed it partly to the laſt Endeavours partly to the Mother's Preſence and of departing Virtue. He impatiently deſired to be alone with her, wherefore the Abbot and Mother left them. But how great was his Surprize, to ſee the young Woman fall down at his Knees, full

 of

of Tears, embrace them, and with a lamentable Voice intermixed with frequent Sighs and Groans conjure him to have Pity upon a young Woman of Quality, who was then by a barbarous Mother ſacrific'd to vile Intereſt! 'Great Prince, (ſaid ſhe 'to him) I am now wholly in your Pow-'er, and my only Hope is placed in your 'Generoſity; which I implore, and am 'perſuaded to be in Greatneſs not inferior 'to your Birth. Abuſe me not, I beg of 'you in the Name of God, in this miſe-'rable Condition, to which my Mother 'has reduc'd me.' A Shower of Tears interrupted her Voice; and obliged her to deſiſt. The Prince touch'd with the Miſery, which he ſaw this young Woman ſubject to, lifted her up. 'Fear nothing, 'Madam, (ſaid he when he raiſed her) I 'am ſo far from abuſing the Authority 'your Mother has given me over you, that 'I will even protect you againſt that ſame 'Mother; only tell me, what you deſire 'me to do.' A condemned Malefactor, to whom Pardon is declared at the laſt Approaches of Death, could not be ſenſible of a greater Joy, than was at this Time this virtuous young Woman. She again threw herſelf at the Prince's Feet; but was incapable of producing a Word; and continuing to embrace his Knees, ſeem'd to adore him, as her Guardian Angel; but the Prince raised her up, and after having given her Time to regain her Senses, he desired to know, why, since she refused to satisfy his Desires, she had consented to be left alone with him. She related to him all that had passed between her Mother and herself, and concealed not from him, that the Fear of being deprived of a Lover, who was very dear to her, had induced her to consent to her Mother's Orders. 'I 'pleased myself with the Hopes, Sir, '(said she) that my Miseries would touch 'you, and if I had been deceiv'd in my 'Expectation, (continued she pulling out 'a Dagger) this should have prevented my 'Infamy; for I should have plunged this 'Dagger into my Breast.' The Prince 'was astonish'd and charm'd to find so 'much Courage in a person not seventeen 'Years of Age. 'Madam, (said he) I 'admire your Beauty, and cannot but re-'spect your Virtue. I am heartily glad 'that I am capable of contributing to 'your Happiness, and shall even endeavour 'to obtain your Mother's Consent to your 'Marriage with that person to whom you 'have promised Fidelity; and fully to 'convince you of my Esteem, be not, I 'beg of you, displeased at my settling 'upon you an annual Pension of a Thou-

'fand Crowns for your Life-time.' These generous proceedings enliven'd the young Lady with Gratitude, and she gave the Prince fresh Assurances, that her Lover and she should for ever gratefully acknowledge his Munificence. 'May Heaven (said she to him) endue you with the greatest and best of its Blessings.' The Prince answer'd, that his Obligations to her for those Wishes, were exceeding great, and begg'd she would call up her Mother, and leave him alone with her. This Woman had no sooner enter'd the Room, than she was loaded with the Prince's Reproaches for the great Injury she had done her Daughter. He continued to persuade her to consent to her Daughter's Marriage, which if she refused, she must not expect him to perform the Contract, he had made with her for the payment of a Thousand Pistoles. 'You must (said he when he saw her irresolute) consent to my Demands, or else be content with being shut up in a Convent. I intend to ask that Favour of the Great Duke, and am well assured, that the Share I have in his Friendship will not suffer him to deny it me. For I tell you again, that I shall not consent to let your Daughter remain with you.' The mention of a Convent put the Mother in a Fear, equal to that, which

which ſhe had put her Daughter in before, wherefore ſhe ſubmitted to the Prince's Deſires. A Notary and the Bridegroom were directly ſent for, the Marriage-Contract was drawn and ſign'd the ſame Hour. The Prince paid the Thouſand Piſtoles to the Mother, and ſettled the promiſed Penſion upon the Daughter. This generous Act being thus ended, the Prince departed from thence for Rome.

CHAP. VI.

Of the Prince's Arrival at Rome, his Reception and Entertainments there, he gains the Affection of the High-Conſtable's Wife, ſeveral other Amours, his Voyage to Naples, from thence to Sicily, his happy Deliverance of the Ship in the latter Voyage; his Journey to Germany, his Campaign on the Rhine; his Marriage of the Princeſs of Bareith, Death of Mademoiſelle Netſch, *of the Elector of Saxony, of the Counteſs of Rochlitz, and of the new Elector's Fidelity to his Spouſe.*

THE Prince of Saxony arriv'd at Rome, the Metropolis of all the World at a Time, when it was viſited by Strangers from

from all parts to attend their Devotion and to ſatisfy their Curioſity. *Anthony Pignatelly* was then poſſeſſor of St. *Peter*'s Chair, by the Name of *Innocent* XII. The Prince paid his ſubmiſſive Reſpects to the Pope, and though he made his Appearance there as Count of Miſnia, yet did he receive Honours from the Pope equal to thoſe that are paid to a Prince. He entertain'd him a long while with an Account of his Voyages, the State of the Spaniſh Court, and the deplorable State of the Catholick Religion in Saxony. His Holineſs recommended thoſe, that adhere to the Doctrines of that Religion, and the Prince promiſed to protect them as far as it was in his power. The Pope, tranſported with Joy, embrac'd his Gueſt, and, as if he had been inſpired with a Spirit of Prophecy, 'God will 'retaliate your Virtues, (ſaid he) he will 'cauſe your Return to the Boſom of the 'True Church, and bleſs you with a long 'Series of Proſperities.' At every Ceremony in the Holy Week, the Pope gave careful Orders, that the Prince might be conveniently placed. He gave him ſplendid Preſents, and ſent every day a Cameriero d' Honore to enquire into the State of *Auguſtus*'s Health. On Corpus Chriſti day, His Holineſs perceiving the Prince at a Window of the Palace Occoramboni, gave him

him the Benediction of the Blessed Sacrament. All the Inhabitants of Rome were not a little displeased at this Action, *Pasquin* said *That His Holiness was become Lutheran, and the Prince of Saxony a Papist.* The Cardinals imitated the Pope, and remitting of their haughty Ceremonies, were eager to pay him all due Civilities. The Nobility in Imitation of their Example were no less forward in procuring him Pleasures of all Kinds. They envied each other in entertaining him, he was constantly diverted at Frescati, Tivoli and Albano. No House in Rome laid the Prince under greater Obligations for their Civilities than that of Colonna, which he also frequented more than any other. The High Constable's Lady could not boast of very great Beauty; but possessed an Air of Majesty, and so charming a Genius, that it procured her a much larger Number of Adorers, than those whom Nature has endow'd with more inchanting Attractions. She was more skilful than any other person in retaining her Lovers; and without giving any particular sign of preference to any one, amused them all with equal Hopes. Her House was at the free Use and ever ready for the Reception of all Persons of Distinction of either Sex. That free and unconstrained Behaviour once introduced by the

Lady

Lady High-Conſtable *Mary Mancini* was ſtill practiſed there. They entertained all Rome with frequent Concerts, Balls, grand Feaſts, and Diverſions of all kinds. The Prince of Saxony ſpent almoſt every Evening there; the great Pleaſure every one that frequented that Place received in the Lady High-Conſtable's Company, induced him to go thither, who was no leſs pleaſed with her delightful Converſation, than ſhe with the Delicacy of his Expreſſions. She diſcharged all her other Adorers, to have the more Leiſure to entertain herſelf with him; and was ſo little capable of hiding her Sentiments in Regard to him, that the High-Conſtable ſoon perceived them. His Jealouſy permitted him not to conſent to his Lady's further Reſidence at Rome, at leaſt not whilſt the Prince of Saxony was there; he pretended, that Affairs of ſome Importance called him to Naples with Speed, obliged the Lady to accompany him, and then retired with her to one of his Eſtates.

The Prince was eaſily comforted at the Departure of the Lady High-Conſtable, for his Sentiments for her were limited within the Bounds of a common Eſteem. His Heart was determined in Favour of Madame *Monti*, who was then reckon'd the greateſt Beauty in Rome. The Prince made

made his Addresses to her, and she gave a willing Ear to them; it is even said, that his Victory would not have been very laborious, but the Flame of his Passion was almost as suddenly extinguished as it had taken Rise, for the dull and insipid Deportment of Madame *Monti* occasioned the Loss of her Conquest.

The Prince's Heart was now at his own Disposal, roved for a considerable Time from one Beauty to another, nothing was capable of fixing it upon one amiable Object. He took no small Advantage of this Leisure-time his amorous Disposition allowed him, for he employed the greatest part of it in viewing the antient and modern Rarities, which Rome is so well known to abound with. In this Interval he acquired that exquisite Taste in Painting and Architecture, that uncommon Knowledge of Antiquity, and that solid Judgment, which enabled him to act and speak so judiciously of all the polite parts of Learning.

His Curiosity being thus fully satisfied he departed for Naples, and made as long a stay there, as was requisite to see the Rarities of a Town, whose situation renders it so singular and renowned. From thence he embarqued for Sicily, and though the Wind seemed at his Departure to favour

him,

him, yet did they undergo a horrible Tempest, which lasted five Days, and deprived the Sailors of all Care and Resolution, and the Passengers of all further Hope. The Pilot almost positive of the Impossibility of a Deliverance, tired with the hard Labour he had been at, and terrified at the Danger they were in, had left the Helm, and given up the Ship to the Mercy of the Winds and Waves. The Prince seeing the Disorder the Ship's Crew seemed to be in, undertook the Management of the Steer; and by performing the Pilot's Office during the space of a Day and a Night, had the good Luck of saving the Vessel and arriving at Palermo.

His Stay in this Place and in all Sicily was very short; but his Curiosity would not suffer him to neglect the Sight of the principal Towns, it even carried him as far as Mount Ætna, the fatal Grave of the proud Giant *Typhœus*, and the Cavern where the unmerciful *Vulcan* resides. He was at length at Messina, from whence he embarqued to pass the Streights, and landed at Reggio. He crossed Calabria, reviewed Naples, and at length returned to Rome. The Pope admitted him to two or three Visits before his Departure from thence for Venice. He was heartily glad, when he arrived at Venice, to see himself returned

turned to a Place, where he had before led ſo pleaſant a Life, and the Inhabitants of that City were overjoyed at his Preſence. He again propoſed to ſpend ſome Time there, but being informed that *Lewis* XIV had declared War againſt the Emperor *Leopold* and the whole Empire, he forſook the Pleaſures prepared for him at Venice, and undertook for his future Employment the Acquiſition of Glory. He made his Appearance at the Army, and there ſignalized that intrepid Valour, which in all Emergencies he was capable of making uſe of, and was even the Admiration of his profeſſed Enemies.

The Campaign ended, the Prince deſigned to return into Italy, but the Electreſs his Mother †, and his Brother the Elector were ſo earneſt in their Intreaties for his Return into Saxony, that he could not poſſibly refuſe them that Comfort. He paſſed in his Journey through Nuremberg and Bareith, and was in this latter Town detained by the Margrave of Brandenburg, who gave him a very ſplendid Reception. He ſaw at this Court the Princeſs *Eberhardine* Daughter of the Margrave. This Princeſs's Beauty ſeemed to

* *Ann Sophia*, Daughter of *Frederick* III. King of *Denmark*.

him

him to exceed all that he had ſeen in his Travels: He became more enamoured with her, than he had yet been with any other of his Miſtreſſes, and reſolved here to ſtop the Courſe of his roving Amours, and to ſecure the Poſſeſſion of her, which ſeemed to him the greateſt Felicity imaginable.

The Princeſs of Bareith was in Reality one of thoſe Perſons, the Sight of whom cauſes a delightful Admiration. The Fairneſs of her Complexion, and her beautiful dark-brown Hair ſet off her whole Perſon in a manner that was never ſeen, but in her. Her Features were all regular, her Face and Perſon were full of Graces and Charms. A certain Modeſty and Goodneſs of Nature rendered her Company exceeding pleaſant. All the Blame ſhe was ſubject to, was for more Gravity, than was commonly experienced in a Lady that had not yet attained the fifteenth Year of her Age.

The Prince of Saxony ſtudied to pleaſe her and when he thought his Endeavours in that Reſpect were not diſpleaſing to her, he offered her his Fidelity. The Princeſs anſwer'd, that ſhe was at the Diſpoſal of a Father and Mother, and ſhould make no Choice without their Approbation: but that ſhe would ſubmiſſively accept of the

Huſ-

Husband they should present to her. The Prince therefore applied to the Margrave and of him demanded the Princess in Marriage; she was promised to him, the Ceremony of betrothing was performed, and a little while afterwards the Nuptials were celebrated with all the Grandeur and Magnificence usual on the like Occasions.

The Prince conducted his Spouse to Dresden, where they were received by the Mother Electress and Elector with all the Marks of a most lively Tenderness. During some Months nothing was heard of but Treats and Rejoicings. The Saxons who lov'd the Prince far more than the Elector, did their utmost Endeavours to testify their Affection for him and the Joy his Return had caused.

All these publick Rejoicings were soon after changed into Sorrow; for Mademoiselle *Neitsch*, whom the Elector always lov'd with an Ardency not to be equall'd, fell sick of the Small-Pox and died. The Elector was hereat in a Despair, not to be appeased. He could not be persuaded to leave the Body of the Deceased; but continued to embrace her, and express himself in numberless affectionate Terms to her, and called Death to deliver him from a Life which was tedious to him, since the Decease of his Mistress.

Every

Every one imputed the Elector's Despair to some supernatural Cause; and as the Saxon Court of Judicature is not of an equal Opinion with the Parliament of Paris, which admits of no Sorcerers, they doubted not, but that Mademoiselle *Neitsch* had employ'd some magical Art in gaining the Elector's Love. A Report was thereupon indiustriously spread, that a Cloth dipp'd in Blood and in it a Piece of Paper, on which were writ very singular Characters, had been found under her Left Arm, and that, as soon as this Paper was taken away from her, the Elector had been pacify'd, and had recover'd his Reason, which he seem'd before to have lost. I cannot assert the Reality of this Fact, but it is very well known, that the Elector's Obstinacy in refusing to leave his Mistress, gave him the Small-Pox about five days afterwards, of which he died the seventh day. He was less regretted by his Subjects than he would have been, had any other except *Frederick-Augustus* succeeded him.

The Condition of the Countess of *Rocklitz*, Mademoiselle de *Neitsch*'s Mother may be easily imagin'd. The Prince suffer'd her not to approach the Elector during his Illness, and sent to her to demand that Prince's Seals and Jewels, which had been committed to her Care. She asked whether the

the Elector was dead, and when she was answer'd in the Negative, 'I have no other 'Master than him, (answer'd she) and no 'one shall oblige me to deliver up that, 'which his Confidence has deposited in 'my Hands.' *John-George* was no sooner expired than the Elector imprison'd the Countess, and prosecuted her according to the utmost Rigour of the Law. She was not so unfortunate, as to survive her Sentence, which was given the same day, on which she died. This Sentence condemn'd her to be drawn on a Hurdle, then to be hang'd, and her Body to be expos'd without any Burial. But the Elector mitigated the latter part of it, and permitted her Kindred to interr her. He said his Reign should not begin with putting so grievous an Affront on a noble Family.

Frederick-Augustus's Promotion to the Electorate entirely changed the Face of the Saxon Court. That Prince gave the Command of the Army to the Field-Marshal *Schoning*; the Management of the Exchequer, together with the Great Seal was given to Mr. *Beichling*, Mr. *Hauchwitz* was nominated Great Marshal; he discharged all his Brother's Officers, and retain'd no others, but those who had been faithful in the Service of the Elector his Father.

The

The Funerals of the deceaſed Elector were ſolemnized in an extraordinary pompous manner, and his Corps was carry'd to Torgau the Place appointed for the Burial of the Electors of Saxony. *Frederick-Auguſtus* was preſent at the Ceremonies of the Funeral, and ſeem'd more ſenſible of his Brother's Loſs than thoſe commonly are to whom by Right of Inheritance the Supreme Power devolves.

The new Elector liv'd in perfect Unity with the Electreſs his Spouſe; he was ador'd by her, and lov'd no other Perſon but her; and that Princeſs eſteem'd herſelf the happieſt Perſon on Earth. The Courtiers doubted not but that ſhe had for ever fix'd the inconſtant Heart of *Auguſtus* upon one Object, and even that Prince himſelf thought he had now renounced all Gallantry; but the Event proves their great Miſtake, and that his Heart was never deſign'd for Conſtancy.

CHAP. VII.

Of the Elector of Saxony's Intrigue with Mademoiselle Keſſel, *his Viſit to her, the Electreſs's Jealouſy, the happy Conſequence of it, and Mademoiſelle* Keſſel's *Marriage.*

THE Elector's Mother, who by reaſon of her eminent Birth, being Daughter of *Frederick* III. King of Denmark, was diſtinguiſhed by the Title of Royal Highneſs, had among her Attendants, a young Lady named Mademoiſelle *Keſſel.* This Lady induced the young Elector to break the Promiſe of Fidelity he had made to his Spouſe. The Chancelor *Frieſe*'s Lady gave the firſt Riſe to this Paſſion, by raiſing in the Elector a Curioſity of ſeeing and knowing Mademoiſelle *Keſſel*, by the Commendations ſhe gave him of the young Lady's Genius and Merit: This good and virtuous Woman deſigned by praiſing Mademoiſelle *Keſſel*, to perform an Act of Charity, I mean to procure her a Penſion; ſhe being born very poor, and incapable of maintaining herſelf at Court with the Salary of a Maid of Honour.

nour. The Elector had indeed before been pleafed, but never yet converfed with her.

One Day he went to pay a Vifit to the Electrefs his Mother, and met in the Anti-Chamber Mademoifelle *Keffel*; he fpent a confiderable Time in her Company, and was fo charm'd with the Excellencies of her Mind, that he inftantly felt a Paffion for her. He ftaid but a very fmall fpace of Time with the Electrefs, return'd thither the next day and proceeded thus for a whole Month. The Courtiers were of Opinion that fome Affairs of great Importance call'd him fo frequently to the Electrefs's Chamber, to afk her Advice. But during this Time he had but few Opportunities of fpeaking to his Beloved; for this virtuous Creature perceiving his Tendernefs for her, and not thinking of making any Anfwer to the Signs of it, carefully avoided him. The Elector, not willing to lofe his Time writ her the following Billet.

THO' my Regard to Madame Friefe's *Recommendations is very great, yet I beg you would not attribute to her the Two Thoufand Crowns of which I here fend you a Bill. It is to yourfelf you owe this Token of my Efteem; and be perfuaded that it is not the only Kindnefs I defign to do you. Shun me*

not

not therefore, as you have done, nor refuse me I beg of you the great Pleasure of your Conversation; perhaps, when you are better acquainted with me, you'll not continue to refuse me your Esteem, the Acquisition of which can only make me happy.

Mademoiselle *Kessel* thought it improper to answer this Billet. She desired *Fitztuhm*, the Bearer of it, to tell the Elector, that she was full of the most grateful Acknowledgment, and that she would not fail to return him Thanks for his excessive Goodness. *Fitztuhm* endeavour'd in vain to persuade her to write a Line or two; but she excused herself by saying it would look much more respectful to shew her Gratitude to the Elector by Word of Mouth. The same Evening, that Prince came to Supper to the Electress his Mother, and was met by Mademoiselle *Kessel*. 'Your 'Electoral Hignes has given me so infallible a proof of your Magnanimity, (said 'she to him) that I am dubious what 'Terms to make use of to express my 'Acknowledgment of it. Permit me, Sir, 'to shew it by a respectful Silence, and to 'be contented with wishing sincerely that 'you may for many future Years cause the 'Admiration of those that approach your 'noble Person, and be the Delight of all

'your Subjects.' —— 'The Favour I have
'done you, Madam, (reply'd the Elector)
'is so trivial, that it scarce deserves your
'Notice. I beg your Acceptance of it,
'as proceeding from one, that is desirous
'of doing Justice to your Merits, and who
'valueth his Supreme Power for no other
'Reason but because it enableth him to
'oblige you.' The Electress appearing at the same Time, this Prince was obliged to discontinue a Conversation, in which he was only engag'd to express the Sentiments of his Heart.

For two days after that he could not meet with any favourable Time to tell her some particular Things. He saw her at the Apartment of the Electress his Mother, and the more frequently he saw her, the more he became enamour'd with her. These two days seem'd to him to exceed the length of an Age. His Impatience at last induced him to consult with Mr. *Beichling* (who was at that Time his chief Confident) about the means of procuring a Meeting with the Person only, for whom he had conceiv'd so great a Tenderness. *Beichling* overjoy'd at the Confidence the Elector reposed in him, made so many Enquiries, that he was at last informed, that Mademoiselle *Kessel* was for some days to retire to a Country-Seat belonging to Madame

Friese,

Frieſe, about] two Miles Diſtance from Dreſden. The Elector went out to hunt in a Foreſt adjacent to one of Madame *Frieſe*'s Grounds, feigned to loſe his Way there with *Biechling*, and unexpectedly to find himſelf near the Houſe of Madame *Frieſe* in which was Mademoiſelle *Keſſel*; and as if Fortune delighted in favouring him, he met his dear Beauty diverting her ſelf in a long Walk before the Houſe. He alighted as ſoon as he ſaw her, and having tied his Horſe to a Tree; he ſaluted and gallantly aſk'd her whether ſhe was not apprehenſive, that ſome Gentleman acquainted with her Merits ſhould come to take her away. She anſwer'd him, That ſhe had no Reaſon to be in Fear of Adventures of that Kind; and eſpecially in Saxony, under the Reign of a Prince whoſe Subjects, in Imitation of his Example, ſcorn'd to commit any Violence. The more attentive the Elector was to her Words, the more he delighted in hearing her. He enquired after Madam *Frieſe* and was told that ſhe was alone.

When he drew nearer to her Houſe, Madame *Frieſe*, looking out of her Cloſet-Window was not a little ſurpriz'd to ſee Mademoiſelle *Keſſel* with the Elector. She ran down to meet them and begg'd of the Elector to come into her Houſe. This

Prince engaged himſelf in his beloved Lady's Company, whilſt *Beichling* was converſing with the other, or ſhe giving Orders for a Repaſt, which ſhe deſign'd to treat the Elector with. Mademoiſelle *Keſſel*'s Aſpect was more agreeable to the Prince than her Words, for ſhe accompanied all her Diſcourſes with ſo much Modeſty, that he could not help blaming her for beiug ſo little ſenſible of it. She excuſed herſelf for having given Occaſion to this Blame, by the Eſteem ſhe had for His Electoral Highneſs. ' O! (cried the E-
' lector) your Eſteem would flatter me,
' was I as indifferent as you are. Your
' Heart, Madam, is all I deſire and the
' longer you refuſe me the Affection of it,
' the more unhappy you will make me.
' How! is it offenſive to you, adorable
' *Keſſel*, to tell you, that your Merit cauſes
' my Inability of living any longer but
' for you; and that, if you pleaſe, you
' will by loving me find a ſincere Lover,
' and a ſubmiſſively reſpectful Sovereign?'
——— ' Sir, (ſaid ſhe) I cannot ſo far
' flatter myſelf as to be perſuaded, that
' Your Electoral Highneſs ſpeaks ſeriouſly.'
——— ' Yes, I proteſt before you, (reply'd the Elector in falling down at her Knees) ' that my Words expreſs the real
' Sentiments of my Heart.' Mademoiſelle

Keſſel

Keſſel lifting him up, ‘ For God's Sake, ‘ Sir, (ſaid ſhe) riſe up ; what would be ‘ Madame *Frieſe*'s Opinion of me, was ‘ ſhe to find you at my Feet ? ’ ---- ‘ She'll ‘ think, (reply'd the Elector) that I adore ‘ you, and perhaps I ſhall be more ca- ‘ pable of moving her pity than yours.’ ‘ How unjuſt (anſwer'd ſhe, changing her ‘ Colour) is Your Electoral Highneſs's ‘ Opinion of me! Could you but pene- ‘ trate my Heart, you would find it ‘ touch'd with the moſt lively Acknow- ‘ ledgment, and’ Madame *Frieſe* enter'd the Room the ſame Minute, and the Elector begun to talk of ſeveral indifferent Things. As he was in Fear of her perceiving too early the pleaſure, that detain'd him at her Houſe, he roſe up to take his Leave of her ; and having joined a large Number of Courtiers, who had been in Search after him, he could not help frequently mentioning Mademoiſelle *Keſſel*, as being far the moſt beautiful of her Sex, and they were in Reality, without being prevented by his Commendations, obliged to own, that ſhe was exceeding amiable. She was tall, beautifully brown, her Eyes were exceeding bright, and agreeably weak, her Complexion was charming and the Beauties of her Mind incomparable, tho' ſhe was a little melancholy.

Three

Three days after this meeting Mademoiselle *Kessel*, being returned to Court, the Elector had a Meeting with her, in which he told her all, that a tender and violent Love could inspire a Man of Gallantry and one subject to that Passion with. Mademoiselle *Kessel* desisted to be any longer reserved, she owned, that her Heart was sensible of his passion for her. The Elector transported with Joy thought he could not sufficiently repay an Acknowledgment, which was solely conducive towards his Happiness. He had no sooner left her, than he sent her Jewels to the Value of a Thousand Crowns, several pieces of Silk, and in short, a Collection of the most magnificent Presents. These acquir'd him that Favour, which is the greatest degree of Happiness a Lover can enjoy.

Mademoiselle *Kessel* begg'd he would conceal his Conversation with her, and told him that she had great reason to fear the Resentment of the Electress. He was desirous of drawing her away from his Mother, but she refused her Consent to that; thus was he constrained to see himself deprived of the Enjoyment of his Mistress's Company, which renders the Lover's pleasure more disagreeable. In the mean while the young Electress perceiv'd that the Elector had not so great a Regard for her as he for-

formerly had, and highly mortified at it. She endeavoured a long while to conceal her Grief, not knowing where to expect any Affiftance: but one day when the Elector's Birth was celebrated at Court, fhe faw Mademoifelle *Keffel* enter in a Drefs equal in Richnefs to that of a Queen and fhining all over with Diamonds. She eafily conjectured, that fo fplendid an Appearance could come from no other but the Elector's Hands, and unable to overcome her Jealoufy, fhe afked who had prefented her with all, that fhe faw? Mademoifelle *Keffel* was in great Confufion for want of a proper Anfwer. Her Diforder confirmed the Electrefs's Sufpicions; 'I fee '(faid fhe) from whom you received this 'magnificent Apparel: but you may be 'affured, that your Boldnefs to me to ap'pear thus in my prefence furprizes me.' Upon thefe Words fhe left her there and went to the Electrefs her Mother-in-Law to communicate her Sufpicions and Uneafinefs to her. The two Princeffes after having confulted well about the matter refolved upon examining Mademoifelle *Keffel* with all poffible Rigour. They fent for her, and after having obliged her to confefs that the Elector was enamoured with her, they reprimanded her feverely, and the Elector's Mother threatned to caufe her to be ſhut up in a Houſe of Correction. The poor Girl retired ſnedding numberleſs Tears ahd her Heart filled with Deſpair. In this Condition ſhe happen'd to meet the Elector, who preſſed her to acquaint him with the Cauſe of her Affliction. She inſtantly told him that ſhe had been ill-uſed by the two Electreſſes. The Elector went in Rage and Fury like a young Lion to the Apartment of the two Princeſſes. 'Every one (ſaid he at his Entrance) endeavours to offend me, but I ſhall make 'Uſe of proper means to render all my 'Subjects ſubmiſſive to the Perſon I love.' The Electreſſes were troubled to the very Heart and began to weep bitterly; the young one eſpecially was nearer to Deſpair; 'How! Sir, (ſaid ſhe, overwhelmed in Tears, and caſting a tender Eye upon him) 'dare you tell me that you 'love any other Perſon but me.' The Elector looking at her diſdainfully, 'Madam (ſaid he) you are a very talkative 'Woman; by whom you have been inſtructed I know not, but it would be 'far better (continued he, looking at his 'Mother,) if every one obſerved his own 'Affairs.' He was going to leave them, when he had finiſhed theſe Words, but the young Electreſs ſtopt him, and throwing herſelf at his Feet, 'Dear Sir, (ſaid

ſhe)

' ſhe) either return me your Affection, or
' eaſe me of my Life; I love and ſhall
' never ceaſe loving you.' ——— ' Pity
' your Spouſe, (ſaid at the ſame time the
Electreſs his Mother) ' remember how
' much you diſapproved of your Brother's
' Eſteem for Mademoiſelle, *Neitſch*, and
' will you imitate an Example that was
' once ſo hateful to you?' The Elector
ſenſibly touch'd with theſe Reproaches
rais'd up the Electreſs, and embracing her,
ſaid, ' Yes, Madam, I do and ever ſhall
' love you, and am now in great Deſpair
' for having cauſed this Grief in you. Tell
' me in what manner you require me to
' give you ample Satisfaction.' ---- ' Marry
' Mademoiſelle *Keſſel*, (replied the Elec-
' treſs) and remove her to a place far
' diſtant from Court for ever.' ---- ' Very
' well, (anſwered the Elector, being put
' to a Stand) you need only procure her
' a Huſband, I am not acquainted with
' any.' The Mother-Electreſs promis'd to
procure her one. The Elector anſwered
not a Word, but retired to his Chamber,
his Eyes full of Tears. A little while afterwards he ordered his Coaches to be got
ready and ſet out out for Mauritzburgh,
taking with him only *Beichling* and *Fitztuhm*, his two Favourites. Before he went
away he writ to Mademoiſelle *Keſſel*, aſk-

ing her pardon for forsaking her; and conjured her to submit to the Fate's Will, and accept of whatever Husband the Electresses should offer to her. 'This (said 'he) is the only method of preserving you 'from the incessant persecutions of the 'Electresses.' Mademoiselle *Kessel* was ready to die with Grief at the perusal of this Letter. 'O the perjured Traitor! '(cried she) yes, I will marry: but to no 'other person but him, that will have 'sufficient Courage to plunge a Dagger 'into the unfaithful Man's Breast.' At these Words she swooned away, and her Servants recovered her again with great Care and Pains. Madame *Friese* came to see her, whilst she was recovering, and officiously counsel'd her to the utmost of her power; she put her in mind of her former Innocence, Religion, and her Reputation. Mademoiselle *Kessel* submitted to her Intreaties, and though she did not forget the Injury the Elector had done her, yet she prevailed upon herself not to shew her Resentment of it. She petition'd the Mother-Electress by Madame *Einsiedel* Maid of Honour to that Princess, for Leave to retire from Court. Her Request was easily granted, and Madame *Friese*, who did not forsake her during her Distress, took her to her own House.

The

The next day the Electresses sent her several Offers, but Mademoiselle *Kessel* made Answer, That she could not make any particular Choice, but would accept of him for her Husband, whom the Elector would be pleased to nominate as such. The Electresses very much troubled sent Monsieur *Miltiz* to the Prince, desiring him to name the Person whom he designed to present with the possession of Mademoiselle *Kessel*; but the Elector refused to chuse any, and replied, That the Electresses ought to be satisfied with the Liberty he had already given them in that respect; but that he should be much obliged to them, if they would not too forcibly resist Mademoiselle *Kessel*'s Inclinations.

The Princesses little satisfied with this Answer, knew not what method to take to. The Mother-Electress went at last to Madame *Friese*, and having sent for Mademoiselle *Kessel*; 'You know, Mademoiselle, (said she) that I have always given 'you the preference to any of my other 'Attendants, and have frequently intimated, that I desired no greater Happiness, than to see you fortunately disposed 'of. You have since that time given me 'some Reasons to disapprove of your Conduct, but all those shall be buried in Oblivion, provided you will instantly chuse

'a

'a Husband. I have made several advan-
'tageous Proposals to you, but you have
'refused them all; can you think of any
'other? If you can, I comply with your
'Desire. But speak, Mademoiselle, for I
'am resolv'd not to leave you till you have
'given me a positive Answer.. Please
'not yourself with the Hopes of my Son's
'protection; for he has forsaken, and is
'resolved never to return to you. Be per-
'suaded by me, let all the Court be sen-
'sible that, though you have departed
'from the path of Virtue, yet you have
'found it again. The Electress my Daugh-
'ter in Law and I have agreed to return
'you our Esteem, and shall be so far from
'remembring what is past, that we shall
'even contribute to that Person's future
'Welfare, whose Happiness it will be to
'be chosen your Spouse.'

Mademoiselle *Kessel*, who had remained silent, and as it were petrified, during the time that the Electress had spoke to her, answered at last in a trembling Tone, That she was so little acquainted with those, that had been offer'd to her in Marriage, that she could not herself determine which to chuse, she would however make some Choice, but required a month's time to consider of it. The Electress in Fear of offending her Son dared not refuse her. 'I

'com-

'comply (ſaid ſhe) with your Requeſt;
'but if, when that time is paſt, you ſtill
'think to amuſe me, be aſſured, that I
'ſhall find ſome means of making you
'repent of your Obſtinacy.'

The ſpace of Time, that had been allowed to Mademoiſelle *Keſſel* was almoſt expired without her having yet made any Choice. She, like a ſecond *Penelope*, expected the Return of her dear *Ulyſſes*. She pleaſed herſelf with the Hope, that the Elector, who liv'd retiredly and mortally grieved, at Mauritzbourg, would at length return and deliver her from the Tyranny of the Electreſſes. Madame *Frieſe* ſeeing, that ſhe deceived herſelf with theſe vain Hopes, undertook to cure her of her fooliſh Paſſion. She ſo excellently deſcribed the ridiculous and horrible nature of it, ſpoke with ſo much Eloquence and ſo much Judgment, and gave her ſo advantageous a Character of Monſieur *Hauchwitz* Marſhal of the Field in the Elector's Service, that the young Lady was at laſt perſuaded to determine to take him for her Spouſe. Madame *Frieſe* went directly to report the News to the two Electreſſes, who were equally rejoiced at it as if ſhe had informed them of ſome Victory carried by the Elector.

The

The Mother-Electreſs was at the Expence of the Wedding, and heaped the new-marry'd Lady with Preſents and Endearments. Some days afterwards Monſieur *Hauchwitz* conducted his Lady to Wittemberg of which he was Governor. He had ſo great an Affection for her, that he gained her Love, and cauſed her to forget the Elector. This Prince returned to Dreſden, ſoon after Madam *Hauchwitz*'s Retirement from thence. Grief was eaſily perceived in his Face, but he did not in the leaſt blame the Electreſſes. Time at laſt, which blots out the Memory of all Things, cauſed the Oblivion of his Miſtreſs, and him to recover his Liberty.

CHAP. VIII.

Of the Arrival of the Counteſs of Koningſmark *at the Saxon Court, her Character, the Elector's Intrigue with her, and ſeveral Conſequences of this Amour.*

THE Elector did not long enjoy the Benefit of his Liberty, for the Heart of *Frederick-Auguſtus* was by Fate deſigned never to be free from Paſſion. A young Beauty come from the furthermoſt part of the

the North was capable of perplexing it again, and inflamed it more vehemently than it had ever been before. This was *Aurora* Countefs of Koningfmark, who to an eminent Birth joined the moft exquifite parts and all the bodily Graces imaginable. Her Size was moderate, and her Shape free and eafy. An unparallel'd Delicacy and Regularity were feen throughout the Features of her Face. Her Teeth were fo nicely placed and of fo beautiful a Colour, that they could fcarce be diftinguifhed from a Row of Pearls. Her Eyes were black, bright, full of Fire and Tendernefs. Her Hair, that was of the fame Colour fet off moft exquifitely her beautiful Complexion, where an exceeding fine Carnation was feen fparkling. Her Neck, Breaft, Arms and Hands were of a Whitenefs, whofe parallel was never feen. In a Word, Nature feemed to have exhaufted all her Charms in this Lady's Favour. To all thefe uncommon bodily perfections fhe joined as uncommon Faculties of the Mind, fhe had an engaging Addrefs, her Jefts were diverting, her Banters pleafant, fhe had lucky Sallies, a bright and lively knack either in defcribing the Character of, or ridiculing a Perfon; uncommon Ideas expreffed in an uncommon manner; was incomparably gallant; no Inftance of Generofity rosity or Disinterestednefs could be produced equal to her; she possessed a benevolent Mind, always ready to serve, and never thought herself too much troubled; no Animosity, no Spleen could ever take place in her Heart, she forgave and forgot all Offences; was humble, modest, and no way prepossessed in Favour of her extraordinary Merits. She spoke the French, Italian and German Languages as well as she did the Swedish; was not even ignorant of the Latin Tongue, and had a fortunate knack at Poetry; she loved Musick, publick Shews, Grandeur and Diversions; delineated exquisitely, was well acquainted with History, no less with Geography, and understood all the Fables and Fictions of antient Writers: In short, she was Mistress of that, which may properly be called polite Literature. The World, I presume, will be no longer surprized, that she captivated the Heart of *Frederick-Augustus.* This amorous Prince conceived instantly a great passion for her, for when his inconstant Disposition induced him to forsake her, he never lost the Regard he had at first expressed; and she was the only one of all his Mistresses, for whom he seemed to have always retained a great Esteem.

The young Countess of *Koningsmark* had quitted Sweden with her two Sisters the Coun-

Counteſſes of *Lowenhaupt* and of *Steinbock.* They were come into Germany to take poſſeſſion of an Eſtate left them by an only Brother, who died ſome Months before at Hannover. This Nobleman had depoſited conſiderable Sums of Money into the Hands of the *Laſtrops* Merchants at Hamburgh. As the Count's Treaſure had been privately carried away ſoon after his Death, his Siſters could produce no other proofs of this Depoſitum, than the frequent mention their Brother had made of it both by Words and Letters; and as ſoon, as they heard of his Death they demanded theſe Funds. The *Laſtrops* informed, that they had not the Receipt, which they had given the deceaſed Count, denied, their poſſeſſion of any other Effects belonging to him, but Diamonds to the Value of Forty Thouſand Dollars. They offered to remit theſe to the Counteſſes, provided they would prove the Death of the Count, and that he had not ſigned any Will before his Death. One of their Clerks betrayed them, and told the Counteſſes, that the *Laſtrops* had Four Hundred Thouſand Dollars, the property of the deceaſed Count of *Koningsmark.* The three Siſters applied to the Magiſtrates of Hamburg, but the Reputation of Meſſieurs *Laſtrops*, well known to every Member of the

the Senate, was far prevalent above the just Cause. The Countesses not daring to address themselves for certain good Reasons to the Directors of the Circle of Lower Saxony, went directly to Dresden to implore the Protection of the young Elector. They had been presented with Letters of Recommendation by the King and Queen of Denmark to the Mother-Electress. This Princess gave them as kind a Reception as can be imagined. She was easily acquainted with the Merit of the three Sisters, but perceived rhat *Aurora*, who was the youngest deserved the Preference; and both she and the young Electress entered into an inviolable and most affectionate Friendship with that Lady. The Elector was at the Fair of *Leipzig* when the three Sisters arrived at Dresden. At his Return he made some stay to divert himself with the Chace at Meissen, and consequently the Princesses could not make their Complaints to him till a Month after their Arrival. When he was returned to Dresden the Mother-Electress presented them to her Son. 'Behold, my 'Son, (said she) I present to you three 'Sisters of the House of *Koningsmark*, who 'are come to implore your Protection; 'of which both their Merit and Birth 'render them deserving. I join with them 'in

'in intreating you not to neglect any-
'thing, that may in the least contribute
'to their Satisfaction.'

The Elector was really amazed at the Beauty of the three Countesses; but his Eyes were instantly fixed upon *Aurora*. He made his first Address to her, and she for that Reason spoke for her Sisters. 'Your
'Electoral Highness (says she) sees three
'Sisters of the Count of *Koningsmark*,
'whom you have honoured with your
'Kindnesses, and Company in some part
'of your Travels. We are come, Great
'Sir, to implore your Assistance in pro-
'curing us Justice against some Merchants
'at Hamburgh, who undertake to deprive
'us of the Funds, which our unfortunate
'Brother has intrusted them with. Those
'that approach you are sensible of your
'great Munificence, the nature of a Re-
'fusal is utterly unknown to you: What
'may not we hope for then, we, who are
'come from the furthermost part of the
'Universe to crave your Aid?' --- 'You
'may be persuaded, Mademoiselle, (an-
'swered the Elector) that I shall see your
'Case proceeded with according to strict
'Justice; and if I am so unfortunate as
'not to succeed in my Undertaking, I
'shall resent any Injury the Senate of Ham-
'burg will dare to do you. In the mean
'while

'while I beg you would be pleaſed with
'your Siſters to reſide in my Court. I
'ſhall give proper Orders, that you may
'be ſerved according to your Merits, and
'by my own Example ſhall teach my
'Courtiers how to reſpect you.'

The young Electreſs's ſudden Entrance into the Room made an End of that particular Converſation, the Elector made ſome polite Addreſſes to the Ladies of *Lowenhaupt*, and *Steinbock*, and after that they converſed about general Matters. Every one admired the exquiſite Wit *Aurora* ſeemed to poſſeſs: She could have no Sounds round about her, but what were cauſed by the Courtiers Praiſes of her. She heard and received them with ſo noble a Modeſty, that ſhe ſeemed even not to hear them.. In regard to the Elector he was ſo affected with her Beauty and the modeſt Air, which he had obſerved as a Concomitant of all her Actions, that from that moment he conceived a great Paſſion and an extraordinary Eſteem for her.

His Impatience for an Opportunity of expreſſing his Love was extream. The next day he paid a Viſit to the Counteſſes, but could find no method of procuring a private Converſation with *Aurora*, the Counteſſes of *Lowenhaupt* and *Steinbock* being always preſent. His Eyes could not reſiſt

reſiſt his great Deſire to expreſs himſelf, and *Aurora* ſoon perceived the Effect her Perſon had upon the Heart of *Frederick-Auguſtus*. The Counteſſes of *Lowenhaupt* and *Steinbock* obſerved it no leſs than ſhe, and bantered their Siſter on that Account, after the Elector was retired. 'We are 'compared to the three Graces (ſaid jeſt- 'ing the Counteſs of *Steinbock*) nor is that 'Compariſon altogether unjuſt. It is 'however not the Prize of Beauty we are 'in ſearch of, and the *Paris* that decides 'it, ought at leaſt to wait till we deſire 'him to give his Opinion of us.' *Auróra* bluſhed at her Siſter's Railleries; ſhe looked at her and ſaid not a Word. 'You 'bluſh, dear Siſter, (replied in the ſame 'manner the Lady *Steinbock*) you ſeem 'more humble than *Venus*, in not triumph- 'ing at your Conqueſt and our Abaſe- 'ment. But when you become a little 'more proud of it, I doubt whether my 'Siſter *Lowenhaupt* and I ſhall not be as 'much perplexed at it, as were formerly 'the two Goddeſſes.' ---- 'As to that (an- 'ſwered the Counteſs of *Lowenhaupt*) I 'aſſure you, dear Siſter, that I ſhall ne- 'ver be in Competition with you for 'Beauty, and if a *Paris* was to preſent 'me with the Prize, as your Superior, I 'ſhould have but an ill Opinion of his

'Taſte

‘ Tafte and Judgment.-- I beg, Sifters, (re-
‘ plied the young Lady *Koningsmark*) you
‘ would defift fpeaking thus allegorically.
‘ What have I done, that you fhould thus
‘ infult me? Of what *Paris* do you fpeak,
‘ and what Conqueft can I boaft of?’----
‘ How! (faid Lady *Lowenhaupt*) is it not
‘ fufficient, that we give Way to you
‘ without Jealoufy, do you pretend fur-
‘ ther to oblige us to name the Perfon,
‘ who gives you fo notorious a Prefe-
‘ rence before us? By no means, Sifter,
‘ our Kindnefs fhall not extend to that
‘ degree; we cannot name, without prai-
‘ fing him, and we are feldom eager in
‘ praifing thofe that abafe us.’ --- ‘ I affure
‘ you, (anfwered the young Lady *Konings-
‘ mark*) I fhall be not a little difpleafed,
‘ and forgetting the Deference I owe you,
‘ as my eldeft Sifters, I fhall impofe you
‘ Silence.’ ------ ‘ If you are difpleafed at
‘ our Difcourfe, dear Sifter, (replied Lady
‘ *Steinbock*) you will undoubtedly filence
‘ us: But you cannot hinder us from
‘ thinking of what you have obferved no
‘ lefs, than we, I mean, the Preference
‘ the Elector has been pleas’d to give you
‘ in regard to us.’ -- ---- ‘ I know not in
‘ what you have been capable of obferving
‘ it, (anfwered Lady *Koningsmark*) for he
‘ feemed to give us all an equally gallant
‘ Re-

'Reception.' ---- 'I own he did, (replied 'Lady *Lowenhaupt*) but did he give us 'all an equally reſpectful Look?' -------- 'You are more capable of making Ob-'ſervations than I, (anſwered Lady *Koningsmark*, with a ſerious Air, by which ſhe ſhewed her Diſlike of Converſations of that kind:) 'and as you are both mar-'ried, and your Huſbands have been Lo-'vers, I ſuppoſe you have been joined 'together by the Language of the Eyes, 'I, who have never yet been enamour'd, 'cannot comprehend, that I am loved, if 'I am not told ſo by the enamoured 'Perſon.'

Some Perſons of Quality, that came to viſit the Counteſſes made an end of the Diſcourſe. They went in the Evening to the Mother-Electreſs's Court; the Elector came thither, and after having ſpoke ſome Words to the Electreſſes he went to Mademoiſelle of *Koningsmark*'s Seat, and giving himſelf over to the Violence of his Paſſion; 'I know not, Madam, (ſaid he) 'whether it will not be offenſive to tell 'you, that your Merit has ſo affected me, 'that I can no longer live, but for you, 'and ſhall be the moſt unhappy of all 'Mankind, if my Reſpect, Endeavours, 'and Homage prove diſagreeable to you.' ------- 'I pleas'd myſelf in coming hither

(an-

(answered she) 'with the Hopes of having
'nothing to boast of, but Your Electoral
'Highness's Generosity; and never ex-
'pected, that your Kindnesses should make
'me blush. I humbly beg therefore, that
'you would abstain from Discourses of that
'kind, which can only lessen my Grati-
'tude and the great Esteem I had con-
'ceived for your Person.' After this she
called her Sister, the Lady *Lowenhaupt*,
who was not far from her. 'The Elector
'is asking me some Questions (said she)
'relating to the Court of Sweden, to
'which you are more capable of return-
'ing Answers, than I.' The Confusion
and Perplexity of the Elector was such as
cannot be imagined. In the mean while,
thinking himself capable to conceal it, he
propos'd some Questions to Lady *Lowen-haupt* before he retired from thence.

When he was alone in his Chamber with
his Favourite *Beichling* he could not help
saying, 'That if ever any Person's Condition was deplorable, he was well assured,
his was. 'I adore, (said he) an ungrate-
'ful Beauty, who hates, and perhaps de-
'spises me; and believe, I shall never
'cease loving her.' Mr. *Beichling* perceived his Master's extreme Passion, assured
him, that his Fears were groundless, and
addressing him with the Freedom he had
him-

himſelf acquired: ‘ Muſt you, Sir, (ſaid he) ‘ becauſe a Lady of Quality complies not ‘ with your firſt Deſires, inſtantly begin to ‘ deſpair? By no means, Sir, Mademoiſelle ‘ of *Koningsmark*, does not at all deſerve ‘ your Blame; her Anſwer to you was ‘ ſuch, as well became a Lady of her ‘ Birth. It was the only Method of in‘ducing you to join Eſteem to your Love. ‘ What would you have ſaid, if ſhe had ‘ ſurrender'd herſelf to you at your firſt ‘ Addreſs? you would have deſpis'd, and ‘ perhaps no longer lov'd her.’ ---- ‘ No, ‘ (cried the Elector) I ſhould have loved ‘ her more, if ſuch a Thing was practi‘cable. But endeavour not to juſtify a ‘ cruel Woman; invent for me ſome means ‘ of convincing her of my Love.’

After this the Maſter and the Confident conſulted together, and the Reſult of their Conference was, that the Elector ſhould write to Mademoiſelle of *Koningsmark*, and Mr. *Beichling* ſhould carry the Billet. The Project was executed the next Day. Mr. *Beichling* went to the Counteſſes at a Time, when he knew, that Perſons of the greateſt Diſtinction at Court were there. As his Favour with his Maſter procured him a Paſſage every-where, he found it an eaſy matter to place himſelf near the Counteſs of *Koningsmark*. He converſed with her for a considerable Time about several indifferent Things, and insensibly fell into a Discourse concerning Poetry. I mentioned before, that she delighted in that Art, and compos'd Verses herself. Mr. *Beichling* happening to be very expert in that respect, as well as she, repeated her an Ode of his own Composition; and when he saw her pleased with and attentive to them, he told her, that he was utterly impatient to shew her a Copy of Verses he had made on the Elector's Amours with Mademoiselle *Kessel*; but that he could not shew them except they were together in some private place. She rose directly and retired with him to the Chamfretting of a Window. Having actually repeated some Verses he had made on that Subject, he took Occasion to mention the Elector's Passion, and gave her so lively and moving a Description of it, that Mademoiselle *Koningsmark* seemed to be moved at it. Mr. *Beichling* made use of this happy Minute to present her the Billet: She took it and having put it into her Pocket, told him he might wait for an Answer. She then returned to the Company, but a little while afterwards went to her own Chamber, and there read the Elector's Billet, the Contents of which were these:

Ma-

Madam,

IF you was in the least acquainted with my Despair, I am well assured that whatever your Aversion be to me, the natural Benevolence of your Heart would not suffer you to refuse me your Pity. Be persuaded, Madam, that no Person's Affliction can be equal to mine, in daring to declare that I adore you. Permit me to expatiate the Crime I have committed at your Feet; and since you desire to hasten my Death, refuse me not the Comfort of hearing my Sentence pronounced by your Mouth. The Condition I am in suffers me not to give you any further Account of it, believe Beichling's *Words, he is my second Self; he can truly tell you, that my Life and Death are in your Hands.*

Mademoiselle of *Koningsmark* found herself very much moved after the perusal of this Letter; she knew not what method to take, whether to be pliable or severe would more become her; that fatal Ascendant, which drew her away against her Content, occasioned her to make the following Answer:

SIR,

SIR,

IT is ſo little becoming a private Perſon, to give their Judgment concerning Sovereigns, that I know not what Means to take in Regard to Your Electoral Highneſs. We cannot eaſily condemn the Perſons we eſteem, much leſs can we deſire to haſten the End of their Lives. Judge, Sir, whether I am capable of acting thus by you, I, who join to my Eſteem, a grateful Acknowledgment and due Reſpect.

Having finiſhed this Billet ſhe returned to Mr. *Beichling*, and giving it to him, 'Here (ſaid ſhe) are the Verſes you de-'ſired to ſee. I beg you would ſhew 'em 'to no other Perſon.' She had no ſooner done this, than numberleſs Thoughts perplexed her. The Company being inconvenient to her, ſhe feigned Sickneſs, retired to her Chamber, and went to Bed, where, having reflected upon what ſhe had done ſhe blamed herſelf for it, as if it had been a Crime. 'I am overcome, 'I am conquer'd by an Inclination that 'had drawn me away to do a Thing againſt 'my own Conſent, (cried ſhe) all my Re-'ſolutions are vain and uſeleſs. I have not

'been

'been capable of refusing a Billet sent to
' me, nor of resisting my Desire to an-
' swer it: can I ever prevail upon myself
' to conceal my Passion? I must retire
' from this Place, and return into Sweden;
' and if my Sisters persist in refusing me
' that Satisfaction, to be informed of my
' Reason, I can do no otherways than ac-
' quaint them with it.' She retained this
Resolution, and passed the rest of the Day
and Night in resisting a Passion, of which
she was no longer Mistress.

Whilst she was thus afflicting herself the
Elector enjoy'd no greater Tranquillity. He
was not at all pleased with the Lady *Koningsmark*'s Billet; the Word Respect,
which ended it, perfectly shock'd him. ' It
' was that Respect, (said he to *Beichling*)
' which she thinks due to my Rank, that
' caused her to receive my Letter, and
' has procured me this cold and disagree-
' able Answer.' Some Minutes afterwards
he took the Billet and kiss'd it tenderly,
because it was writ by the Countess of *Koningsmark*'s Hand. At length, after having
for a long while tormented himself, *Beichling* prevailed upon him to rest satisfied
till the next Day and to go himself and
learn how Fortune designed to favour him.

The next Day the Lady *Koningsmark*
knowing that her Sisters were risen, desired

 them

them by a Servant to paſs the Morning in her Bed-Chamber, ſhe told them that the Air of Dreſden was ſo little agreeable to her Conſtitution, that ſhe could not help begging they would depart inſtantly; ſhe moreover inſiſted upon it, becauſe ſhe thought their Preſence at the Saxon Court would be uſeleſs, ſince the Elector could be of no further Aſſiſtance to them, than by interceeding with the Emperor to oblige the Senate of Hamburg to do them Juſtice in regard to the Treachery of the *Laſtrops.* The Counteſſes of *Lowenhaupt* and *Steinbock* were much ſurprized at their Siſter's unexpected Requeſt; they told her, that they could not be perſuaded, that the Preſervation of her Health was the motive, that induced her to remove from Dreſden, ſince ſhe had never before been indiſpos'd there; and preſſed her to confeſs the real Reaſon of ſo precipitate a Reſolution. 'Is 'it not rather, dear Siſter, (ſaid Lady '*Steinbock*) what my Siſter and I truly 'conjectur'd ſome time ago, I mean that 'you are apprehenſive of the Elector's 'Preſence?' The young Counteſs would willingly have made a Reply, ſhe was very deſirous of confeſſing ſincerely the State of her Heart; but a Torrent of Tears interrupted her Voice, and her manifeſt Grief ſufficiently explained her Mind. Her Siſters

ters ſhewed a ſincere Concern for her Trouble; they renewed their Intreaties, and begg'd of her to acquaint them with the Cauſe of her Grief. ' Force me not ' (ſaid ſhe) to tell you a Thing which I have not Strength, tho' Will enough to declare. Conſider only that Prudence will not permit a Perſon of my Age, and one, that is at her own Diſpoſal, to remain expoſed at the Head of this Court. The Counteſs of *Steinbock* ſenſibly touch'd with her Siſter's Miſery, told her that ſhe was very ready to depart from thence inſtantly; and begg'd ſhe would conceal her Grief. ' Let us, if poſſible, deſerve the ſame E-' ſteem, that has been hitherto ſhewn us by ' the Saxons.' The Counteſs of *Lowenhaupt* ſpoke not a Word. Her Heart was at no more Eaſe, than that of her Siſter Mademoiſelle *Koningsmark*; the Thought of departing from the Saxon Court entirely ſhocked her. She was entered into inviolable Engagements with the Prince of *Furſtemberg*, who was next to the Elector the moſt amiable Gentleman at Court. He was tall, graceful, his Deportment was extreamly noble, no one exceeded him in Gallantry and Politeneſs; his Taſte was exquiſite, his Expreſſions fine, and he had the happy Art of perſuading whomſoever he pleaſed: He would certainly have been

 an

an accomplifhed Gentleman, had Sincerity accompanied his bodily Graces, and had he been more fcrupulous in his Amours.

He had no fooner feen the three Counteffes make their Appearance, than he was enamoured with Mademoifelle *Koningsmark*; but his penetrating Genius foon difcovered, that the Elector's Heart was captivated by that Lady's Charms. He was too obliging a Courtier to become his Mafter's Rival; Love gave way to Reafon; and as he was not inclined to any other Lady at Court, he was enamoured with the Countefs of *Lowenhaupt*. She was well acquainted with his Merit, and they were foon united by a ftrict Alliance. Their amorous Intrigues were juft begun, when the young Lady *Koningsmark* intended to return into Sweden. The Countefs was far from confenting to her Sifter's Demands, though fhe promifed them to be at any time ready for Departure; but fhe refolved not only upon ftaying, but even upon perfuading them to ftay. Mademoifelle *Koningsmark* was more fatisfied, when her Sifters promifed to conduct her into Sweden. She rofe and was the remaining part of the Day in her Defhabille, as if fhe had been indifpofed. The Heavinefs that appeared in her Eyes, gave her a weak Air, which did not in the leaft diminifh her Charms. The Counteffes

re-

received the whole Day the usual Visits of the most polite Persons of the Court. The Elector went in the Evening to see them; at his Entrance the Countess of *Koningsmark* retired to write a Letter. He was apprehensive, that she designed to avoid him, and his Heart was in great Uneasiness about it, he was scarce capable of making his Addresses to the Ladies. The Countess of *Lowenhaupt* soon knew the State of *Augustus*'s Heart; she drew near to his Person, and in a low Tone addressed him, saying, 'You are at present shunn'd, 'Great Sir, but you would not be thus 'avoided was you an Object of Hatred.' These few Words supplied the Elector with Hope. 'How, Madam, (answered he) 'have you been informed of the Perplexities I am under? —— Your Grief is 'utterly unnecessary, Sir, (replied she) you 'are beloved, confide in me; and I shall 'be serviceable to you with the utmost of 'my Power.' Mademoiselle *Koningsmark* appeared in the Room, as soon as her Sister had ended these Words; her Presence and Lady *Lowenhaupt*'s last Words gave the Elector so great a Joy, that all the Courtiers were instantly sensible of it. The young Countess, ignorant of that Prince's Arrival, seemed to be at a Loss, whether she should see him or not; She colour-

ed, and paid him all due Refpects, without daring to look at him. 'You appear
' fo beautiful, Madam, (faid the Elector
' when he embraced her) that I cannot be-
' lieve I had any juft Caufe to fear your
' Indifpofition, at the News of which I was
' greatly troubled. I now imagine you
' defigned to make a Trial of your Friends
' by this pretended Diftemper. Can I, if
' my Conjecture proves true, be fo fortu-
' nate, as to be one of that Number? I
' dare undertake to fay, that I am deferving
' of fuch a Preferment, by the Mifery I
' have been in fince the firft Report of
' your Sicknefs. —— I am too fenfible, Sir,
' replied the Lady) of my Duty to your
' Highnefs, to prefume to place you
' among my Friends, the Perfon, whom
' I ought to refpect as my great Sovereign,
' and reverence, as the fole Protector of
' my Family. I am neverthelefs incapable
' of Ingratitude for your Electoral High-
' nefs's Pleafure to be concerned for my
' Indifpofition?

The Courtiers knowing the Elector's Delight in private Entertainments with the Ladies, and more particularly thofe, whom he was enamoured with, retired moft refpectfully. The Prince of *Furftemberg* pleafed himfelf with Lady *Lowenhaupt*'s Company, and Chancelor *Beichling* difcourfed

with

with the Counteſs of *Steinbock*, about their Differences with the *Laſtrops*.

The two Lovers in the full Enjoyment of the Liberty of diſcovering the true Sentiments of their Hearts to each other, made an advantageous Uſe of it. The Elector's Expreſſions were ſo tenderly perſuaſive, that the Counteſs of *Koningsmark* experienced the Impoſſibility of retaining the Reſolution ſhe took before to conceal her tender Affection for him. They mentioned numberleſs pleaſant Things, that were equally agreeable to both, and at laſt promiſed a conſtant Love to each other. The enamoured Lady required her Lover to acquaint no-body with their future Correſpondence, and eſpecially to hide it from the Counteſs of *Steinbock*, whoſe rigorous Virtue ſhe was very much in fear of. The Elector told her, what he had heard the Lady *Lowenhaupt* ſay, and they reſolved to repoſe all their Confidence in her. At laſt they parted extreamly ſatisfied with ſo fair an Opportunity of converſing together.

Before the Elector retired he ſpoke to the Counteſs of *Lowenhaupt*; informed her of the great Succeſs he had met with in his new Amour, and begg'd ſhe would endeavour to promote his Intereſt in that reſpect, and prevail upon Lady *Konings-*

mark.

mark to conſent to his profeſſing a publick Adoration of her. She made freſh Aſſurances of her Integrity in ſerving him, and he retired with all the Satisfaction imaginable.

The Counteſs of *Lowenhaupt* laboured ſo effectually for the Elector, that ſhe removed all her Siſter *Koningsmark*'s Doubts and Fears. She informed the Elector of the Succeſs of her Negotiation, and in a private Meeting between them aſſured him of the Infallibility of his Conqueſt: But one Objection was ſtill remaining to perplex them, which was, that he could not ſee his beloved Lady without the knowledge of Lady *Steinbock*. The Elector, who never wanted Expedients in his amorous Intrigues, told her, that ſhe muſt perſwade her Siſters to retire with her to Mauritzbourg, that he could there procure an Apartment for the Lady *Koningsmark*, in which they could converſe together, without any knowledge of the Counteſs of *Steinbock*. The Confident-Lady gave a ready Approbation of the Project, ſhe propoſed it to her enamoured Siſter, who directly made ſome Objections to it, but at laſt ſubmitted to her Siſter's Deſire and the Elector's Intreaties, who came to viſit them at the ſame time, that they were conſulting about the Journey to Mauritzbourg.

The Elector never appeared more satisfied, than at having obtained the Lady's Consent to depart from thence; and in this same Conversation they promised each other upon Oath an everlasting Affection, and the Pleasure Mademoiselle *Koningsmark*'s Company gave him was by reason of her charming Addresses so great, that, whilst he was with her, he employed all his Time in renewing all the Protestations of a most tender Passion. They at last quitted the Room, and the Lady *Koningsmark* took an affectionate Leave of her Lover, and left him the most enamoured Person on Earth.

The Countess of *Steinbock* was highly displeased at the Promise her Sisters had made to depart for Mauritzbourg. She represented to them the Injury such a Proceeding, which the Electresses were undoubtedly averse to, would do them in regard to their Friendship with those Princesses. 'Whilst I thought (said she to the 'Countess of *Koningsmark*) that you re-'ceived the Elector's Passion for you with 'a Coldness, that becomes your Birth and 'Virtue, I never made mention of it in 'your Presence; I acquiesced in your Pru-'dence: but now am sorry to find that 'you forget the Austerity you at first pro-'posed to yourself; I think, dear Sister,

'my

'my Duty obliges me to advise you of
'the Precipice you are going into. Your
'Inclinations are certainly at free liberty,
'I pretend to no Authority over you, but
'am perswaded that your Virtue guides
'your Actions, and let me conjure you
'never to resist its Injunctions. Consider
'even the Obligations you are under to
'yourself, and consider that you are going
'to sustain the irreparable Loss of the Re-
'putation you have hitherto so justly ac-
'quired. Let your former Courage and
'Vigour appear, and let us, dear Sister,
'depart from hence for Sweden; follow
'me; and fear not to undertake too au-
'stere and hard a Task: for however dif-
'ficult it may at first appear, you will
'soon afterwards find the Effects of it far
'more convenient, than the Misfortunes
'Amours are constantly subject to.'

The Countess of *Koningsmark* was instantly overwhelmed with Tears, and made no Reply to her Sister, but embraced her tenderly, and went to shut herself up in her Chamber; the Lady *Lowenhaupt* follow'd her thither, and, like a dangerous Confident, found it an easy matter to withstand and surmount all those Emotions of Virtue, which the Lady *Steinbock* had but just before rais'd in her. She represented the Elector submissive, respectful and amorous; the

the Deſpair he would be in, was ſhe to forſake him, and the juſt Cauſe he would have to complain, if, after their Promiſe to go to Mauritzburg, they were not to perform it. ‘ It is a Civility (ſaid ſhe) due ‘ from us for the Inſtances of Generoſity ‘ we have already experienced in him. ‘ My Siſter, the Lady *Steinbock*, is un- ‘ doubtedly unwilling to do it, but I ſhall ‘ do my utmoſt Endeavours to obtain her ‘ Conſent.’ Mademoiſelle *Koningsmark*, who had loſt all the Command over her Paſſion, was fully overcome by the irreſiſtible Power of Love, made but few and very weak Objections to her Siſter's Arguments, and at laſt conſented to depart for Mauritzburg.

The Counteſs of *Steinbock* was highly afflicted, when ſhe ſaw her Siſters perſevere in their fatal Reſolution, and finding herſelf incapable of diſſuading them from it, pretended Sickneſs, to excuſe her of the Journey. Before the Elector quitted Dreſden, he ſent the Lady *Koningsmark* an extraordinary rich Dreſs, with a Trimming of the choiceſt Jewels. His munificent Diſpoſition was not altogether forgetful of the Counteſſes of *Lowenhaupt* and *Steinbock*; the Preſents he ſent them were very ſplendid, though far inferior to thoſe deſigned for their Siſter Mademoiſelle *Koningsmark*.

The

The Counteſs of *Lowenhaupt* being accompanied by the moſt beautiful Ladies of the Court, dreſſ'd in *Amazones*, departed a little while after the Elector, who diverted them in an extraordinary manner. They had no ſooner made their Entrance into the Foreſt belonging to Mauritzburg, than they ſaw a Palace moſt magnificently built. The Coach ſtopp'd at this Palace, that they might have Leiſure to take a particular View of the Magnificence of this Edifice, and whilſt they were viewing it, they ſaw the Gate open on a ſudden, where *Diana* preſented herſelf, ſurrounded by her Nymphs. She addreſſed herſelf to Mademoiſelle *Koningsmark*, and, alluding to the Name of *Aurora*, invited her, as if ſhe had really been that Goddeſs, to enter the Palace, there to receive the Homages of the Wooden Deities.

The Ladies ſtepp'd out of their Chariots, and *Diana* conducted them into a large Hall, adorned with ſeveral Paintings, that repreſented that Goddeſs's chief Actions. Tender *Endymion* and raſh *Actæon*'s Death, were painted there with all the Art a Workman could be capable of. *Diana* enjoined her Nymphs to divert *Aurora* and all her Attendants. Soon afterwards the inlaid Floor open'd, and on a ſudden a Table covered with the moſt delicious

licious Sweetmeats was ſeen to riſe from out of the very Earth. The Ladies placed themſelves, and inſtantly heard the Sound of Fifes, Hautbois, and other muſical Inſtruments. At the ſame time the God *Pan* made his Apperrance, followed by the Gods of Fields and Woods; theſe were repreſented by the Elector and the moſt graceful Perſons of his Court. *Diana*, whoſe Part the Lady *Beichling* acted, invited *Pan* to ſit down by the beautiful *Aurora*. The God entertained her with the moſt delightful Diſcourſes, inſiſted preſſingly upon being ſerviceable to her, endeavoured carefully to pleaſe, and convince her of his Paſſion. They often told each other reciprocally, of the amiable Charms they poſſeſſed, of their mutual Affection, and promis'd an endleſs Continuance of the ſame.

The Repaſt being at laſt ended; they heard the Horns blow and Hounds crying as if ſome Huntſmen were near. The Ladies ran in great Surprize to the Window, and ſaw a Stag run by to eſcape the Purſuits of the Huntſmen; they were deſirous of following the Chace, and had no ſooner expreſſed their Deſire, than they ſaw ſome Horſes ready, with open Chaiſes for the Reception of thoſe that were unwilling to mount on Horſeback.

The

The Stag being at laſt ſurrounded by the Huntſmen was obliged to throw himſelf into a Pond near the Caſtle of Mauritzburg, the Hounds purſued him, and the Ladies being arrived at the Waterſide found Boats ready for their Reception, that carried them to an Iſland in the middle of the Pond. They arrived here at the Death of the Stag, and ſaw the Dogs rewarded immediately.

At the further-end of the Iſland they ſaw a magnificent Tent built after the Turkiſh manner. They enter'd it and found, that all the Furniture was no leſs Turkiſh, than the Structure of the Tent. Whilſt they were in Admiration of the Beauty of this Place, they ſaw twenty-four young Turks richly dreſs'd, who preſented them with all kinds of Refreſhments in large Silver Diſhes. Few Moments afterwards they ſaw all the Officers of the Grand Seraglio appear from another Tent; in the midſt of theſe was the Grand Signor, adorned with the moſt pretious Stones: This was the Elector, who came to join the Ladies, and having thrown a richly embroider'd Handkerchief at Mademoiſelle *Koningsmark* ſat down by her upon a Sopha. The Ladies were preſented with delicious Cakes, and as ſoon as they were ſat down, ſeveral Dancers came in, who by their

their Leaps, Poftures and Turkifh Dances diverted them for fome time. At laft the Company rofe, and the Elector handed the Lady *Koningsmark* into his Boat. The Elector, the Lady *Lowenhaupt*, and the Prince of *Furftemberg* followed her, the other Ladies took their refpective Gentlemen into their Boats. In this manner they diverted themfelves for fome time upon the Water, entertained with the harmonious Sound of a Concert of Mufick. The Company being all landed the Elector ftepp'd into an open Chaife with the Lady *Koningsmark*, furrounded by Janizaries and the great Officers of the Seraglio. The Ladies followed in feveral Chaifes, and thus they arrived at length at the Palace of Mauritzburg. The Elector conducted Mademoifelle *Koningsmark* into the Apartment defigned for her Ufe, which was furnifhed in an uncommon rich manner. The Bed was in particular furprizingly fplendid, whofe Furniture was of yellow Damafk embroider'd with Silver. It was adorned with Reprefentations of the Amours of *Aurora* and *Tithon* in feveral Compartments. Pictures of Amours fupported the Curtains in Feftoons, and feem'd to ftrew Poppies, Rofes, and Wind-Flowers upon that incomparably beautiful Bed. ' This is the Place, Madam, (faid the

' gal-

'gallant Elector) in which you are truly
'sovereign, and in which a great Lord, as
'I was, now becomes your Slave. ---- Sir,
'(replied Mademoiselle *Koningsmark*) what-
'ever Condition you present yourself in,
'you shall be ever dear to my Eyes.' The Elector kiss'd her Hand, and left her alone to change her Dress, and himself to put on another Habit. Mademoiselle *Koningsmark* dress'd herself in that Habit, which the Elector had given her, and never did her Person seem more beautiful than it did then. The Elector on the other hand, seemed by his Apparel, which was enrich'd with Diamonds and Pearls, to have taken the Pains of a Person, whose sole Endeavour is to please. When he was informed that Mademoiselle *Koningsmark* was dress'd, he went to her, and was extreamly pleased at her graceful Appearance. He conducted her to the Theatre, where *Psyche* and all her Charms were display'd.

The Comedy was no sooner ended, than Supper was ready, and Mademoiselle *Koningsmark* when she sate down to Table found upon her Napkin a Knot of Diamonds, Rubies, Emeralds and Pearls, by which she perceived, that she was the Queen of the Ball that was to follow the Supper. She did effectually open it with the Elector, and the amorous Couple drew

upon

upon themſelves the Regard and Admiration of every Spectator; every one was ſurprized with Wonder and Delight at the Sight of them; all the Ladies envied her Happineſs in the Enjoyment of ſo amiable a Lover, as the Elector, and the Gentlemen wiſh'd they were in Poſſeſſion of a Miſtreſs equal to Mademoiſelle *Koningsmark*. This great Day ended at length to the entire Satisfaction of both the Lovers, and they unexpectedly diſappeared from the Ball-Room, but no one of the Company ſeemed to obſerve their Abſence, ſince they knew very well, that they deſired to be alone. The Elector enjoy'd the moſt alluring Pleaſures with Lady *Koningsmark*, which gave him the moſt eſſential Tokens of her Tenderneſs.

This great Feaſt was during the ſpace of a Fortnight, ſucceeded by Games and Diverſions of all kinds. Dancing was more particularly practis'd, and Mademoiſelle *Koningsmark*'s Appearance was always amazing, for her Perſon was ever diſtinguiſhing among any of the reſt.

Whilſt nothing but Pleaſure was the Employment of the Noble Company of Maurzburg, the Lady *Steinbock*, highly diſpleaſed at her Siſter's Conduct, reſolved to depart from Dreſden. She pretended to have received Orders from her Spouſe

to

to return into Sweden, but the Electreſſes eaſily perceiv'd the real motive of her Departure, and thought her for that Reaſon more deſerving of their Eſteem. She writ a Letter to the Elector, in which, without making the leaſt mention of her Siſters, ſhe returned him hearty Thanks for the Civilities ſhe had received from his Hands.

This Prince, not in the leaſt dubious, but that Lady *Steinbock*'s ſo ſudden Departure would cauſe great Grief in Mademoiſelle *Koningsmark*, concealed it from her, and taking Horſe inſtantly, ran to Dreſden, in order, if poſſible, to diſſuade the Counteſs of *Steinbock* from the performance of her Reſolution; but his Precaution was unneceſſary, for he found, that ſhe was gone that ſame Morning, which ſo mortified him, that he forgot to viſit the Electreſſes. Theſe Princeſſes were informèd, that he had been at Dreſden, and extreamly grieved at his indifferent Behaviour towards them. The young Electreſs cried bitterly, and the Mother-Electreſs proteſted, that ſhe would no longer be expoſed to ſuch Affronts, but retire to the Caſtle of Lichtenberg, which had been ſettled upon her, as a Dowry. At the ſame time ſhe gave immediate Orders to prepare her Equipages.

Made-

Mademoiselle *Koningsmark*'s Grief at the Lady *Steinbock*'s Departure was excessive; but it was greatly increased, when she heard of the Injury the Elector had done to the two Princesses. She reproached him severely for his rude Deportment, and told him, that the greatest proof she expected of his Love would be a Continuation of all the Regard he had formerly had for the Electress, and of which that Princess's Virtues rendered her so deserving; she even threaten'd, that if he acted otherwise, she would directly retire from his Country; and to alleviate the Electress's Trouble, she desired he would return to Dresden, saying, that she would not occasion that Princess to be deprived of the Pleasure of seeing him. The Electress, informed of these Proceedings, was charmed at them, and renew'd her Esteem for the Lady *Koningsmark*. This Favourite has certainly always made the most surprizing Returns for that Esteem, she has always used the Electress with all the Respect and Deference imaginable, and was so far from dissuading the Elector from the Sight of that Princess, that she frequently told him, that the Loss his Spouse sustained of his Heart was so great, and that it could not but so sensibly affect her, that it was impossible to him sufficiently to comfort her in her Distress,

treſs, or to uſe her in too obliging a manner.

The Electreſs hearing of Mademoiſelle *Koningsmark*'s generous Concern for her, ſaw the Favour ſhe was in without Jealouſy. 'I am pleaſed (ſaid ſhe ſometimes) with 'having a Rival, ſince ſhe is a Perſon of 'great Merit.' The Mother-Electreſs, whoſe rigorous Virtue always ſupported in her an Enmity againſt all kinds of Gallantry, could not diſapprove of her Son's Paſſion for ſo amiable a Perſon. The two Electreſſes ſaw, and entertained her with great Familiarity. The Courtiers had a Reſpect for her, whoſe ſole Foundation was a great Eſteem: Even the Ladies could not think her an Object of Hatred. Her Modeſty, Sweetneſs of Temper and uncommon Politeneſs never forſook her; her Favour was not diſagreeable to any one, and ſhe prevented the approaching Calamities of the Unfortunate Her Memory is ſtill had in Veneration by all thoſe that knew her Merits.

The Elector being returned from Mauritzburg to Dreſden order'd a Houſe to be prepared for Mademoiſelle *Koningsmark*, lodg'd her there, and furniſh'd it very richly. A little while afterwards he prevailed upon the Canoneſſes of Quedlinburg, all Princeſſes or Counteſſes, to chuſe her

Abbeſs

Abbeſs of the Chapter. By this Promotion ſhe obtained the Title of *Madame.* The Elector ſupped with her every Evening, and gave her ſplendid Treats, of which all the Court partook. Strangers came from all parts of the World to Dreſden, and returned in full Admiration both of the enamour'd Elector, and his amiable Miſtreſs.

In the mean while Madame *Koningsmark*'s Happineſs was leſſen'd by the Departure of the Counteſs of *Lowenhaupt*, who having for a long while reſiſted her Huſband's Orders, who deſired her Return, was at laſt obliged to depart.' ' Now behold me ' in Solitude, (ſaid with a tender Air Madame *Koningsmark*, addreſſing herſelf to ' the Elector) for your Sake I renounce all ' that is moſt dear to me. How unfor- ' tunate ſhall I be, if you forſake me! ' ------- No, Madam, (cried the Elector) ' you need not fear that: I am totally ' yours for all my Life-time. Be aſſured ' thereof, and that thoſe Perfections, that ' have long ſince charmed me, and can ' only be found in you, are ſure Guards of ' my Fidelity. In you only can I find, ' that excellent and charming Mind, which ' occaſions my thinking myſelf in your ' Preſence the moſt happy Mortal on ' Earth Ceaſe therefore to harbour a

'Suspicion, that afflicts and vexes me. In
'you, my dearest Countess, I adore not
'only the most perfect Beauty; but also
'that virtuous Soul, that exalted Mind,
'that benevolent Heart; and in short, all
'those great Qualities, that distinguish you
'so advantageously among all the Women,
'that I know, and which I cannot pos-
'sibly find any-where else. ---- How ami-
'able are you, my dear Prince, (replied
'she) and how capable are you of re-
'moving the Fears of a Heart, that is
'only apprehensive because you are too
'fond of it! Preserve these Sentiments,
'they only affect my Happiness, my Joy.
'Yes, my Dear, for I can no longer
'give you any other Appellation, since
'Love banishes all Constraint, I prefer
'your Tenderness, to your Grandeur and
'Sovereign Power. I find you much
'greater by your Sentiments, than your
'Rank. You are Master of my Person,
'my Heart and my Life.' Our two
Lovers having entertained each other with
numberless more Discourses of this kind,
supped and remained together till the latter part of the Night.

They made so good a use of their Time,
that nine Months afterwards Madame *Koningsmark* was deliver'd of a Son, who was
the true Picture of his Father, whose Air,
Strength,

Strength, Behaviour and manner of thinking he ſtill poſſeſſes. The Birth of this Child rejoiced the Elector extreamly. He was denominated *Mauritz*, (*Mauritius*) in memory of the Victory, that had been gained over his Mother at *Mauritzburg*. He was afterwards honoured with the Title of Count of Saxony. This is the ſame Perſon, who by his Merit has acquired the Eſteem of all Frenchmen, for whoſe Benefit he ſerves as Lieutenant-General in a Regiment of Infantry.

The Elector did not leave his Miſtreſs during the Time of her Illneſs; he paſſed whole Days at the Bolſter of her Bed, and as her Illneſs was at firſt extream, he inceſſantly conjured the Phyſicians to take care of her, and to employ all their Art for the preſervation of her Health; but, notwithſtanding all the Pains they took, Madame *Koningsmark* retained an almoſt continual Sweat, very diſagreeable to the Senſe of Smelling, and which not even the ſtrongeſt Scent could exceed. This unfortunate Diſeaſe was inſtantly the Cauſe of an inexpreſſible Grief in the two Lovers, but it at laſt gave the Elector ſo great a Diſguſt, that by inſenſible degrees he avoided his formerly beloved Counteſs, till having entered into other Engagements, he entirely ceaſed to live with her

 as

as her Lover, but visited her daily, and always testified a very great Esteem for a Person, well deserving of it.

CHAP. IX.

Of the Elector of Saxony's Behaviour at the Imperial Army in Hungary, his Return from thence to the Court of Vienna, his Passion for the Countess d' Esterle, *her Answer, the Entertainment prepared for him at Court, his Success in his new Amour, an extraordinary Adventure at the Imperial Court by the Fallacies of a Roman Catholick Priest, the Interruption the Count d'* Esterle *gave the enamoured Couple by surprizing them in Bed together, and the Consequence of it, the Reception the Lovers met with from Madame* Koningsmark *at Dresden, the Mother-Electress's Displeasure at her Son's Passion for the Countess d'* E-sterle, *and her Retirement to Lichtenberg.*

FEW Months after the Birth of the young Prince the Court of Vienna made the Elector an Offer of the Command

mand over the Imperial Army in Hungary. This valiant Prince, who begun to ſhake off thoſe Chains, that confined him to the Company of Madame *Koningsmark*, and whoſe Love of the Female Sex after all gave way to that of Glory, almoſt innate to him, readily accepted of the Emperor's Offer, he departed for the Army, and there behaved himſelf in a manner, that perfectly anſwer'd the great Opinion all Mankind had conceived of his Courage.

When the Campaign was ended, he went to pay his Reſpects to the Emperor, by whom he was received with all the diſtinguiſhing Civilities, due to a Perſon of his Rank. Vienna was the fatal Place, at which this glorious Conqueror of the Turks was again overcome by the powerful Arms of Love, and the Counteſs *d' Eſterle* was the fatal Perſon that occaſioned the reiterated Loſs of his Liberty. His Heart in full Conformity to his Eyes, cauſed him to fix them upon her, as the moſt accompliſhed Perſon on Earth, and a Miracle of Nature. The firſt time he ſaw her was at a Ball given by the King of the Romans, Son of the Emperor. The Sight of ſo beautiful a Woman had ſo great an effect upon him, that notwithſtanding the Boldneſs he was frequently blamed for, he ſeem'd ſpeechleſs. He undertook to addrefs her, but was in fo great a Diforder, that he was at a lofs for Words to exprefs himfelf; all his Difcourfe was only a confufed Number of Words, the Senfe of which was unintelligible, nor would fhe have comprehended it had fhe had a lefs knowledge of the Language of the Eyes; for by his fhe perceived all the effects her Charms had produced in his Heart.

As the Countefs *d'Efterle* did not pretend to any referved Virtue, and defired nothing more than to hear an Expreffion of the Sentiments of his Heart, fhe retired to the Chamfretting of a Window. The Elector followed her thither, and fhe directly fpoke to him of the Grandeur of the Entertainment; but he anfwered not a Word. She thought hereupon that he was indifpofed, and prefenting him with fome Hungary-Water, 'Sir, (cried fhe) do you 'underftand me? ---- Yes, Madam, (replied he giving a doleful Sign) I underftand and fee you very well, and am as 'fenfible, as I ought to be of the Af'fiftance you are defirous of giving me. 'But Hungary-Water is not capable of 'recovering me. You have other Reme'dies, vouchfafe, I beg of you, to make 'ufe of thofe, and fuffer me to wait for 'my Cure from you, who are the only 'Caufe of my Indifpofition. -------- I am
'ig-

'ignorant (anſwered laughing the beau-
'tiful Counteſs) of any Diſeaſe, I have
'been able to infect you with, for no
'contagious Diſtemper perplexes me. I
'am moreover but little expert in the
'Uſe of Remedies. Was I however but
'acquainted with your Diſtemper, I ſhould
'with Pleaſure employ the little Know-
'ledge, I can boaſt of, to recover your
'Health, which cannot but be precious
'to all Europe. ------- If all Europe neg-
'lects me, Madam, (ſaid the Elector) and
'you will but condeſcend to have a Re-
'gard to my Concerns, I ſhall eſteem
'myſelf the happieſt of all Mankind. Yes,
'adorable Counteſs (continued he with a
'Tranſport that eaſily diſcovered his Paſ-
'ſion) my Diſeaſe is no other, than the
'moſt lively and moſt tender Affection I
'have for you. Nothing can cure me of it;
'unleſs you afford ſome Comfort to the
'Pains I undergo. I aſk my Life of you
'for no other Reaſon, but to devote it
'wholly to you, and to adore you as the
'moſt deſerving Perſon of my Admira-
'tion in the Univerſe. ----- I promiſed be-
'fore, Sir, (anſwered the Counteſs *d' E-
'ſterle*) to employ all the Remedies I have
'any Knowledge of, to procure your Re-
'covery. I am too exact in the perfor-
'mance of my Promiſes, and too faithful

'a Subject of his Imperial Majesty, not
' to return you a Health, which is cer-
' tainly very precious to him. Enjoy
' therefore your wonted Tranquility, and
' allow me sufficient time to consider upon
' what will be requisite for me to do.'

The Countess spoke so eagerly, that the King of the Romans, who came to accompany the Elector was at the distance of some Steps, when she saw him. His sudden Presence gave her not the least Disorder; for, as if she had been answering the Elector, 'I love Musick (said she) and more particularly Singing.' The King of the Romans was perswaded, that the Subject of their Discourse was no other but this; he intreated the Elector to go into an Apartment hard by, in which a grand Entertainment was prepar'd for Supper. The Table was in the Form of a Piece of Fortification; the Inside of it was hollow, in the Form of a Bason of Water, in the middle of which *Zephyrus* and *Flora*, to whom the Gods of Love presented Flowers. The four Corners of the Room were adorn'd with artificial Waterfalls of an agreeable Smell, which gave a charming Prospect, with the Light of a thousand Wax Candles upon branched Candlesticks of Crystal. At one end of the Room was a Theatre, whose Curtain

re-

represented *Psyche*, in a magnificent Palace, which *Cupid* had caused to be built for her. Laughing, playing and Diversions of all kinds surrounded her. Nothing ever appeared more beautiful, than did this young Princess: She was in short such, as was capable of increasing the Flame of Love itself. The King and Queen of the Romans, and the Elector of Saxony being seated, the Curtain was drawn, which discovered a magnificent Stage, representing the Heavens, where all the Gods were assembled. *Jupiter* presented the Council of the Deities with the Picture of the Elector of Saxony, and desired that a Stop might be put to his Life, as Mortal, and he be received among the number of the Gods. The Gods gave an universal Applause to *Jupiter*'s Proposal, and afterwards by Dancing and Singing shew'd their Joy at the Resolution that had been taken.

After Supper, whilst the Tables were removing, the Court approaching towards the Window saw an excellent Firework display'd. After this the Ball was open'd, and this grand Entertainment was not ended till the next Morning, after Sunrising.

The Elector would have been exceedingly well satisfy'd with this Feast, had he been capable of finding means of continuing the Difcourfe he had begun with Madame *d' Efterle*, but fhe fhunn'd his Addreffes; for though fhe did not pretend to oblige any one to be a long while in purfuit of her, yet would fhe keep at a fufficient Diftance to lay the Perfon under an Obligation, to whom fhe furrender'd herfelf.

Two Days paffed in which the Elector could not fee his beloved Lady. He met with her at the Apartment of the Queen of the Romans, but could not converfe with her, becaufe, as was before obferved, fhe kept at a Diftance from him. At laft the King of the Romans happened to come in and propofe to the Queen and Elector to play at Cards. Madame *d' Efterle* was defired to make a Party, and was by Chance placed next to the Elector. The Prince was careful not to lofe a moment, but ufing numberlefs fhort and gallant Expreffions, in as low a Tone as poffibly he could. He was obliged for that purpofe to take Snuff, and frequently to make ufe of his Handkerchief to hide the motion of his Lips when he fpoke to her. He did not look at her, being in Fear, that the Count *d' Efterle*, who, as Chamberlain in waiting, ftood behind the King's Chair of State, fhould perceive his Paffion: but he ceafed not however in that manner to tell

her

her that he adored her, that all the Recompence he was desirous of was a Permission to serve her with a Deference due to the Gods, and that his Disinterestedness deserved some kind Return. Tho' she feigned not to understand, yet did she comprehend his Expressions very well. The Elector's Eagerness in speaking to her was such, that he did not at several times regard nor hear the Queen's Words, when her Majesty spoke to him. The Countess was charmed with the Elector's Addresses, but made very few Answers, fearful of being observed by the Queen of the Romans and the Count *d' Esterle*. The few Words however, that she spoke, signified to him, that nothing should be wanting as to her part, if she could soon compleat his Felicity.

The next Morning the Elector, who was desirous of seeing her persevere in her Resolution, writ to his Dear whatever Words his Heart inspired him with, as a Person enamoured to a great degree, and pleased with the Hope of not being despised. As a certain inexpressible Delicacy and Vivacity accompanied all his Thoughts, so were they expressed in Terms so choice, so natural, and so noble, that his Mind was no less inchanting than his Person. He was ready to die for Impatience for the

happy

happy Hour in which ſhe would give him Leave to pay her a private Viſit; he begg'd this Favour of her, and to render his Intreaties more effectual, encloſed in the Billet a pair of Ear-Rings to the Value of Forty Thouſand Florins. The golden Shower had not a more ſeducing effect upon the Heart of *Danae*, than the Ear-Rings had upon that of Madame *d'Eſterle*. All the Arguments, that oppoſed her Inclination to ſurrender herſelf, inſtantly vaniſhed, and to be deficient in her Acknowledgment to ſo generous a Prince, was in her Opinion the only Fault ſhe could commit. She anſwered him in Terms that required no Explanation, and gave him Notice, that ſhe ſhould expect him at Eight o'Clock at Night.

The Elector waited upon her at the expected Hour. He found the Counteſs lying negligently upon a Couch of Gold Brocade, in an Apartment where nothing was ſeen but Gold, Paintings, and rich Brocades: it ſeemed to be the Dwelling-place of the Mother of *Cupid*. Madame *d' Eſterle* was charming. Her Hair, that were of the moſt lively Colour, that ever was ſeen, fell in Buckle upon her Shoulders, and were tied up with green Ribbons. Her Dreſs was of Roſy-Colour mixed with Silver, ſet off with Flowers, that

that truly imitated natural ones. A rich Lace added to the natural Beauty of her Neck and Breaſt; her red and white Complexion might be compared to a Parcel of Roſes and Lillies joined together. She ſeemed to be in great Diſorder at the Elector's Arrival, either through Fear or Joy; which was no ſmall Addition to thoſe Graces ſhe naturally poſſeſſed. The Prince look'd at her with a certain Pleaſure, a Deſcription of which I ſhould find as impracticable, as of all that paſſed between the two happy Lovers. It is certain that the Elector was ſo well ſatisfied with his Viſit, that when he retired from her, he ſpent the beſt part of his time in thinking of her.

In theſe delightful Thoughts he had employed the greateſt part of the Night, and begun to take a little Reſt in the Morning, when he was informed, that the King of the Romans was deſirous of his Company in his Apartment. He aroſe inſtantly and waited upon the King. But how great was his Surprize, when he ſaw that Prince, whom he had before left in a perfect ſtate of Health, at preſent lying in his Bed pale, waſted, and in the poſture of a Man, deprived of the right uſe of his Senſes! 'Good God! (cried the Elector) what do 'I ſee, and what has befel your Majeſty?

'The

‘ The moſt cruel of all Adventures, (an-
‘ ſwered the King of the Romans) I am
‘ threaten’d with a ſudden Death, but
‘ what perplexes me moſt, is, that you
‘ are to undergo a more terrible Fate. ---
‘ What frightful Dream (ſaid the Elector)
‘ has diſturbed your Reſt, and what un-
‘ fortunate Reaſon have you, Great Sir,
‘ to foreſee a Thing of ſuch Incertainty ?
‘ ---- Sit down a little while (replied the
‘ King) my dear Couſin, hear me, and
‘ you will perhaps after having given Ear
‘ to my Narrative have as great Reaſon to
‘ be in fear, as I at preſent have.’ The
Elector being ſeated, the King related the
Subject of his preſent Miſery. ‘ I have,
‘ ſaid he) had a more frightful Appari-
‘ tion this Night, than perhaps ever any
‘ Mortal has been ſenſible of. Two Hours
‘ after I had begun to take my laſt Night’s
‘ Reſt, I heard my Chamber-door open
‘ and ſome-body enter. Suppoſing the
‘ Perſon to be one of the Gentlemen of
‘ my Bed-Chamber, I mutter’d at their
‘ diſturbing me in the Night. But judge
‘ how great my Surprize muſt have been,
‘ when I heard a great Noiſe of Chains.
‘ I look’d out and ſaw a Ghoſt all over
‘ white, which in a dreadful Tone ſaid :
*Joſeph, King of the Romans, I am a Soul,
that now undergoes the Pains of Purgatory !*
I

I am come by Order of the Gods to ſeek for thee, to give thee Notice of the Precipice, that is ready for thy Deſtruction, by reaſon of thy Alliance with the Elector of Saxony. Deprive him of all Pretenſions to thy Friendſhip, and do thou renounce his or prepare thyſelf for eternal Damnation. ‘ Here the Noiſe of ‘ Chains was increaſed, and as the Fright ‘ had render'd me ſpeechleſs, the Appari- ‘ tion repeated his Threats, and ſaid : *Doſt thou not think fit to anſwer me, Joſeph? Art thou ſo unfortunate, as wilfully to reſiſt God? and is the Friendſhip of a human Creature more dear to thee, than his, to whom thou art beholden for every thing? I give thee Leiſure to form what Reſolution will ſeem beſt to thee. In three Days I ſhall return for thy Anſwer; and if thou doſt perſiſt in converſing with the Elector of Saxony, both thy Ruin and his will be inevitable.* ‘ At theſe Words ‘ the Ghoſt diſappeared, and left me, I ‘ aſſure you, in a ſtrong Uneaſineſs. I ‘ had not ſufficient Strength to cry out, ‘ and the firſt Gentleman of my Bed- ‘ Chamber found me thus terrified by this ‘ uncommon Adventure. I am a little ‘ more eaſy, ſince I have taken a Reſolu- ‘ tion to change the Courſe of my Life. ‘ I hope to receive Pardon for my Sins. ‘ You, my dear Couſin, are the only Per- ‘ ſon I am in a deep Concern for; where-

‘ fore

'fore let me conjure you to embrace our
'most holy Religion, and with me to me-
'rit everlasting Life.'

The Elector had heard the King of the Romans with Attention; but could not at last contain himself from saying: 'Are
'you positive, Sir, that you was awake,
'and was it not rather a Dream of which
'your Majesty has still retained an Im-
'pression?' The King assured him, that he did not sleep, and protested that no part of his Relation was the effect of a Dream. 'Then I cannot comprehend it,
'(cried the Elector) for no Person shall
'be capable of perswading me, that an
'Apparition should appear in, or carry
'Chains. I cannot however imagine that
'any Person can be guilty of so much
'Rashness as to impose upon your Ma-
'jesty in this manner. --- How could they?
'(answer'd the King) is there any Proba-
'bility of an Imposition? Who would
'dare to make use of such a Deceit upon
'me? ------ What can we say after all?
'(said the Elector) you have Priests about
'you, Sir, that are not only able but
'even fertile in Frauds; their Power at
'this Court is great. They imagine per-
'haps that when I have the Honour of
'conversing with your Majesty, I make
'Religion the Subject of our Discourse,
'and

'and then expoſe their Impoſtures. Per-'mit me, Sir, to aſk Your Majeſty, 'whether your Father-Confeſſor has not 'given Riſe to ſeveral Scruples in you 'upon the Honour you do me of your 'Friendſhip?' The King owned, that his Confeſſor had threaten'd him with a Refuſal of the Abſolution, if he continued to converſe with the Elector. 'Since I 'find the Caſe to be ſo, (replied the E-'lector) we ſhall ſoon diſcover the Appa-'rition. I beg, Sir, you would give me 'Leave to undertake the Care of ſo im-'portant a matter. I will be reſponſible 'for the Event, provided your Majeſty 'will promiſe to continue your uſual Good-'neſs to me, and let no-body know that I 'am acquainted with the Adventure.' The King promis'd to keep the Secret, and the Elector to be the better aſſured of his Fidelity ſtaid with him; at Bed-time he went to his own Chamber, was un-dreſs'd, and went to the King by a private Door.

The third Night the King of the Romans and the Elector heard a Motion of Chains, and a Voice, that ſaid, *Joſeph, King of the Romans!* The Elector would not hear any more, but leap'd out of Bed, and ſeiz'd the pretended Ghoſt, who was on the other hand in a much greater Fright,

than

than the King of the Romans had before been in, cried *Jesu Maria!* and upon his Knees begg'd his Life, and said he was a Prieſt, but the Elector, deaf to his Cries, carried him to the Window, and throwing him down, *Go*, (ſaid he) *return to the Purgatory from whence you came.* But the pretended Apparition's laſt Hour ſeemed not to be come yet, for though he fell from a high Room, yet did he only break one of his Thighs. He was very deſirous of concealing his Adventure from the Knowledge of the Common People, but could not reſiſt the Pain; for he cried out for Aſſiſtance, the Guard came up to him, and he was known to be Aſſiſtant to the King's Father-Confeſſor. This Prince was greatly diſpleaſed at having been thus highly impos'd upon, he ſwore he would one day baniſh all the Jeſuits from his Country: but after he was informed by whoſe Perſwaſions the Prieſts executed this Project, he pardon'd them, and forbid any further mention of the Adventure.

Whilſt this Affair was tranſacted at Court the Elector was deprived of the Sight of his dear Counteſs, and ſhe, ignorant of the Cauſe of his Abſence, ſuſpected him guilty of Infidelity. She was even ſo impatient, that ſhe could not wait for an Opportunity of ſpeaking to him, but writ a Billet in which

which ſhe deſired him to come to her. The Elector, no leſs impatient than ſhe, waited upon her. She was in a rich Deſhabille; her Head-dreſs, though it ſeem'd to have been put on with a careleſs Air, was very genteel; ſhe carried the Elector's Picture in her Bracelet. In this Dreſs ſhe received the Prince. When he enter'd the Lady was playing upon a Spinet and ſinging a doleful Tune. She no ſooner ſaw him than her Eyes were overwhelmed with Tears; ſhe remained, as it were deſtitute of Motion in her Chair. The Elector, ſurprized to ſee her in that Condition, deſired to know the Cauſe of it. 'How dare you 'ſaid ſhe ſighing) deſire to know the Sub-'ject of my Grief? does not your Heart 'check you for being the occaſion of it? 'have I not ſufficient Reaſon to ſhed theſe 'Tears, when I conſider, that another 'Perſon has been capable of robbing me 'of your Tenderneſs, and thoſe Moments 'you are come to ſpend here are only ſtol-'len from her, and which you think you 'cannot yet refuſe me.' The Elector ſenſibly touched with her Reproaches, threw himſelf at her Feet, took hold of her hands and ſqueez'd them between his, kiſs'd them inceſſantly, and aſſured her upon Oath, that he had no Object of Love but her. 'Do you love me (ſaid ſhe looking on

him

'him tenderly) and can you leave me 'three Days without giving any Assu- 'rances of your Love!' The Elector related to her the Adventure that happen'd at the King's, which Relation, together with the Assurances he gave her of his Love and Fidelity, appeas'd the Countess, and renewed her former pleasant Humour. As she was naturally very hot in her Passions, she fell about his Neck, embraced, kissed, and addressed him often with the Appellation of her Dear and Adorable Prince. The Elector, who was never backward with his Mistresses in Tokens of Tenderness, gave the Countess most lively ones. She could not prevail upon herself to let him go, and though he had promis'd to sup with the King of the Romans at the House of Mademoiselle *Palsi* his Mistress, she obliged him to break his Promise and to sup with her. The Elector consented to it, provided she would let him spend the whole Night with her, which the Lady did not refuse, and he thereupon occupied the Place of the Count *d' Esterle*, who by the Advice of the Physicians had not lain with her for a considerable time. ---- Our Lovers had so many agreeable Subjects to discourse upon, that Day-light surprized them before they had slept a Minute, at last they fell asleep, and had not awaked at

Ten

Ten o'Clock had not the Count *d'Esterle* diſturbed their happy Repoſe. This Nobleman having ſome Buſineſs to conſult with his Lady, went to her Bed-Chamber. As the Chamber-door was ſhut he opened it ſoftly, and walked along very ſlowly, intending to have the Pleaſure of ſurprizing her; but he was ſorry to find the Reverſe, for he was himſelf greatly ſurprized, when approaching to the Bed, he there ſaw the Elector reſting on the Counteſs's Arms, and his Head leaning upon her Breaſt. O thou perfidious Wretch! (cried he) and inſtantly awaked the two Lovers. The Elector leap'd out of the Bed, took hold of his Sword and ſo frightened the Count, that he ran away and left the two Lovers in great Confuſion at their unexpected hard Fate. ------- The Counteſs was in great Deſpair, not knowing what to do, and very apprehenſive of her Spouſe's Reſentment. The Elector who knew that her Fear was not ill-grounded, begun to invent ſome method to ſecure the Counteſs from any Abuſe, and could think of none better, than to take her to the Houſe of his Envoy, which the Law of Nations renders a ſafe and privileged Place. The Counteſs objected ſome Difficulties, but the Elector repreſented to her, that their private Familiarity had reached the Knowledge of a Per-

Perſon, that ought to be moſt ignorant of it, and that, ſince the effects of his Reſentment would in all probability be dreadful, ſhe ought no longer to heſitate about the matter. She at laſt conſented to it, and having taken a Box, in which were her Jewels, ſtepp'd into a Hackney-Coach, and the Prince conducted her to the Houſe of his Envoy, and recommended her to him as a Depoſitum, that was extreamly dear to him. --- Whilſt Madame *d' Eſterle* was abſent from her Huſband, the unfortunate Gentleman was in the Emperor's Anti-Chamber; there he expos'd his Shame, and publiſhed his Deſpair. His Friends afforded him what Comfort they were capable of, in telling him that he had no reaſon to be ſo highly afflicted at ſo trifling a matter. They quoted Inſtances from the Fictions of the Poets and both antient and modern Hiſtory. ' *Amphytrio*
' (ſaid they) was in a Rage, no ways in-
' ferior to yours at preſent, at his Wife
' *Alcmena*'s perfidious Behaviour, but in-
' ſtantly pacified when told that *Jupiter*
' himſelf had been his Rival. How many
' Huſbands do we read of in the Ro-
' man Hiſtories, who willingly gave up
' their Wives to the Emperors? In France
' Mr. *Monteſpan* deliver'd his to *Lewis* XIV;
' and in England, where the Royal Power
' is

'is more limited, numberleſs Huſbands
'ſuffered King *Charles* II. to converſe with
'their Wives. ---- All the Arguments you
'have advanced (replied innocently the
'Count *d'Eſterle*) are both true and pre-
'vailing, but *Amphitryo* ſubmitted to the
'Pleaſure of a God, and the Others to
'that of their Sovereigns. -------Very well,
(anſwered the Count of *Martinitz*, who was
at that time Ambaſſador from his Imperial
Majeſty to Rome) 'that you may imitate
'the Examples of thoſe Huſbands we men-
'tioned to you, enter into the Elector of
'Saxony's Service; and he may lye with
'your Wife without your being obſtructed
'by any Perſon on that Account.' The
whole Aſſembly gave a general Applauſe
of this Advice, and the Count *d' Eſterle*
was ſo well pleas'd with it, that he went
directly to Mr. *Beichling*, and deſired his
Intereſt in procuring him ſome Office under the Elector.

This Prince was in great Surprize when
Mr. *Beichling* delivered the unexpected
Meſſage; he thought that it was a Whim
of his own, but the Favourite proteſted,
that the Count *d' Eſterle*'s Intreaties had
induced him to petition his Highneſs for
that Favour. The Elector by a Billet directly acquainted the Counteſs with it, and
deſired to have her Advice about the matter.

ter. She anſwered, that ſhe begg'd his Electoral Highneſs would not take the Count *d'Eſterle* into his Service; but allow him a Penſion upon the Conditions ſhe would require of him. The Elector told her, that he left the management of that matter entirely to her Diſcretion, and that he would allow the Count Twenty Thouſand Florins as a Preſent. Hereupon the Counteſs obliged her Huſband to ſign the following Treaty, which ſhe compos'd herſelf:

I. *That he ſhould conſent to her Return to her former Apartment.*

II. *That he ſhould never mention what was paſſed in her Preſence.*

III. *That he ſhould renounce all the Right of a Husband, and no longer live with her.*

IV. *That ſhe ſhould be at liberty to ſet out on what Journey ſhe ſhould judge convenient.*

V. *That he ſhould come in his Coach to fetch her from the Houſe of Mr.* Gerſtorff, *Envoy of Saxony, and conduct her to his own Houſe.*

She

She would have begun these with an Article, That her Husband should ask her Pardon in the Presence of Mr. *Gerstorff* and his Lady for daring to surprize her, but Mr. *Beichling* pitied the poor Count, interceded for him, and prevailed with her to mitigate the Articles by omitting that, but he added, *That the Count* d' Esterle *should acknowledge those Children to be his of which his Wife should after that be deliver'd, and that both the Sons and Daughters should have the Name and bear the Arms of* Esterle. This Treaty was signed by both Parties, and every Particular of it was rigorously observed. The Elector related the whole Matter to the King of the Romans, who was very much diverted with it, and from that time the Countess *d' Esterle* passed publickly for the Mistress of the Elector. That Prince, the King of the Romans, Mademoiselle *Palfi*, and Madame *d' Esterle* supp'd together frequently by several Turns. At one of these Meetings the King by a promissory Note laid himself under an Obligation, if he had any Daughters, to marry the eldest to the Electoral Prince of Saxony. By virtue of this Note that Prince did obtain the eldest Archdutchess of the Emperor *Joseph*, to the Prejudice of the Elector of Bavaria his Rival.

The new Amour of the Elector being known at Dresden, Madame *Koningsmark* willingly gave up her Place, she instantly thought of a Retreat, but an honourable one, and one that could be expected of none, but a Person of her Prudence and Conduct. The Publick thought she designed to go to her Abbey, or to return into Sweden; but she acted more wisely, for she staid at Dresden to see the Elector and her new Rival make their Appearance. She did not in the least reproach the Lover, and received his Mistress with uncommon Civility. By these means she preserved a Reputation sufficient to retain the Veneration of the Courtiers, who were all extreamly concerned for her, and highly troubled at her Disgrace. She experienced more, than perhaps ever any Mistress did before her: She retained the Friendship of many, and knew no Enemy, whilst she was out of Favour. — Madame *d'Esterle* had not so excellent a knack at procuring the publick Affection and Esteem. This Favourite was haughty, revengeful, her Sincerity in Friendship equall'd that in Love; Interest had the first place in all her Undertakings; she had a large number of Followers, whom she sacrificed one to the other, but always to her own Profit; her Expences were excessive,

and

and no Miſtreſs ever prov'd more expenſive to *Frederick-Auguſtus*.

The Electreſs gave no ſign of a Diſpleaſure at her Arrival, and when Madame *Brandſtein* told her that the Elector deſired ſhe would ſuffer the Counteſs *d'Eſterle* to viſit her, 'The Elector is the Maſter, '(anſwered ſhe) let him bring to me 'whomſoever he will.' But though this Princeſs ſo prudently concealed her Uneaſineſs, yet did ſhe reſolve never to converſe with the Elector again, except in a publick manner. Which Reſolution ſhe carefully obſerved, and when the Elector expreſſed a Deſire of performing his nuptial Duties, ſhe always had ſome pretence, to excuſe herſelf.

The Mother-Electreſs refuſed abſolutely to receive the Counteſs *d' Eſterle*, ſhe refuſed it in a manner, that ſeemed very inſolent to that Lady, and as little obliging to the Elector. She then put her former Intention of retiring to Lichtenberg in execution, and took with her the young Prince her Grandſon, who lately ſucceeded his Father, and educated him with a Care, that teſtified an extream Tenderneſs.

CHAP. X.

Auguſtus *is choſen King of Poland, and crowned at Cracow, his Conſtancy to the Counteſs* d' Eſterle, *her Infidelity, and Baniſhment from Warſaw, ſhe cheats the King of his Jewels, he is enamoured with* Fatima *a young Turkiſh Lady, the event of this Amour. The King is again enamoured with the Princeſs* Lubomirſki, *he ſucceeds in this Amour, and being afterwards tired with her, entered into Engagements with the Lady* Hoyhm, *who is divorced from her Husband, the King is oppoſed by the Cardinal-Primate, and the King of Sweden advances with an Army towards Poland.*

THE Heart of *Frederick-Auguſtus* was not ſufficiently employed in amorous Intrigues, to neglect the Care of Glory. *John Sobiesky* King of Poland's Deceaſe gave the Elector of Saxony Hopes of ſucceeding him. His Competitors were indeed great and renowned Men, but equalled by him

him in Merit, and exceeded in Riches and Power. He did not want for Men that favoured his Party in Poland, and among the rest *Brebendorfsky* Governor of Culm, who had married the Daughter of Count *Fleming* Field-Marshal in the Service of the Elector of Brandenburg, and formerly Field-Marshal in Saxony, promoted his Interest. The Elector sent the Chevalier *Fleming*, Cousin-German to that Palatine's Lady, to him. ——— Whilst *Fleming* was making all necessary Preparations for his Embassy, the Elector changed his Religion privately in the Presence of the Prince of *Sax-Zeitz*, Bishop of Javarin. It is well known what passed in Poland at that Election of a King; that the Cardinal *Radziowsky* chose the Prince of *Conti*, and the Bishop of *Cujavia* proclaimed *Frederick-Augustus* Elector of Saxony, who at last was chose to the Prejudice of his Rival.

This Prince having received the Diploma of his Election departed for Cracow, where he was crown'd with Royal Splendor. The Countess *d'Esterle* accompanied him thither, and her Lover's Coronation was a kind of Triumph for her. She saw the Ceremony in a Gallery that was built on purpose for her, and made her Appearance there, shining all over with Jewels. It was observed, that when the King drew nearer to the Offertory, he looked at his Miſtreſs, as if he was deſirous of ſaying, that ſhe was the Perſon to whom he offer'd the Incenſe and his Heart. The greateſt part of the Polanders, being extreamly ſuperſtitious were highly diſpleas'd at it, and dubious of their new King's Sincerity in regard to his Religion.

The Ceremony of the Coronation being ended, the King and his Miſtreſs went to Cracow, where the new Sovereign receiv-ed the Homages of the Palatinates. The Nobility eager to pleaſe him, honour'd him even in his Miſtreſs. Madame *d' Eſterle* became ſo proud of the Deference ſhe was uſed with, that ſhe was unmindful of any Perſon, except thoſe, that had obtained her Favour.

Of this number was the Chevalier *Flemming*. This Gentleman made his future Proſperity his only Aim; and though the King had declared him Marſhal of the Field in his Army to the Prejudice of Officers ſuperior to him in Age and Experience, yet did he endeavour to procure more Employments. His Couſin Madame *Brebentau*, advis'd him to engage himſelf with the Counteſs *d' Eſterle*, and if poſſible to gain her tender Affection. Mr. *Flemming* repreſented to her, that to deprive his King of his Miſtreſs's Heart would ſhew a

want

want of Fidelity and Acknowledgment to his great Benefactor; she objected, that those, that always strictly regard Decency, could never make any great Advances in the Road to Fortune, that she should never be accessary to his betraying his King; but that she could not look upon him, as guilty of a criminal Action, if he partook with him in the Favours of a Mistress, who was more beloved, than esteemed, for whom the King would not long retain an equal Passion, and whom he would one day see with Indifference in another's Arms. Mr. *Flemming*, who was by nature of an easy Disposition and quickly to be persuaded, followed his Cousin's Advice, made his Addresses to Madame *d'Esterle*, and met with a favourable Reception. She undertook to make his Fortune, and the King, in regard to her Recommendation, made him Lieutenant-General, Minister of State to the Privy-Council, and chief Master of the Horse over all Lithuania. Mr. *Flemming* adapted himself in every respect to the King's Temper, and his Majesty accustomed himself on the other hand so much to his Favourite's submissive and complaisant Deportment, that he could scarce live without him. —— Mr. *Flemming* behaved himself with so much Caution, that the King never suspected him to be his Rival; and had Madame *d'Esterle* been as prudent as he, ſhe would in all probability have retained the King's Favour, who admired in his Miſtreſſes that haughty Carriage, and has always given the Preference before thoſe, that had an outward ſhew of Modeſty, to Women of that Character. Madam *d'Eſterle* looking upon the King's Favour, as an Inheritance of which ſhe had acquired an everlaſting Poſſeſſion, acted ſo very raſhly, that the King at laſt diſcovered her Infidelity; but as his great and paſſionate Love would not ſuffer him to rid himſelf of her at once, he reſolved to diſſemble with her, till at laſt he ſurprized her with the Prince *Wieſnowisky*. He was in a very great Rage, when he ſaw her, but did not in the leaſt reproach his vile and abuſive Miſtreſs, but ſent her a Meſſage by Mr. *Fitztuhm*, by which he deſired her to go from the Palace within two Hours, from Warſaw within twenty-four, and to quit the Kingdom without Delay.

She obey'd, and was no ſooner gone, than her Enemies, who were innumerable, inſinuated to the King, that he ſhould have obliged her to return ſome of the Diamonds, which he had given her, ſince ſuch a Puniſhment would have affected her more ſenſibly than her Diſgrace. The

King

King, not recovered of his firſt furious Rage ſent a Meſſenger after her. She was overtaken at the diſtance of two Days Journey from Warſaw. A Gentleman of the King's Life-guard, demanded in his Majeſty's Name, her Box of Jewels. She told him, that ſhe was ready to deliver up the Jewels, but as ſhe would not be ſubject to his Majeſty's Suſpicions, in caſe any of thoſe Diamonds, he gave her, ſhould prove deficient, ſhe deſired the liberty of locking the Box, and incloſing the Key in a Letter ſhe deſigned to write to the King. The Gentleman believing he had got the right Box, becauſe he had that, which had been deſcribed to him, and one, whoſe Lock could not be ſeen, made no Oppoſition to the deceitful Counteſs, and thus ſhe ſealed the Box and Key, left them in the Hands of the Gentleman of the Life-guard and continued her Journey with great Expedition. She arrived at Breſlau, at the ſame time, when the Gentleman arrived at Warſaw. He delivered the Box to the King, who having open'd it found only a Heap of Cut-Paper; for Madame *d'Eſterle* foreſaw the Event, and had entruſted an Italian Muſician with her Jewels, who went in Haſte through Dantzig whilſt ſhe took the Tour of Sileſia. The King, ſeeing the Impoſture, could not help laughing at it, and was no longer diſpleaſed at the Counteſs *d' Eſterle.*

His Majeſty was now deſtitute of a declared Miſtreſs: but as Idleneſs was hateful to him, he diverted himſelf with thoſe trifling and accidental Amour, which might properly be only called by the aſtronomical term of *Ignis fatuus*; but in which he found ſo great a Pleaſure that he was tempted to make frequent uſe of them. The firſt, he fixed his Eye upon, was a young Turkiſh Lady, who had been taken Captive at Buda, when the Imperialiſts made themſelves Maſters of that Place. She was at that time but ſix Years of Age, and together with her Liberty loſt both her Parents, who have ſince then never been heard of. Mr. *Schoning* ┼ Lieutenant-General in the Service of the Elector of Brandenburg, to whoſe Share ſhe happened to fall, took her to Berlin and baptized her; but ſhe kept her Name of *Fatima.* Mademoiſelle *Flemming* having a great Value for young *Fatima* aſked Mr. *Schoning* to give her to their Family, which he willingly granted. When ſhe was married to the Palatine *Brebentau*, *Fatima* followed her into

┼ He died Field-Marſhal in the Saxon Service, after having enjoyed the ſame Place under the Elector of Brandenburg.

into Poland. As the Beauties of her Mind equalled those of her Body, Madame *Brebentau* used her with great Tenderness, and introduced her into all Companies. At her House the King had the pleasure of first seeing *Fatima*. Though he thought her Beauty great, at the time of his Amour with Madame *d'Esterle*, yet was his Engagement with that Lady so inviolable, that he looked at the other with Indifference, and could scarce prevail upon himself to speak to her. But the Countess *d'Ester'e* was no sooner banished from his Heart, than he sought for an Opportunity of making his Addresses to *Fatima*, which he procured, and had a long Conversation with her one day, when he was so charmed with her excellent Genius, that from that Moment he became enamoured with her. He then went daily to Madame *Brebentau*, all the Court resorted thither, and the most beautiful Ladies endeavoured to please him. But his Eyes were only fixed upon *Fatima*: he could not be satisfied without dropping now and then a gallant Expression, which was only understood by her. *Fatima* answered him with Modesty and Politeness. She avoided the Passion of loving for a long while: but what Slave can be capable of resisting the pursuits of an amiable, magnificent and generous King?

King? That Prince gave her ſo lively Aſſurances of a laſting Tenderneſs, and made ſo ſeducing Promiſes to her, that the young and innocent *Fatima* was at laſt overcome. —— It is not known how ſhe could poſſibly eſcape Madame *Brebentau*'s vigilant Care, but moſt certain, that ſhe did; the Change of her Shape diſcovered her Intrigue, and Madame *Brebentau* perceived inſtantly; ſhe was ſo incenſed againſt the poor Girl, that ſhe would have baniſhed her from her Houſe: but the King, informed of her Proceedings, begg'd ſhe would take care of the young Lady, and look upon her as a Depoſitum, which he had a greater regard for, than even his Life. Madame *Brebentau* very deſirous of obliging the King, kept *Fatima*, who was ſome Months afterwards delivered of a Son, who by reaſon of his extraordinary Beauty the King acknowledged as his, and whom he has ſince thought fit to educate as ſuch, and to give him the Title of Count *Rotofski*. —— The King, who could never be long attach'd to one Miſtreſs, and was chiefly pleaſed with married Women, and thoſe who diſcovered a nice Capacity for intriguing, ſhewed an early Diſguſt to *Fatima*: She was too ſoft, too modeſt to ſuit his Taſte. However as he eſteemed her, he thought a ſpeedy Settlement

ment would render her happy, and gave her in Marriage to one *Spiegel* Lieutenant Colonel in his Troops. *Fatima* willingly promised that Officer her Fidelity, with whom she has led so happy a Life, that a Person most given to Detraction has been obliged to respect her. The King had not with *Fatima* totally forsaken Love; but another Beauty of a more eminent Rank took possession of his Heart. This was the Princess *Lubomirski*, Wife of the Great Chamberlain of the Crown, and Niece of the Cardinal *Radziowsky*, Primate of the Kingdom. It was a common and received Opinion in Poland, that the King pretended a Passion for this Lady to procure her Favour, and to make use of the great Influence she had upon her Uncle's Mind, who did ever oppose him. But if a political View induced *Frederick-Augustus* to court the Princess *Lubomirski*, it is certain, that that Lady's uncommon Merit render'd the amorous King at last in Reality her Adorer. ------ He attacked the Heart of Madame *Lubomirski* according to all the formal Rules and Ceremonies of Courtship; and she on the other hand encountered him as a true Heroine, pretending neither to understand his Sighs, nor tender Looks. When his Majesty addressed her, she answered respectfully, but at the same

time

time like a Princeſs of a free Kingdom. This increaſed the Royal Paſſion. The Princeſs loved Diverſions, and a profuſe Method of living, and herein to indulge her Inclination no Expence was thought too great; the French Comedians and Muſicians were ſent for from Dreſden. Their daily Diverſions were Plays, Balls, Feaſts, Hunting, Games, Entertainments upon the Viſtula, and other Pleaſures of equal Splendor; never had Warſaw made ſo bright an Appearance.

One day, as they were running at the Ring, after the King, whoſe Dexterity was ſuperior to any other, had won the Prize; he ordered ſome young Horſes, which he had lately ſent for from Turkey to be brought to him. Tho' theſe Horſes had had no Inſtructions, yet would he mount them, and order'd others to be mounted by the firſt Lords of the Court. The King and Mr. *Fitztuhm* happened to mount the moſt unruly ones: theſe were wont to hit their Heads together, but the King pull'd him briſkly back, and rid ſo violently againſt a poſt of the Riding-Houſe, that the Blow made the Horſe throw him. The Spectators ran directly to his Aſſiſtance and thought he was much wounded. Madame *Lubomirski* thought him more hurt than any of the reſt. The Concern ſhe had

had for him, gave her a Trouble and an Apprehension which ſhe could not conceal. She drew nearer to him, and obſerving ſome Drops of Blood was ſo terrified, that ſhe ſwooned away in the Arms of the Counteſs *Tobianski* her Couſin. When the King was recover'd and had lifted up his Head, the firſt Object, that ſtruck his Sight, was his dear Princeſs *Lubomirski.* The Condition he ſaw her in, revived him; he roſe and ran to her Succour. She happened at the ſame time to open her Eyes and in a languiſhing Tone to ſay to her Couſin, *Is the King dead?* She ſaw the ſame Moment that Prince beholding her in a manner, that ſignified ſufficiently, how ſenſible he was of her Condition. She was ſo rejoiced at the bad ſtate of Health, and the Preſence of her Huſband, to whom ſuch Behaviour ſeemed undoubtedly indecent, ſhe cried out, 'Great Sir! do you live? do 'I again enjoy the Happineſs of ſeeing 'you, has God returned you at my humble Intreaties! ----- -Yes, Madame, (anſwered the King) but I beſeech you to 'believe that I am more grateful for the 'Tokens of Compaſſion you have expreſſed, than even for my Life itſelf.' The Great Chamberlain's Preſence hindered her from ſaying any more.

Ma-

Madame *Lubomirski* retired from the Riding-Houſe to the Princeſs *Conſtantine Sobiesky*, who had invited the King to a Ball that Evening. His Mind was wholly employed upon what was paſt, and notwithſtanding the late unfortunate Adventure, he went thither in a ſplendid Dreſs, and made the Appearance of a Man inſenſible of the Accident, that had happened but a little before: He even appeared with more Gaiety than uſual, and his Joy at what he had that day ſeen gave him an Air which was no ſmall addition to his other endearing bodily Perfections. All the Aſſembly was amazed at his Entry, and every-body congratulated his happy Deliverance, except Madame *Lubomirski*. The King after having given the Ladies a polite Salutation, and paſſed ſome Moments in diſcourſing with the Princeſs *Sobiesky*, went to Madame *Lubomirski*, whom he addreſſed in a low Tone, 'Madame, (ſaid he) this Day I may juſtly 'call the happieſt of all my Life, ------- I 'think (replied the Princeſs, who would not give him time to expreſs himſelf) 'that your Majeſty may add it to the 'number of your moſt fortunate Days, 'ſince you have eſcaped ſo great and imminent a Danger.---The Danger (anſwer'd 'the King) is but trifling in competition

'of

'of the Benefit it has procured me. I
'only recollect the Danger I was in, to
'call to Mind the Condition I ſaw you in.
'But, Madame, is that, which was then
'the only Cauſe of my Felicity to ceaſe
'already, and will you repent of having
'given me Tokens of your Affection at
'that time? For God's Sake, Sir, (re-
'plied Madame *Lubomirski*) be contented
'with what you have ſeen, and exact not
'of me the Confeſſion of a Thing, too
'well known to you, and which I am in
'vain deſirous of hiding. Conſider the
'Preſence of my Huſband, and that I
'muſt not explain my Sentiments before
'him.' The King could ſcarce contain
the Tranſport of Joy this Anſwer cauſed
in him; however that he might not expoſe his Miſtreſs, notwithſtanding his Royal
Authority, he obey'd and retired from her.
----- He opened the Ball with the Princeſs
Sobieski, and had no ſooner danced once,
than he fell very ill, and was obliged to be
carried away; when he arrived at his Palace, he was let Blood, and found himſelf
much better. The Phyſicians imputed this
Accident to his Fall and Refuſal of bleed-
ing immediately after the Misfortune, as
they had adviſed him (but he was far from
conſenting to it) apprehenſive of being
deprived of the Sight of his Miſtreſs at the
Ball.

Ball. His Diſeaſe was however ſoon cur'd, and what contributed chiefly to his ſpeedy Recovery, was a Billet deliver'd to him by his firſt Phyſician in the Name of Madame *Lubomirski.* It was expreſſed in the following Terms:

WHAT Uneaſineſs. hath not your Majeſty given me in one Day! Be aſſured, Sir, that this laſt has been the moſt miſerable Night I ever had in my Life, and the Danger I thought you to be in, has almoſt broke my Heart. I have juſt now been informed, that you are better. May you be ſpeedily capable of witneſſing the Joy that Report has occaſioned in me! Yet I ſtill tremble, O! if I love my King --------- my Lover ----- what Advantage will a temporal Life afford me?

The King peruſed this Billet frequently and with great Care; he read it to Mr. *Fitztuhm*, whoſe Intereſt begun to be more prevalent, than that of the Chancellor *Beichling*. This Favourite was not ſparing in his Praiſes of the Stile. ‘ She wiſhes ‘ (cried the King) that I could be Witneſs ‘ of the Joy the Recovery of my Health ‘ has cauſed in her. Wherefore, dear *Fitz-* ‘ *tuhm*, I ought to go to her, I ought to ‘ make her Witneſs of the Joy her Kind- ‘ neſſes

'nesses have caused in me, such a Mistress
'deserves, that I should hazard my Health
'for her Sake. --------- The Princess *Lubo-
'mirski* deserves all the Favours you can
'confer on her (replied Mr. *Fitztuhm*) but
'I am perswaded your Majesty will offend
'her, if you expose your Health to see
'her. Let me manage the Affair, Sir,
'I hope to be capable of inducing her to
'come hither; that will be more advan-
'tageous both for her and you. ------ O!
'dear *Fitztuhm*, (cried the King) if you
'procure me that Happiness you shall ask
'nothing of me, but what I shall give
'you, and you may expect the best To-
'kens I am capable of shewing my
'Acknowledgment.' Mr. *Fittzuhm* thank'd
the King for his excessive Goodness, and
begg'd he would write an Answer to Madame *Lubomirski*, and to make him the
Bearer of it. The King writ the following Billet:

PARDON me, dear Princess, for all the Uneasiness I give you. But what do I say! I should have been sorry had I not given you any; I should still have remain'd ignorant of your Sentiments for me. You should certainly see me at your Feet, to re-turn you Thanks for your obliging Behaviour to me, did not my Physicians, and Fitztuhm *him-*

himſelf confine me to my Chamber. I am ever ſenſible, that it is impoſſible for me to live without you. Whatever they do I am reſolved to eſcape their vigilant Care to enjoy the Happineſs of your Converſation. If my Life is in Danger, I will at leaſt loſe it, for which I ſhall have a moſt plauſible Reaſon.

Mr. *Fitztuhm* found a large Aſſembly of Gentlemen and Ladies in Madame *Lubumirski*'s Apartment; but told her nevertheleſs, that he deſired to confer with her about ſome private Affair. She went into a Cloſet, and he followed her, where he delivered the Billet, and told her, that the King would die, if ſhe did not come to viſit him. ' How, or what can I do? ' (ſaid ſhe) I cannot go to ſee the King ' without ſubjecting myſelf to my Huſ-' band's Reſentment, and the Cenſure of ' the whole Court. ------ Every Affair may ' be managed by ſome method or other, ' Madame, (anſwered Mr. *Fitztuhm*) and ' provided you will follow the Rule I ſhall ' propoſe, every-body except the King, ' you and I ſhall be ignorant of this Vi-' ſit. ---- Speak then, (replied the Princeſs) ' what muſt I do? ---- Retire into a Con-' vent under a Pretence of a devout Diſ-' poſition, (ſaid Mr. *Fitztuhm*) for Retreats ' of

'of this kind are very cuſtomary at the
'preſent Seaſon of the Year, this being
'the firſt Week in Lent. When you are
'in the Convent, you are to leave it at
'Ten o' Clock at Night; to ſtep into a
'Coach, which I ſhall take care to prepare
'for your Reception; you are to ſtep out
'of this Coach at the Door of my Lodg-
'ing, and I ſhall conduct you to a private
'Stair-caſe, only made uſe of by me, and
'from thence to the Royal Apartment.----
The Princeſs found the Project extreamly
well laid and promiſed to follow him the
next day. She then left Mr. *Fitztuhm* and
returned to her Company. Her Huſband,
who obſerved her Abſence aſked where
ſhe had been; ſhe told him inſtantly, that
ſhe had been in Conference with Mr. *Fitztuhm*, and couſulted with him about Matters which the King deſired her to communicate to the Cardinal-Primate. The Prince
believed that no other Affair had detained
her, and ſhe afterwards began to diſcourſe
about the Devotions of the Lent-Seaſon.
'As for me, (ſaid ſhe) I ſhall not make
'uſe of any corporal Auſterities, becauſe
'they will be inconſiſtent with my Health;
'but ſhall mortify myſelf by ſeeing leſs
'Company. In order thereto I intend to
'paſs four Days in each Week in a ſolitary
'manner in a Convent,' This religious
'Zeal

Zeal was admired by every one, and Mr. *Lubomirski* was the firſt Perſon, who gave his Approbation of it.

The Princeſs executed her Reſolution the next Morning, and at Ten o' Clock at Night ſhe followed Mr. *Fitztuhm*'s Directions in every reſpect, and arrived at his Majeſty's Bed-Chamber; who waited for her with an Impatience, which no Pen can poſſibly deſcribe. Mr. *Fitztuhm* being retired, Madame *Lubomirski* ſate down upon the Bed. She was in a negligent Dreſs, but as amiable as ſhe had ever appeared before. The two Lovers were together for ſome time without ſpeaking a Word to each other. The Princeſs looked at the King with a languiſhing Air, which ſufficiently told him, that her Heart was entirely devoted to him. The King was ſo tranſported, that after having returned her Thanks for the Favour ſhe did him, he kiſs'd her Hands for a quarter of an Hour, telling her inceſſantly, that he was the happieſt Man on Earth, and look'd upon himſelf as the greateſt Monarch in the World in the Enjoyment of her Love. 'I think 'myſelf no leſs happy (anſwered ſhe) in 'the poſſeſſion of the Heart of ſo great a 'King, and ſo accompliſhed a Man. Let 'us therefore love each other always, dear 'Prince; be not unfaithful to me: May

'Hea-

' Heaven punish me, if ever I love any
' other Person but you!' They proceeded
at that time no farther than tender Expressions;
the King indeed was desirous of a
further Enjoyment; but Madame *Lubomirski*
to whom his Majesty's Health was
very dear, suffered him not to run the Hazard
of it again. The King insisted upon
her Promise to return in the same manner
the next Day. It was near Four o' Clock
in the Morning when she retired. When
she was arrived at the Convent, she endeavoured
to preserve the Character of a pious
Woman by attending at the Morning-Prayers
and Masses, after which she took
the Repose her Body was in great need
of.

She returned to the Palace the two next
Days, and the King was no sooner able to
go out, than he begun to visit her in the
Convent. With these delightful Meetings
the two Lovers passed the whole Lent-Season,
but could not do so after Easter. The
King however continued to visit Madame
Lubomirski, and her Husband had Intelligence
of the Matter, he mentioned it to
his Wife, who answered him in a very arrogant
manner. The Prince not a little
dissatisfied with his Wife's Conduct, happened
to drop some Words, that were
highly offensive to the King, whereupon
he

he was forbid to appear at Court, this obliged him to resolve to retire to his own Estate, and desired his Wife to follow him thither, which she presumptuously refused; he summoned her after this Refusal to appear before the Pope's Nuncio, and there demanded a Dissolution of his Marriage-Bonds, and as she consented to it, the King, who was glad to meddle in this Affair, obtained for them a Divorce from his Holiness, and to this Effect, that either Party could marry again. ---- As no other Obstacle hindered the two Lovers from doing what they pleased, the King departed for Saxony. Madame *Lubomirski* followed him soon afterwards, accompanied by her two Sisters, one of which was married to Mr. *Vopofski*, a Polish Gentleman. The other was unmarried, but soon afterwards entered into a conjugal Life with Mr. *Glasnap* an Officer in the Life-guards, a Gentleman of eminent Birth, and no less eminent Merit, but without a Fortune which he designed to procure by this Alliance, but was deceived in his Expectations, and saw himself at last reduced as well as Mr. *Vopolfski* to dissolve his Marriage, since which time he has married another Woman. ---- The King desirous of appearing in as magnificent a manner as possible in his own Country, shewed his Mistress the chief Towns

Towns of Saxony. When he was arrived at Wittenberg he left her to go and see the Queen, who had resided some time since at the Castle of Pretsch at the distance of two or three Leagues from that Town. Tho' he was to leave her but for the space of two Days, yet were both Parties unwilling to be separated. The Mistress sigh'd and wept. 'How! (said she) will you leave 'me? shall I live two days without seeing 'you? and will you spend all that Time 'with the Queen? whom, notwithstanding the Respect I owe her, I cannot look 'upon any otherways, than as my Enemy, 'since she cannot but hate me, who deprive her of the most perfect Heart in 'the Universe. O! what should I do, if 'she was on the other hand to deprive 'me of it? even the Idea of that Misery 'gives me a mortal Uneasiness, judge 'then, dear Prince, what a Condition I 'shall be in, if you forsake me. I own, 'that I should rather see you return to 'the Arms of the Queen, than in those of 'any other Rival: but in short whatever 'way I lose you, Death only can procure 'me Comfort.' The King touch'd with these Words embraced his Mistress, and begg'd her not to be afflicted about a Thing, that could not possibly happen. 'How can I be unfaithful to you? (said

'he) where ſhall I find ſo accompliſhed a
'Perſon as you, and one that can love
'like you? No, my Dear, you need not
'be apprehenſive of any thing. Your
'Accompliſhments will for ever ſecure my
'Fidelity.' This Diſcourſe revived Madame *Lubomirski*; but ſhe intreated the King neverthleſs to delay his intended Journey three Days longer. This Prince incapable of making her a Refuſal, conſented to it, and that Interval of Time was employed in Diverſions, Balls and Feaſts, in which the King's Politeneſs and Grandeur were over conſpicuous. ---- At one of theſe Entertainments the King preſented his Miſtreſs with a little Box of a precious Stone full of Jewels of all kinds, and in the midſt of them the Emperor's Diploma, declaring her Princeſs of the Empire by the Name of *Teſchen*. 'How much am I
'obliged to you, Sir, (ſaid ſhe) and what
'Tokens can I give of my Acknowledg-
'ment? ------ The only one I deſire, (re-
'plied the King) is an endleſs Continuation
'of your preſent Love. The Rank, by
'which his Imperial Majeſty is pleaſed to
'diſtinguiſh you, is far inferior to your
'Deſerts; what reaſon have you then to
'to be grateful to me. I wiſh a Crown
'was at my Diſpoſal, with what Pleaſure
'ſhould I ſee you wear it!' In this man-
'ner

ner did they divert themſelves with ſuch pleaſant amorous Diſcourſes, till they thought proper to retire and meet again in private. The Night would have ſeem'd to be of too tedious a length, had the Lovers been in ſeparate Apartments, wherefore they agreed to paſs it together.

The next Morning his Majeſty departed for Pretſch, where he met with a ſubmiſſive and obliging Reception from the Queen's Hands; but her Heart had received too bitter a Wound by the long courſe of his unlawful Amours, to give him any ſenſible Tokens of Love, and tho' the King addreſſed her in all the affectionate terms, natural to a Huſband, that reſpected her Virtues and unparallel'd Merit, yet was ſhe reſolved to continue that cold and indifferent Behaviour, which ſhe had long ſince accuſtomed herſelf to.

The King was too impatient for the Sight of his Miſtreſs, to ſtay any longer than one Night at Pretſch, he ſet out the next Morning, and met her in a Wood between Wittemberg and Pretſch. She was dreſs'd in a Riding-Apparel, the Body of which was yellow, and the Petticoat blue embroidered with Silver; thoſe Colours were at that time in Faſhion in Saxony. Her Hat was adorned with a blue and white Feather. This Dreſs gave the

Princeſs ſo enchanting an Air, that no other could have ſet off her Charms more advantageouſly. The King haſtened to her as ſoon as he ſaw that ſhe was coming, and when he had approached her, he ſtepped out of his Chariot, ſhe offer'd to anſwer this Civility by diſmounting, but her tender Lover would not ſuffer her, he kiſs'd her Hand with Eagerneſs, and ſhe complimented him in an endearing manner on his Return. His Majeſty having aſked for a Horſe, mounted, and propoſed a Hunting-Match to his Miſtreſs, and as he had the day before given Orders for the Preparation of this Match, the Hounds were ready. The King was in fear leſt any unfortunate Accident ſhould happen to this new Huntreſs, intreated her to keep at his Side, and he would not forſake her. After having given her the Pleaſure of ſeeing the Stag, that was hunted, run by her, he retired with her to the moſt hidden part of the Wood, to take a ſmall Refreſhment with her. The Gentlemen and Ladies of the Court ſoon perceived their Retirement, but would not interrupt their quiet Fruition of the ſolitary Pleaſures. The Event has ſufficiently manifeſted, that this was in reality the occaſion of an agreeable Converſation between the King and his Miſtreſs; for ſince that time ſhe was perplexed with

with Pains in her Stomach, and frequent Vomits, which raiſed a Suſpicion, that the King and ſhe had not made a trifling uſe of their time. She was in due time deliver'd of a Son, who is at preſent diſtinguiſhed by the Title of Prince of *Teſchen*, and reſembles his Mother's Lover in every reſpect.

The day after this Hunting-Match the King and his Miſtreſs ſet out for Leipzig, which was at that time, by reaſon of the Fair, frequented by a large number of Perſons of Diſtinction. The Queen went thither to aſſiſt her Conſort in receiving the King of Pruſſia, who was come to viſit them. Madame *Teſchen* ſaluted the two Queens at the Redoubt, and the King himſelf preſented her to thoſe two Princeſſes, who gave her a very different Reception. The Queen of Poland received her with an Indifference, not agreeable to her Rival, and aſked her how long ſhe had been in Saxony. ' I am come hither with ' the King, Madame, (anſwer'd the Fa- ' vourite) and hope ſoon to return from ' hence with him again.' The Queen was ſo mortified at this Anſwer, that her Eyes were filled with Tears. She pretended Sickneſs to excuſe her Retirement.

The Queen of Pruſſia on the contrary was extreamly obliging in her Deportment to Madame *Teschen*, but as that Prince was only diverted at the Expence of another Person, she invited the King to sup with her in private, pretending that the Noise and Grandeur a Court is perplexed with, was very inconvenient to her. 'But 'if you please (said she to the King) I'll 'name those Persons, that I design to invite, which number your Mistress is to 'be excluded from. I long to see you 'once without her, and to have the sole 'possession of you. I know that she occupies all your Thoughts; but shall 'chuse Persons, whose Conversation will 'be capable of diverting you from her; 'and if they do not, I shall rather have 'you think of, than always speak to your 'Mistress.' The King promised an entire Compliance with all her Desires, and permitted the Queen to invite whatever Persons should seem most agreeable to her.

She invited the Ladies *Koningsmark*, *Hauchwitz* and *Esterle*, the three disgraced Mistresses of the King, whom Chance and some particular Affairs had occasioned to meet at Leipsig. The Queen of Prussia was attended by both the Princesses of *Hohenzollern* and *Henrietta* Princess of *Anhalt-Dessau*. The young Princess of *Hohenzollern* could boast of a most beautiful Person; but her tender Years gave her too

inno-

innocent an Air to suit the Taste of *Frederick-Augustus.* The Princess of *Dessau* was not altogether so beautiful in her Person, but was possessed of that *Je-ne-sçai-quoi*, which does equally please and affect; her Shape, Graces, Behaviour and entertaining Discourse could not be exceeded; and the King could not but give her the Preference before the Princess of *Hohenzollern*, whose Mother was so mortified, that her Daughter did not gain the Conquest over the King, (as she expected) that she mutter'd at her Daughter all the Evening, whose Eyes were constantly filled with Tears.

Madame *d'Esterle*, to whom his Majesty had granted a Pardon for her Treachery and Deceit, endeavoured to gain the Superiority by forced and artificial Charms, and seemed not to have lost all Hopes of recalling the King to her Arms. Madame *Hauchwitz* sate in a pensive and doleful posture; in short, no one behaved in a more indifferent manner than Madame *Koningsmark*, and with that Lady her Prussian Majesty was pleased to divert herself in observing and reflecting upon the various effects the King's Presence produced in that Assembly:

In the mean while the King conversed for a considerable time with the Princess of

Dessau, whose Charms had so great an effect upon his Heart, that she may truly be said to have been the first occasion of Madame *Teschen*'s Disgrace. But that Princess answered all his tender Expressions in very cold and disagreeable terms. 'Your Majesty (said she) is incapable of promoting 'me to the Royal Dignity, and was it in 'your power, you would perhaps think 'me unworthy of so great a Promotion, 'but let me perswade you that I think 'my Birth too eminent to be your Mistress.'

At Supper-time Madame *Koningsmark* observed to the Queen, that Madame *Teschen*'s Presence would be no small addition to the Pleasure of the Entertainment, and the Queen pretended to be sorry for not having invited her, which occasioned the other Lady to say that it was not too late for the Pleasure of her Company, that they need only open a Ball after Supper and admit all the Masques. 'Be assured, Madame, (continued she) that the Princess 'of *Teschen* will not fail to come.' The Queen gave a ready Approbation of the Expedient, and offered a Dance to the King; after whose Consent the Musicians were called in; and her Prussian Majesty ordered one of the Servants in waiting, without the King's Knowledge, to acquaint

the

the Masques that they might be admitted. The Noble Company rose from Table and the King opened the Ball with the Queen of Prussia. After having danced his Majesty placed himself by the Princess of *Anhalt*, whose reserved Behaviour had not discouraged him from making his Addresses to her. He spoke to her in so lively and eager a manner, that he did not perceive three masqued Ladies, approaching near enough to hear whatever Words were spoke. One of these Masques listened for some time and then broke out in these Words to the Princess of *Anhalt*; 'O! 'Princess, the King made use of the same 'Expression to me but this Morning, be-'lieve him not, I conjure you ---- 'Alas! '(answered the amazed King) it is the 'Princess of *Teschen!* ------------ Fear not, 'masqued Lady, (replied the Princess of '*Dessau*) the King has a Fluency of 'Speech, but all Princesses do not resem-'ble you.' She then rose up, and the King was doing the same, when Madame *Teschen* stopped him, saying, 'You shun 'me, notwithstanding all your Promises 'this Morning never to love any other 'Person.' The King, apprehensive of undergoing the Censure of her Prussian Majesty, was desperately vexed at this Accident. 'For God's Sake, Madame, (said

'he) let us not be the Jeſt of all the Stran-
'gers here preſent, for we are taken notice
'of. Go to your own Houſe, I ſhall fol-
'low to reaſſure you, that you ſhall ever
be the ſole Object of my Love.' Madame *Teſchen* well ſatisfied with the King's Anſwer, departed, and the King would have followed her, had not the Queen of Pruſſia, who deſigned to divert herſelf at the Expence of that Favourite, as ſoon as ſhe ſaw him going, propoſed to join in a Country-Dance with him, which, as he conſented to, ſhe occaſioned to laſt very long; after theſe Dances ſhe diſcourſed with him upon ſeveral Subjects, jeſted about his amorous and inconſtant diſpoſition, and, as if ſhe had not ſeen Madame *Teſchen*, told him, that ſhe was heartily ſorry for not having invited that Lady to Supper.
'Perhaps, (ſaid ſhe) the poor Lady is at
'this very Inſtant mortally uneaſy, and
'your Majeſty ought to let her know,
'that I hinder you from going to aſk her
'Pardon, for the Preference you have
'this Evening given the young Princeſs of
'*Deſſau* to her in Beauty.' Theſe Railleries diſordered the King very much, he endeavoured to anſwer her, but all his Words teſtified his Confuſion; and the more Diſorder he diſcover'd the more the Queen perplexed him. 'My Inconſtancy,
'Ma-

'Madame, (answered he at last) doth in
'some measure deserve a free Pardon. If
'I might boast of a Spouse, permit me to
'say a Mistress, equal to your Majesty,
'you may be assured, I would not occa-
'sion my Enemies to censure me for be-
'ing too fickle ------ If your Majesty is in-
'clined to wheedle me (replied the Queen
'of Prussia) I shall directly send for the
'Princess of *Teschen*; it will however be
'in vain, for Day-light appears, and the
'Masques are all retired. Come hither,
'Princess (cried she to the Princess of *An-*
'*halt*) the King mistakes me for you.'
With these and other Discourses of this
kind she detained the King till Seven o'
Clock the next Morning.

He then went to Madame *Tescen* whom
he found in a deplorable condition. She
was sitting in a flood of Tears, her Sisters
sate by and comforted her, but she gave
no ear to their Words, and found no other
Comfort but in her Despair. The King
was so transported at this sight that he
asked her Pardon in the most submissive
terms, and kissed her Hands for a considerable time. She cast a tender look upon
him and said; 'How great will be my
'Misery, Sir, if you refuse me your Pity!'
The King made all the Excuses he could,
complained of the Queen of Prussia, whom
he

he accused of being the occasion of all that had happen'd, and added to these Excuses, that all he said to the Princess of *Dessau* was designed for an Amusement. As we are most apt to believe what we wish for, Madame *Teschen* gave ready Credit to the King's Words. The two Lovers were happily reconciled, and parted at last in a very amicable manner.

In the mean while the King was in reality pleased with the Princess of *Dessau's* great Merit, and greatly afflicted at her Departure. The Queen of Prussia perceived his Melancholy, and the cause of it, and told him with that pleasant Air, natural to her, that she advised him to quit that pensive posture. 'Believe me (said she) 'you shall accompany me to Orangen-'baum, where I design to remain some 'days with the Princess-Dowager of *An-*'*halt-Dessau*. You will be at more li-'berty there; a Wife and three or four 'Mistresses, to whose Humour you are 'here obliged to adapt yourself, cannot 'but be very troublesome.' The King consented to the Proposal, and that the Princess of *Teschen* might not oppose his Design, he pretended that State-Affairs obliged him to have a private Conference with the King of Prussia. He begg'd she would go and wait for him at Dresden, he would

would there return to her in few Days. This Separation grieved Madame *Teschen* mortally; but the King represented to her in so perswasive a manner, that it was absolutely necessary for the Interest of his Kingdom, and swore so often that he would return to her with a faithful Heart, that she at last consented to it.

The King then set out on this small Journey, and arrived some Hours afterwards at Orangen-baum. The Princess *Henrietta*, displeased at seeing him there, gave him a very cold Reception. She related to her Mother all the King's Words, and begg'd her permission to keep her Chamber under pretence of Sickness. ' No ' (answered that Princess) dear Daughter, ' it will directly be suspected not to be a ' real Indisposition. And I have more-' over too good an Opinion of you to be ' perswaded, that you can by no other ' means, than shunning your Lover, se-' cure yourself from answering to a Passi-' on, which can only offend you.'

The Princess *Henrietta* saw herself obliged to submit to her Mother's Commands, but alweys kept at such a distance from the King, that he could not make any private Addresses to her, though he was during the space of four Days in constant search after means, whereby to gain his end.

end. At laſt he departed from thence for Dreſden on the ſame day, that the Queen of Pruſſia ſet out for Berlin. His Return cauſed an inexpreſſible Joy in the Princeſs of *Teſchen*, who notwithſtanding the King's ſolemn Proteſtation, was dubious whether ſhe ſhould ſee him again. The firſt Days were wholly employed upon Endearments on both ſides. But as ſhe ſaw ſeveral Coquets ſtriving to deprive her of the King's Heart, and knowing his inconſtant Mind, ſhe begun to be uneaſy, and Dreſden at laſt proved quite inſupportable to her, for ſhe foreſaw, that ſhe ſhould loſe her Lover, if he made any ſtay there: this induced her to perſwade him to return into Poland, whither the War undertaken againſt Sweden, and carried on with little Succeſs, ſeemed beſides to require his Preſence.

The King's Affairs in Poland, and the Campaign in Livonia, ſeparated him frequently from his Miſtreſs. Theſe Abſences were very advantageous to the Favourite-Lady: they were not of a ſufficient length to occaſion him to forget her; but long enough to create a Deſire in the King to ſee her again, and to meet her, as if lately enamoured with her. Madame *Teſchen* enjoyed his Favour in the mean time for ſome Years without any interruption; this time ſhe ſpent in procuring Riches ſufficient

cient to maintain her ufual Grandeur in her Difgrace. The King's ill Succefs in his War obliged him to fetch a frefh Recruit of Soldiers from Saxony, leaving his Miftrefs at Warfaw. This Departure did not occafion fo many Tears, fhe was accuftomed to his Abfence, and that Vivacity, which is the true Delight of a real and ardent Paffion, fubfifted no longer. The King upon his Arrival at Drefden was refolved to drive all Melancholy away from his Heart, and to that purpofe frequented Places where Debauchery was practifed to a great degree. At one of thefe Converfations, which confifted at that time only of Men, they happened to difcourfe about their Miftreffes. Every one boafted of his, and related Wonders of her. Mr. *Hoyhm*, Minifter of State, of the Privy-Council, who was prefent there told them, that he had no Miftrefs, but that his Happinefs confifted in a Wife, whom he loved as a Miftrefs, and who was much more charming than any that had yet been defcribed. As Wine had deprived him of the free ufe of his Senfes, he delivered fo exact a Defcription of his Wife, that not the moft able Painter could have better fet off her Beauties. The King, not ignorant that Jealoufy occafioned him to confine her to the Country, told him that he could not pof-

fibly

ſibly believe his Aſſertion, that his Diſcourſe was like that of a Man married but three Months before, and ſtill charmed with his Wife's Accompliſhments, and that if Madame *Hoyhm*'s Beauty and bodily Perfections did but in the leaſt anſwer his Deſcription of her, ſhe would have been much more noted than ſhe was. The Prince of *Furſtemberg* maintained the King's Argument, and added, that he would lay a Wager of a Thouſand Ducats, that if Madame *Hoyhm* was to make her Appearance at Court ſhe would not be found ſo beautiful, as he had perſwaded them to believe. Mr. *Hoyhm* laid the Wager, and the King offer'd to decide it; the Gentleman was inſtantly obliged to write to his Wife, and ordered her to come directly to Dreſden; a Servant was at the ſame diſpatch'd with the Letter; and that Mr. *Hoyhm* might not be capable of altering his Mind, they forced him to drink ſo much, that he could ſcarce ſpeak, act or think. He was in a great Surprize at his Wife's Preſence the next Morning at Dreſden, repented of having ſent for her, and would have ſent her back the ſame Hour, had he not been apprehenſive of the Cenſure of the whole Court for his great Jealouſy.

The Queen of Poland was at that time at Dreſden, and Madame *Hoyhm* was preſented

ſented to her Majeſty. The King and thoſe who laid the Wager were at the Queen's Apartment, and found themſelves obliged to acknowledge, that Mr. *Hoyhm* had even been ſparing in his praiſes of the Lady's Beauty. The King condemned the Prince of *Furſtemberg* to pay the Thouſand Ducats. ' I find (anſwered the Prince ' in Jeſt) that we muſt pay dear for your ' Majeſty's Diverſion.' The King extreamly fond of the Prince, deſired him to pay the loſt Sum, and to go and receive Ten Thouſand Ducats of his Treaſurer. The Prince kiſs'd his Majeſty's Hand, and thank'd him, he paid the Debt, and received the Sum which he had been preſented with.

Before I proceed any further in this Hiſtory, I think it not improper to delineate as exactly, as poſſibly I can, the incomparable Beauty of this Lady, and to relate ſome Particulars concerning her. The remarkable Diſtinction ſhe was honoured with at the Saxon Court, requires an Account of her Perſon and Character.

Her Face was of a charming length, her Noſe by reaſon of its fine ſhape the chief Ornament of her adorable Face, her Mouth was beautifully ſmall, her Teeth incomparably fine, her Eyes black, agreeably large, bright

bright and alluring, all her Features were moſt delicate; the Beauty of her Face, when laughing, was unparallell'd and capable of captivating the moſt inſenſible Heart. Her Hair was black, her Breaſts could not but raiſe any Perſon's Admiration, her Neck, Hands and Arms were extreamly graceful; her natural Complexion was ſeldom ſeen, but the Paint was commommonly red and white. Her ſhape could not be conceived to be the performance of Nature, and a majeſtick Air added to the great perfection ſhe had acquired in Dancing.

Such was the Perſon of this young Lady, but her Character was not equal to the other Accompliſhments ſhe had juſt Reaſon to boaſt of. She was lively and pleaſant in her Repartees, but diſcover'd little ſolid Senſe, and leſs Sincerity. She was of an inconſtant Diſpoſition; complaiſant to thoſe, who uſed her with the Deference ſhe claimed as due to herſelf, and very arrogant in her Deportment to thoſe who reſiſted her; ſelfiſh, and nevertheleſs liberal; grateful to her Benefactors, unappeaſeable in Wrath, abſolute in her Commands, and not always deſirous of Things conformable to the ſtrict Rules of Juſtice. Nevertheleſs no Prejudice againſt her was able to defend an amorous Perſon's Heart from being

ing imprisoned by her Charms. Sometimes her Behaviour was charming, and at other times as unpleasant; she would condescend to act the meanest part for Riches and Honour. She was no sooner the King's Mistress, than she endeavoured to secure that Prince from a dangerous Solitude and Tranquillity. She cast off all her unpleasant Deportment, lest it should displease those who were enamoured with her; and constantly preserved Victims to sacrifice to the King's Jealousy; a Jealousy, which she was capable of giving rise to, supporting and refraining, according as she thought most proper. Her greatest Art consisted in concealing her Aim at Glory; her Interest was always hid under the cover of the King's. She pretended to love Feasts and publick Shows, the better to amuse her Royal Lover. That Prince intended by distributing Favours to acquire a larger number of Creatures, but those Favours served only to establish the Power of his Mistress, who, notwithstanding the great Discernment of *Frederick-Augustus*, was the sole Judge of the Merit of those Persons, who received any. Thus did the Subject, who was distinguished by some new Dignity, or heap'd with the Sovereign's Bounty, attribute his Happiness only to Madame *Hoybm.* Notwithstanding the Designs form-

ed

ed for her Destruction, notwithstanding the Hatred of the Ministers, did she support herself in his Favour during the space of nine Years; and may be said to have seen Poland and Saxony prostrate at her Feet during that time.

Madame *de Hoyhm* could, besides her other Qualifications, boast of an eminent Birth; she was born in the Dutchy of Holstein, and had followed the Princess of *Holstein-Ploen* to Wolfenbuttel, when that Princess was given in Marriage to the hereditary Prince of *Brunswick-Wolfenbuttel*; this was the Court at which Mr. *Hoyhm*'s Marriage was celebrated. This Gentleman was for a long time in search after a Wife: he was unwilling, tho' himself a Native of Saxony, to marry a Saxon Lady; he thought them too much inclined to Coquetry and too expensive; was desirous of a beautiful, prudent Wife, and one noted for Oeconomy. One of his Friends, who was just returned from the Court of Wolfenbuttel, acquainted him that all those excellent Qualities were to be met with in Mademoiselle *Brouchstorff*, Maid of Honour to the Princess hereditary of Wolfenbuttel. Mr. *Hoyhm* believed his Friend and departed for Brunswick, under pretence of seeing the Fair, but in effect to see Mademoiselle *Brouchstorff*. He found her

her ſuch as ſhe had been deſcribed to him, and directly thought of being joined to her in Marriage. As he was a Perſon of Quality, poſſeſſed of great Riches, and diſtinguiſhed by an eminent Rank at the Court of Saxony, he met with a favourable Reception, and the Matrimonial Engagements were ſoon afterwards enter'd into. When the Celebration of the Marriage-Ceremony was ended, he conducted his Wife to one of his Seats in Saxony, where he intended to leave her till the King returned into Poland. But as his Deſtiny was inevitable, he happened, as I before mentioned, to be guilty of Indiſcretion in making mention of her before the King, and was obliged to ſend for her to Court, where ſhe had ſoon the Happineſs of ſeeing herſelf the Driſtributer of Royal Favours, and Promoter of the Fortune of private Perſons.

The King at the firſt ſight of her was charmed with her Beauty. He found in her a gay Diſpoſition, which he deſired to ſee in a Miſtreſs. No further Endeavours were requiſite to render him amorous. His Paſſion for Madame *Teſchen* oppoſed for ſome time his Sentiments in regard to the new Rival. ' This will only be a little ' turn of Gallantry (ſaid he to himſelf) I ' ſhall forget Madame *Hoybm* when ſhe's

' out

'out of my ſight.' His Conqueſt ſeem'd very eaſy to him, but when he made mention of Love to that Lady, he found her not ſo pliable as he expected. Never was the Acquiſition of a Miſtreſs more expenſive to him, he was obliged, as it happen'd, to take Pains, Aſſiduity, and ſpend large Sums of Money upon his Conqueſt; but this Reſiſtance only increaſed the Deſire of a Victory over her. When Madame *Hoybm* thought herſelf ſure of the King's Heart, ſhe became more eaſy and compliant, and at laſt ſurrendered hers upon Conditions, whereby ſhe obtain'd an abſolute Command over the Heart of *Frederick-Auguſtus*. This Prince laid himſelf under an Obligation, for ever to forſake Madame *Teſchen*, to diſſolve the Bonds by which Mr. *Hoybm* and his Spouſe were joined together; he obliged himſelf by a promiſſory Note, writ and ſubſcribed by himſelf, at the Queen's Deceaſe to honour her with the Royal Dignity, and to acknowledge thoſe Children, that might be born before or after, to be legitimate Princes of Saxony. To theſe Articles ſhe added an annual Penſion of an Hundred Thouſand Rixdollars.

Upon theſe Conditions Madame *Hoybm* accepted the Title of his Majeſty's Miſtreſs; and leſt her Huſband ſhould have any reaſon to accuſe her of ungrateful and treacherous

cherous Behaviour, went herſelf to inform him of the Reſolution ſhe had taken to leave him. In order thereto ſhe went into his Bed-Chamber one Morning, and finding him there, ' I am come, Sir (ſaid ſhe)
' to return you my hearty Thanks for the
' Favours and kind Tokens of Affection,
' you have hitherto honoured me with,
' which give me leave to aſſure you ſhall
' never eſcape my Memory: but I am alſo
' come to tell you, that, ſince that mutual
' Sympathy, which only cauſes and pro-
' motes the Happineſs of a Marriage-Life,
' was never the concomitant of our Love,
' I deſign to be ſeparated from you. The
' King is enamour'd with me, Sir, and I
' cannot conceal from you my Reſolution
' of anſwering the Honour he thereby con-
' fers on me. I am however not deſirous
' of giving you occaſion to complain of
' me, and therefore propoſe to your Con-
' ſideration a Divorce, which as it will ren-
' der us independent of each other, will
' alſo ſecure your future Reputation. I
' think, Sir, it will moſt become you rea-
' dily to accept of this Propoſal, which if
' you do, be aſſured of my future Friend-
' ſhip, and Readineſs at all times to con-
' tribute, as far as I am able, to your
' Proſperity. If on the other hand you
' give me the leaſt Uneaſineſs, you ſhall

' not

'not only be incapable of forcing me to
'change my Resolution, but will also
'oblige me to forget the Obligations you
'have laid me under, that I may the better
'remember the Opposition I meet with
'to my Desires from your Hands.'

The Surprize Mr. *Hoybm* was in at this unexpected Compliment can neither be described nor conceived. He was ready to break into Reproaches and Expostulations, but his Wife interrupted him instantly. 'I know, Sir, all you can tell me, wherefore you may spare the pains of opposing a Resolution, which nothing shall change. Acquaint me therefore, if you please, with your Intention, and give me a positive Answer, that I may know what Measures to make use of.'

Mr. *Hoybm*, finding himself so strangely abused by a Wife, whom he adored, and was upon the point of losing in so extraordinary a manner, felt in his Heart all the Motions, Indignation, Rage and Despair could raise. He walk'd up and down his Room in a great Passion, lifted up his Eyes and Hands, and seem'd almost render'd senseless by Grief. Madame *Hoybm* waited in the mean while quietly for his Answer. When she found she could not perswade him to speak, 'I see, Sir (continued she) 'you at present want Resolution, and re-
'quire

'quire time to consider what you are to
'do. I beg you will recollect in the mean
'while, that the Establishment or Subver-
'sion of your future Welfare depends en-
'tirely upon yourself.' Upon this she retired without waiting for any further Answer.

The unfortunate Husband remained in a
condition, whose Misery cannot be expressed. He was in the greatest pain imaginable, rose up, sate down, and thought
his Misery so great, that all further Assistance would be useless. His Mind, little
accustomed to yield, was not so greatly
disordered in having the King for his Rival, as his Lady's supposed Passion for
that Monarch. 'O perfidious Wretch!
'(cried he) why did you marry me? why
'did you testify any Tenderness for me?
'Alas! have you promised me your Fide-
'lity with no other Design, than to de-
'ceive and render me the most unhappy
'Man on Earth!'

Mr. *Fitztuhm* found him in this pertur-
bation of Mind, when he brought a Message from his Majesty to the distressed Gentleman. He told him, that the King desired he would resign all further Pretensions
or Claims to Madame *Hoyhm* in consenting
to their immediate Divorce. He assured
him that the King would retaliate his Com-

 plaisance

plaiſance in that reſpect; but if he reſolved to oppoſe an Affair, which he could not obſtruct, and perſiſted therein, the King would remember his Diſobedience, till he felt the effects of his Royal Reſentment. Mr. *Hoyhm* ſeeing himſelf obliged to comply with the King's Demands, conſented to what was exacted of him, and all the Favour he deſired in return was a Permiſſion from his Majeſty to abſent himſelf for ſome time from Court, which the King readily granted.

Fitztuhm had no ſooner carried the Anſwer to the King, than that Prince ran haſtily to his Miſtreſs to inform her of the delightful News. ' I am then (ſaid ſhe) ' entirely devoted to your Majeſty; may ' my proſperous Days be of an endleſs duration. After this ſhe returned her Thanks to Mr. *Fitztuhm*, promiſing never to forget the Service he had done her. She preſented him with a Gold Snuff-Box enrich'd and adorned with Jewels, and deſir'd he would accept of that as a ſlight Token of her Acknowledgment. The King deſired to ſee this Box, opened it, and finding his Miſtreſs's Picture in it, ' No, *Fitztuhm* (ſaid ' he) this is too beautiful, and no other ' Perſon but myſelf ſhall ever have this ' Picture. Let me keep it, and be ſatisfied with Twenty Thouſand Rixdollars ' which I give thee.' The

The Convocation of Dresden being in due time assembled, Mr. *Hoybm* and his Spouse appeared there by Proxy, desiring the Dissolution of their Marriage. Their Inducements for this Petition seemed just and reasonable to the Assembly of Divines, who declared their Marriage dissolved, permitting both Parties to marry again. The King confirmed the Sentence, which was the same day posted upon all the Church-Doors.

Madame *Hoybm* changed her Husband's Name, and took the denomination of Madame *Cosel*. As her Ambition was very great, she desired to be distinguished by some Title; and the King procured her by several Intreaties with the Emperor that of Countess of the Empire. By this Honour she obtained a very large Court, and the Envy of most Ladies of the greatest Distinction.

As by the Divorce the King found himself at liberty to act according to the Dictates of his Passion, he resolved to satisfy and publish it. He lodged Madame *Cosel* in the Neighbourhood of his Palace, and built a covered Gallery by which he might visit her whenever he pleased without any Person's knowledge. Some time afterwards he built a Palace for her, in which were several Apartments only to be made use of at the ſeveral Seaſons. Two were appropriated for Summer, lined with Marble; the two others wainſcotted, inlaid, adorned with the fineſt China-Ware and Brocade-Hangings, were intended for the Winter; he paid Two Thouſand Rixdollars for the Furniture of this Room; and thoſe who ſaw it fancied themſelves in an enchanted place. The Diſhes and Plates were all Silver-gilt, the Veſſels and Tables enriched with Cryſtal; the Beds of Brocade, and finely embroidered. In ſhort, all the Furniture ſhewed ſo exquiſite and uncommon a Taſte in the Buyer, that every thing in the Palace might ſerve for a Model to others.

Madame *Coſel* now ſaw her Favour eſtabliſhed, and the better to ſecure it ſhe thought proper to remove thoſe from the King's Perſon, whom ſhe ſuſpected to oppoſe her Intereſt. The Chancellor *Beichling* was the firſt Victim ſacrificed to her irreſiſtible Ambition of reigning.

He had made too liberal an uſe of his Tongue in ſpeaking of her, and repreſented to the King, that the Sums expended for her Sake might be better employed. This was ſufficient to prove him guilty. She accuſed him of great Miſdemeanours and Embezzlement of the publick Treaſure. The King order'd him to be arreſted,

and

and carried to Koningftein, feizing befides upon his Goods and Eftates, which were very confiderable. By this publick Action did Madame *Cofel* eftablifh her Authority, and let all the World know, that nothing could be more dangerous than to offend her.

After the Chancellor's Difgrace Mr. *Fitztuhm* was the only Favourite, or rather the only Confident of the King's Amours. This Favourite was of a large Size, had a fine Shape, and an amiable Afpect; his Deportment was in every refpect fuch, as became a Perfon of Quality; he was complaifant, fupple, affable, and truly honeft. He refpected the King as his Mafter, and loved him as his Friend. The Prince of *Fürftemberg* and the Field-Marfhal Count *Flemming* were looked upon as Favourites, but all thofe whom their private Affairs or Favour at Court induced to approach the King, could fcarce gain Admittance, without being very fubmiffive to Madame *Cofel.* She governed fo abfolutely, that fhe might be faid to have been Miftrefs both of the King and State.

Whilft all the Court was cringing to her, a Lutheran Prieft boldly reproached her in the Pulpit; he compared her to *Bathfheba*; and left the Auditors fhould miftake the Perfon, he defcribed her in fo nice a manner, that her Picture drawn by the most expert Painter could not have represented her in a better Light. She heard of it, was extreamly enraged, made bitter Complaints to the King, and desired a severe Punishmight be speedily inflicted on the Preacher for his Indiscretion. But the King, who was always a professed Enemy to Violence, could not himself deny the Justice of the Comparison, was not so complaisant to satisfy her: he told her, Preachers have one Hour every Sunday and Holiday, during which time they may speak whatever their Thoughts suggest to them; that he could not deprive them of that Privilege, but if any one was to be wanting in his Respect to her out of those Hours, he would punish them according to their Deserts.

The King was in the mean while called into Poland, and begg'd of Madame *Cosel* to remain at Dresden; but she was too timerous of losing him, to let him go without her. She answered, Nothing but Death should separate them; and he was obliged to take her with him.

Madame *Teschen* was informed, that the King was on his Return to Warsaw, accompanied by Madam *Cosel*, and at that News directly quitted Warsaw, and retired to the Seat of the Cardinal-Primate her Uncle, fully resolved to foment that Prelate's Hatred

tred against *Frederick-Augustus*. But this eager Desire of Revenge was cooled as soon as she received a Letter from her former Lover. In this Letter he made a pleasant mention of their former mutual Love.

MADAM,

IS it possible that Hatred should so immediately succeed an ardent Passion? As for me, I do still, and shall always retain the great Esteem and friendly Regard I have hitherto had for you; such I mean as is capable of forming the strictest Alliance; my Happiness consists in the sight of yours, and am at all times ready to contribute whatever may conduce to your Satisfaction. Can you harbour any other Sentiments of me? You, whose natural Benevolence is not unknown to me, who has loved me, and in whom I never once discovered any other than generous Thoughts? Will you oppose me in Favour of a King utterly unknown to you, and ignorant of the Nature of the Adoration of the Fair Sex? I cannot believe it, Madame; all the Ladies in Poland will, I'm persuaded, promote my Interest in Opposition to you, and blame you for preferring a Savage-King to a Prince, who has always admired you. Suppose therefore, I beg of you, my Interest with the Cardinal-Primate your Uncle: Persuade him not to break the Oath he has ſworn to be faithful to me, to remain favourable to my Party, that we obtain a Glorious Peace for the Benefit of a Nation, of which you are ſo worthy an Ornament, and of a King, whoſe Troubles cannot occaſion the Oblivion of his former paſſionate Love for you.

The King ſent this Letter by a Gentleman to Madame *Teſchen*. She could not peruſe it without burſting into Tears. She forgot the King's Infidelity, and could think of nothing but having loved him. In her Anſwer to him, ſhe concealed not from him, her Intention in retiring to her Uncle's Seat was chiefly to prejudice him: *But, Sir, I am now ſenſible, that it is not wholly in my Power to hate you. I ſhall convince your Majeſty, that I am not in the leaſt unworthy of the Confidence you honour me with; and ſhall not be ſparing in my Intreaties to my Uncle, to conform to your Requeſt.*

She did effectually all, that a diſcreet Woman was capable of doing, to ſupport her Uncle in the King's Intereſt; but the Cardinal had before reſolved to dethrone that Prince. He had for this purpoſe a Meeting with the King of Sweden, and Madame *Teſchen* could never divert him from

from that pernicions Deſign. She gave the King Notice of it, who finding no Refuge, except in his own Courage, guarded himſelf with a patient Conſtancy, and ſent for his Army from Saxony to encounter the King of Sweden, who advanced in great Haſte towards Warſaw.

Here I ſhall, perhaps, be expected to make a ſhort Digreſſion, and relate the Particulars of the War; but, as the Deſign of this Book is not to mention his military Atchievements, but to entertain the Reader with his amorous Adventures; and as thoſe may be read in other Hiſtories, † I ſhall cloſely follow my firſt Intention, and proceed with the other Amours of this Great and Gallant Prince.

† See the Hiſtory of Poland under the Reign of *Auguſtus*, lately publiſhed in Two Volumes *Octavo*.

CHAP. XI.

Of the King's Intrigue with Henrietta *a French Merchant's Daughter, an Accident occasioned by this Amour, Madame* Cosel's *Suspicions. The Swedes invade Poland, and hasten to Warsaw. King* Augustus's *Conduct, he flies into Saxony. Madame* Cosel *is delivered of a Daughter, and* Henrietta *is likewise delivered of a Daughter. Madame* Cosel *is enamoured with another Gentleman, the King is informed of it, and reproaches his Mistress. The King of Sweden advances towards Saxony with the new King of Poland.* Augustus *submits to the Conquerors, and retires to Flanders to make a Campaign under Prince* Eugene, *his Behaviour in the Army, his Return through Brussels, and Amour there with a French Comedian; she follows the King to Dresden, his Intrigue with her there. King* Frederick IV. *of Denmark visits* Augustus, *and meets with a splendid Reception. The two Kings visit King* Frederick *King*

of

of Prussia. Charles XII. *King of Sweden is conquered by the Russians.* Augustus's *Re-accession to the Throne of Poland. His Amour with Madame* Denhoff. *Madame* Cosel's *Disgrace after her third Delivery. Madame* Denhoff's *Disgrace, and the King's new Amour with Madame* Dieskau, *and after that with Mademoiselle* Osterhausen. *The Prince-Royal of Poland is married to the Arch-Dutchess of the Empire, and returns to Dresden, where grand Entertainments are prepared for him. The King renounces to his new Mistress all further Amours; marries his Daughter by* Henrietta, *and continues the usual Gallantry of his Court to the end of his Life.*

KING *Augustus* was now perplexed with State-Affairs, but could nevertheless not subdue his amorous Inclination; Madame *Cosel* was the principal Object of his Passion, but he sometimes disappointed her, to visit another Beauty of an inferior Rank.

There lived at this time in Warsaw a Wine-Merchant Native of France, nam'd *Duval*, who had a Daughter possessed of great

great Beauty, whose Name was *Henrietta*. The brightest young Persons of the Court made their Addresses to her, and no Coquet in Warsaw had so large a number of Adorers; she received all their Addresses with equal Behaviour, and no-body could distinguish which was the Favourite-Lover. This young Lady was the common Subject of Conversation with those, who were called the Gallants of the Court. A Company of these made mention of her one day at his Majesty's Levee. The King overheard them, and asked who was the fair Subject of their Discourse? Mr. *Rantzau*, Aid de Camp to the King, answered, That the Person of whom they were speaking, was the Daughter of a French Merchant, and certainly the most lovely Creature in the Kingdom. The King made no Reply, but was no sooner dress'd, than he ordered *Rantzau* to follow him into his Apartment, where he enquired in a more particular manner after *Henrietta*, and desired he would conduct him to her. This Visit was appointed for the next Night. The King told *Rantzau* he would disguise himself, and desired not to be known by *Henrietta*, or any Person whatever. The new Confident was forbid to mention this nocturnal Intrigue to Madame *Cosel*, and he promised to keep it secret, but begg'd the

the King would alſo promiſe not to expoſe him to the Reſentment of the revengeful Miſtreſs. The Monarch told him his Fears were groundleſs, and ordered him to be in the Anti-Chamber in the Duſk of the Evening. He then went to Madame *Coſel*, and told her, his Preſence had been deſired in a private Conference the next Night with Count *Tobianski* Nephew to the Cardinal-Primate, but that Lord being known by every one, he dared not ſee him in the Palace, therefore they had determined to meet in a private Houſe, where they were both to be in Diſguiſe. 'I intend to take
'*Rantzau* with me (ſaid he) and have the
'more Reaſon to truſt to his Fidelity, be-
'cauſe he is related to, and recommended
'by you.' The King expreſſed himſelf in ſo ſincere a manner ſeemingly, that he ſoon deceived his cunning and penetrating Miſtreſs. 'Though my Couſin is to have the
'Honour of going with you, Sir (replied
'ſhe) yet ſhall I be very uneaſy. A
'thouſand unforeſeen Accidents may hap-
'pen to you; Warſaw is inhabited by in-
'numerable Traitors, who are by Oath
'reſolved upon your Deſtruction, one Per-
'ſon happening to know you may put an
'End to your Days.' The King anſwered her in Jeſt, That he ſhould think thoſe Fears pardonable in any other Perſon, but could

could not excuse them in her. 'Alas! Sir, '(replied she fixing her Eyes tenderly upon him) have we not the liberty of being 'intrepid or fearful of a Danger approaching the Object of our Love?' The King made endearing Answers to those Tokens of Tenderness; but was very much disordered at a whimsical desire of Madame *Cosel* to accompany him in his nocturnal Journey. 'Suffer me, Sir, (said she) to 'follow and guard you; if any one dares 'to make any Attempt upon your Person, *Rantzau* and I may defend you; 'for before you shall be offended, I will 'lose my Life.' The King was touch'd with all the Tokens of Love he received from his Mistress, repented of having undertaken to deceive her, and was tempted to acknowledge the Truth, but thought such an Acknowledgment would only afflict her, he judg'd it most proper to conceal it; begg'd she would not follow him, telling her, he would rather disengage the Conference, than expose her to the Hazard of so fatal an Adventure. Madame *Cosel* submitted to his Desire, she not having yet acquired that Absolute Power, which she has since been seen to make use of.

The impatiently expected Night at last approached, the King disguised himself as well as possible, took Mr. *Rantzau* with him,

him, and went on foot to *Duval*'s House. They desired a private Room, and sometime afterwards Mr. *Rantzau*, one of their best Customers, sent for the young *Henrietta*, and presented the King to her, as if he had been an Officer and Friend of his; the young Person, who had only seen the King go by, and could not expect a Visit from him, was easily deceived. In the mean while they conversed together for some time, the King entertained her with his usual pleasant Discourses, and she look'd at him more attentively. 'The more I 'look at you, (said she) the more I find 'you resemble the King —— I own (re- 'plied he) several Persons have told me I 'had the Honour of resembling his Ma- 'jesty, but I would rather equal him in 'Power than Shape, that I might be ca- 'pable of raising your Fortune. —— 'Interest (said she) is not the sole Guide 'of my Actions; and was I so happy as to 'be beloved by him, I should think myself 'more fortunate by reason of the good 'Character I daily hear of him, than be- 'cause he would make my Fortune —— 'O! Mademoiselle (cried the King) if 'those be your Sentiments, let me beseech 'you to love me in Favour of the Resem- 'blance I bear to his Majesty —— You 'have indeed (replied she) those Graces, 'which

'which the King is diſtinguiſhed by; but
'I doubt whether you can boaſt of ſo ten-
'der a Heart, as his is ſaid to be, which
'can only charm me. ----- Yes, Mademoi-
'ſelle (replied the Prince in a Tranſport
'which deprived him of all Command over
'his Paſſion) I can boaſt of that tender
'Heart, and all the Qualities of that Prince,
'in ſhort, I am the King.' He then caſt
off a great Coat and Periwig, which hid
his dark-brown Hair, and ſhewed her the
Star of the Order of the Elephant fixed to
his Coat. Young *Henrietta* was at the ſight
of this in great Diſorder, fearful of not
having behaved herſelf with due Reſpect in
the King's preſence, but he ſoon removed
her Fears, by aſking her pardon for ſurprizing her in that manner: but told her
he had been informed of her Charms, and
was deſirous of ſeeing, whether they did
in reality correſpond with the Report he
had frequently heard of them; but found
her Beauty far exceeded the Deſcription
given of her, and that he could not enjoy
the ſame Liberty when he departed from
her, which he could boaſt of before he
ſaw her. *Henrietta* fixed her Eyes upon
him, anſwering with great Reſpect, but
ſo diſordered, ſcarce knowing what ſhe
ſaid. The King took Advantage of her
Confuſion, making an Offer of his Heart,
which

which *Henrietta* had not the power of refusing. In this exceſſive Joy he forgot Madame *Coſel* was ſitting up for him, and he ſpending the Night in jeſting and diverting himſelf with *Henrietta*, who being by degrees more familiar, made uſe of her natural Gaiety. She ſung, and plaid; the King would have perſuaded her to let him proceed further, but her Virtue oppoſed any criminal Action, and the Monarch was obliged to conform to her Will. They parted at length, promiſing faithfully to meet again the next Night.

Day-light appeared when the King returned to his Palace, where he found Madame *Coſel* at the Fire-ſide. As his Mind was wholly employed upon the beautiful *Henrietta*, he aſked her with much Indifference, why ſhe was not in Bed before? 'I waited (anſwered ſhe in a doleful Tone) 'and have been very uneaſy for you, Sir. '----You muſt accuſtom yourſelf to bear 'my Abſence more patiently (replied the 'King) when I am at the Head of an Ar- 'my, I ſee no probability of your follow- 'ing me thither ---Why not (anſwer'd ſhe) 'I ſhall follow you every-where, when I 'am near you no Fear ſhall caſt me down. 'But what has happened to you? (conti- 'tinued ſhe) you ſeem troubled -- Nothing 'troubles me (anſwered the King) except

'not

'not finding you in Bed.' The Coldneſs with which he ſpoke gave Madame *Coſel* Reaſon to ſuſpect an Intrigue; but ſhe thought proper to conceal her Suſpicions, till the event proved them to be juſt. She went into Bed, and the King, repenting of having cauſed any Uneaſineſs in her, would not leave her. They teſtified a moſt lively Tenderneſs for each other, which nevertheleſs did not remove Madame *Coſel's* Doubts.

The King roſe early to hold a Council, and ſhe made uſe of his Abſence in enquiring of Mr. *Rantzau* where he had been with the King. This Confident ſhewed no Diſorder at her Queſtion, telling her, they had been in Conference with the Count *Tobianski*. 'I believe your Words (ſaid 'ſhe) but take care not to deceive me, for 'if you do, you ſhall aſſuredly have good 'reaſon to repent of it'.

Mr. *Rantzau* acquainted the King with his Converſation with Madame *Coſel*. 'I 'proteſt (ſaid that Prince) your Couſin 'perplexes me very much. I love her: 'yet ſhe is a deſperate Woman, capable 'of undertaking any thing. But *Henri*-'*etta* does never the leſs pleaſe me. What 'can I do? You may engage yourſelf, Sir, '(anſwered Mr. *Rantzau*) with the Perſon 'who pleaſes you moſt, and no longer

'think

' think of the other.' The King made no Reply, but went to his Miſtreſs, whoſe Eyes he found full of Tears; ' What ' troubles you, Madame, (ſaid he) and ' what occaſions the Affliction I ſee you in? ' ------- Alas! Sir, (anſwered ſhe) I don't ' know what Reply to make, but my Heart ' tells me you are unfaithful.'-----The King did his utmoſt endeavour by endearing Speeches and Aſſurances to hearten her, he conjured her not to load him with groundleſs Suſpicions. And to divert her mind from thoſe perplexing Thoughts, he diſcourſed with her about the State of his Affairs, telling her, he ſhould be obliged to have another private Conference with Count *Tobianski*. ' I readily conſent to it, ' Sir, (anſwered ſhe) but fear Count *Tobi-* ' *anski* is not the Perſon you confer with.' The King, highly diſpleas'd with this repeated Affront, told her Suſpicions and Reproaches were very diſagreeable to him.

In the mean while the Night was coming on, which he impatiently waited for to ſee *Henrietta*, he went, and was pleaſed to find her leſs reſerved, than ſhe was the Night before: She had conſulted her Mother, whom ſhe acquainted with what had paſſed between the King and her, and who had inſtructed her how to behave herſelf; theſe Inſtructions had adapted her much

more

more to the King's Humour, and removed the Doubts ſhe was before perplexed with The King triumphed over her Shame; but ſhe ſhed numberleſs Tears, and no Virginity was ever loſt with more Sighs and Regret. The two Lovers aſſured each other frequently of their mutual Love, and the Aſſurances of both Parties were made in a very different manner.

The Night was almoſt paſt before the King retired. Before he left his dear *Henrietta* he begg'd her Conſent to keep their Amour ſecret. He promis'd to viſit her frequently, and agreed, that ſhe ſhould viſit him in a Man's Dreſs, and Mr. *Rantzau* ſhould conduct her to him.

When the King was going home with his Confident, he met with an Adventure, which almoſt diſcover'd this whole Intrigue. A Gentleman of the Life-Guard was deſperately in Love with *Henrietta*, intending to be marry'd to her. He had been two days out of her Company, when told by a Servant, *Henrietta* had ſpent the two laſt Nights with Mr. *Rantzau* and another Officer. This rais'd a furious Jealouſy in the Gentleman; he reſolved to take away the Perſon's Life, who durſt deprive him of his Miſtreſs, and that his Succeſs might be infallible, he took with him his Brother, a Gentleman of the Life-Guard like him, both waiting for Mr. *Rant-*

Rautzau at ſome diſtance from *Duval*'s Houſe. They no ſooner ſaw him, than they cried out, deſiring him to draw his Sword: but Mr. *Rantzau* in fear of diſcovering the King, thinking the Perſons who threaten'd him were perhaps miſtaken, he having had no Quarrel with any-body, told them his Name, and if he was really the Perſon they intended to fight with, he was ready to give them Satisfaction: but deſired they would allow him half an Hour to go and return an Anſwer to a Meſſage his Majeſty had charged him with. 'By 'no means (cried the other) you ſhall not 'eſcape me: be ready for your own De-'fence. You have deprived me of my 'Miſtreſs, and I will in return occaſion the 'loſs of your Life or mine.' The King ſuffer'd them to fight, whilſt the other Perſon remained a Spectator like him; but when he ſaw him run to his Comrade's Aſſiſtance to kill *Rantzau*, he ran to the latter's Succour with Sword in hand, and aſſaulting the ſecond Lifeguard-man, gave him ſo violent a Blow that he dropp'd his Sword. Whilſt he was taking it up again, a Coach paſſed attended by Servants with Flambeaus. The diſarmed Soldier knew the King, called out to his Brother to deſiſt, throwing himſelf at the King's Feet: 'Sir (ſaid he) I have deſerved Death, and

'ſhould

'for the little Regard you have to my
'Words. I desire you not to go out
'of my Service. Behave yourselves like
'Gentlemen of Honour, and be assured I
'shall endeavour to advance your Fortune.'
Hereupon they were admitted to kiss his hand, and after they were gone, the King sent to each a Present of an hundred Ducats.

In the mean while Madame *Cosel* easily perceived the Ardency of the King's Passion to be much diminish'd. She doubted not but some Mistress caus'd an Alteration in his Heart, but whatever pains she gave herself could not discover the Person. After many useless Enquiries she was informed by one of the King's Valets de Chambre, that the King passed many Hours with a young Man, who by his great Beauty, and the mysterious method by which he was introduced to the King, gave him reason to think the Person might perhaps be a disguis'd Woman. This Information cleared at once innumerable Doubts, which tormented her, but her Condition was not much better. As she was naturally very arrogant, she could scarce prevail upon herself patiently to put up with it: but she had not yet been at Variance with the King, and thought it would look more prudent in her not to exclaim against him, if he could not be convinced, than to ruin herself by a

Re-

'should be too happy, was I to receive it
' from your hands. I desire no Favour,
' because I acknowledge my Crime is un-
' pardonable --- You are mistaken (replied
' the King) with me all Faults are pardon-
' able, provided they were not perpetrated
' with an evil Design. I excuse that which
' you have just now committed, being per-
' swaded you did not intend to offend me,
' but enjoin ye both, to make some Ex-
' cuse to *Rantzau* for having assaulted him,
' and use him for the future with the Re-
' spect due to him from your hands.' He
gave them a slight Reproof for offending
a Person they were not acquainted with,
desired they would be more considerate for
the future, and forbid them under the Pe-
nalty of incurring his Displeasure, to make
any further mention of this Adventure, or
to let any-body know they met him. The
next morning the two Soldiers thought
their Ruin inevitable, applied to Mr. *Rantzau*, and after asking his Pardon for their
late Offence, begg'd he would obtain leave
for them to depart, not being able to believe, after committing so great a Fault,
they could ever hope for Promotion. Mr.
Rantzau deliver'd the Message to the King,
who sent for them both immediately; 'I
' have assured you (said he) of my Pardon,
' and sent for you to-day to reproach you
' for

Resentment. She was thus meditating on what would be most proper for her to do, when the King surprized her in a deep Thought. As she sate in a melancholy posture, he told her she seem'd distressed, and he had for some time always found her bright Eyes drowned in Tears. She answered him by this passage in a Tragedy;

What reason have I not to cry?
My senseless Lover bids me die.

The King blush'd at these Words, and looking with a tender Air; 'What is it 'you mean (said he) by Reproaches, I so 'little deserve?' She soon expressed herself in a lively and sorrowful manner. The King surprized to find her so well acquainted with his Intrigue, assured her in a seemingly sincere manner, no greater Falshood was ever invented. He told her the pretended Woman, mentioned to her, was Nephew to *Brebendofski* Governor of Culm, that That Nobleman had sent him to give Notice of the measures taken by the Polish Rebels; that he had indeed detained him for some time in his Chamber, but no longer than was requisite for an Answer to the Governor; since that time he had never seen the young Gentleman, and if the Person had been a disguis'd Woman, to whom he he had been amorously inclined, it would not have been impracticable to find her again: but to all outward appearance the Persons who reported these Falsities to her, intended to supply her with Arms for her own Destruction, since he hated nothing more than Expostulations and Broils. The Countess, vexed to see him persevere so stedfastly in the Denial of his Infidelity, was highly enraged. 'I believe you (said 'she) but be now assured by me, I am re- 'solved not to undergo the Fate of your 'other Mistresses. I have for your Sake 'quitted a Husband, lost my Reputation, 'and done all this, because you promis'd 'me upon Oath an everlasting Fidelity. I 'will not suffer your Abuses, except your 'Life pays for them; I am resolved to 'break your Head with a Pistol, and then 'make use of it upon myself, as a Punish- 'ment for my Folly in loving you.'

However insolent this Rage of the Countess was, the King pitied her; endeavoured to appease her Anger, and did not leave her till very late. He was considering of the means by which he might extirpate this Mistress's Jealousy, when an unexpected Courier brought him Advice the Swedes were advancing in great Haste towards Warsaw. Other Cares employed his Mind at this time, and he found no other way left, than to take to his Flight, the Polanders being so imprudent as to prefer the Yoke *Charles* XII. was going to impose on them to the pleasant and happy Reign of *Frederick-Augustus*, forsook him; and those few who remained loyal to their King were incapable of keeping him upon the Throne, and ever unwilling to consent to his sending for his Army from Saxony to his Assistance. This magnanimous Prince found only Refuge in himself; he acted as the most refined Politician, when he endeavoured to stop the Progress of his Enemy, retired to Cracaw, there assembled a Body of Soldiers, and sent for the Saxons; and when he saw himself able to compare his Forces to those of the implacable *Charles*, he marched on to encounter him, resolved to hazard all, and leave it to the decision of a Battle. But before he placed himself at the Head of his Army he sent Madame *Cosel* back into Saxony. This Departure was very tender on both Sides, and nevertheless exempt of any Weakness. Madame *Cosel* conjured the King to consent to her Stay near his Person. 'I will cloath my-'self in a Man's Dress (said she) and fight 'at your Side. My Blood and Life are 'but of a very small Value; and I am 'ready to sacrifice either for your Sake --- 'No, Madame, (replied the King)' your

'Days

'Days are too precious to me, preserve
'them. Desire me not to place all that is
'most dear to me, you and my Crown, at
'the Hazard of a Battle. Depart for
'Dresden; that I may be certain of your
'Safety, I shall then fight more vigorously;
'and as the Pleasure of seeing you again
'will be the first Prize I shall gain by the
'Victory, I dare promise myself to enjoy
'it.' The Countess not daring to insist on her Demand any longer, consented to depart: but as those Suspicions, which were first founded at Warsaw, were still inherent in her Mind, she made use of those tender moments which preceded her Departure in asking the King whether she had any just Cause for those Doubts. The King, who no longer thought of *Henrietta*, whom he had left at Warsaw, confessed the whole Adventure. Madame *Cosel* seemed not in the least displeas'd, but her Heart was very much vexed at it, and she fully resolved to sacrifice *Rantzau* to her Vengeance.

At length she departed for Dresden, where she may be truly said to have had a greater Command than the Prince of *Furstemberg*, who was in the mean while Stadtholder or Vice-King of Saxony. The King continued his March towards *Charles* the Twelfth's Army. These two Monarchs met in the Plain of Clissau. The Battle begun, and both exerted an extraordinary Valour, but *Charles* at last prevailed by the Number of his Troops, and carried a compleat Victory. *Frederick-Augustus* retired to Cracaw, but the Conqueror pursued him, and he flew from that Place to Lublin, where he assisted at a Diet, which however came to no particular Resolution. He retired at last to Saxony. When he arrived at Dresden, he found Madame *Cosel* in Labour; but this did not hinder him from running to her. His Presence afforded her Comfort, and some moments afterwards she was delivered of a Daughter. Madame *Cosel* had undergone so much pain, and was so weak, that she could not speak to the King, but squeezed his Hand, and looked at him tenderly. The King was so touched with her Misery that his Eyes were drowned in Tears. Her Pain being a little lessened, she made use of all the most tender Expressions her Fancy could inspire her with. The King asked her whether his Defeat did not occasion her Love to cease. 'I shall love you (cried 'she with more Force than her Condition 'would admit) if I even see you in 'Chains.'

During the forty Days in which she kept her Bed, the King passed his time at her Bed-side, and took all possible care to please

please her. One day, as they were discoursing together, Mr. *Bose*, Minister and Secretary of State, brought the King Word that he had receiv'd a certain Message with a Letter, which came from Warsaw, and which he presented to the King. The King, when he opened the Letter, blush'd, and was in great Disorder. Madame *Cosel* desired to know the Subject of it, and to see it herself, but he refused to shew it her. This rais'd Madame *Cosel*'s Curiosity, she leap'd out of Bed, and pull'd it by force out of his hand. She shewed the King and Mr. *Bose* on that Occasion what no modest Woman would have shewn her Husband without many Perswasions. She found that the Letter came from *Henrietta*, who acquainted the King that she was delivered of a Daughter, and desired to know his Pleasure concerning the Child. 'Let her 'drown it, (cried Madame *Cosel*) and 'would to God it was in my power to 'drown the Mother too!' The King laugh'd heartily at this impertinent Sally, but Madame *Cosel* considered of the matter seriously, and told him, that if he made any Answer to that Creature, or acknowledged the Child of which she said she was deliver'd, she would instantly take Post, and go to Warsaw to strangle both the Mother and Child. The King to prevent any

Diſturbance, promis'd to think no more of either *Henrietta* or her Infant-Daughter. This Child however, which was at that time ſo abus'd, has been ſince acknowledged by the King; ſhe has been to the King dearer than any of his other Children, and he has honoured her with the Title of Counteſs of *Orzelska*, and married her to a younger Prince of the Houſe of *Holſtein-Beck*.

This Miſtreſs was in the mean while, notwithſtanding her great Jealouſy, thought by ſeveral Gentlemen a proper Object of Adoration, and their Offers were very agreeable to her. She did indeed receive them only as Victims to ſacrifice to the King and her own Intereſt. One of theſe Lovers was the Count of *Lecherenne*, a Nobleman of Savoy, whoſe Neceſſity induced him to come with his Brother, a Knight of the Order of Malta to Dreſden, in ſearch after a Lady of Fortune. The two Brothers directly made their Addreſſes to Madame *Coſel*; this they thought would be the moſt proper means to accompliſh their Point, for ſhe had the chief Diſpoſal of Honours and Royal Favours. She admitted them as Gentlemen of the King's Bed-Chamber. Whilſt ſhe was alone at Dreſden, theſe Gentlemen inſinuated themſelves into her Favour; but the Count was

pre-

preferr'd to the Knight: he had a fine Shape, and made a graceful Appearance. As he was a Man of exquisite parts, was witty, complaisaint, had a nice Taste, and was never perplexed with any Doubts. The particular Kindness Madame *Cosel* testified for him, was wrongly censured by her Enemies. As they could do her no greater Prejudice, than set the King and her at Variance, they did their utmost endeavour to perswade him, that the Love he testified for her was too great for the little return he received from her hands. This was certainly no very easy Undertaking, but they took so essential a method to carry their Point, that, except any of 'em were overheard by the King, their Design could not be discovered, nor the Project be in the least suspected. The better to succeed in the Plot they represented to the King, that Madame *Cosel* had shewed but little Deference to his Majesty in certain Assemblies, and seemed to give this Report in so disinterested a manner, that the King, notwithstanding his great Subtilty in Affairs of this kind, could scarce help being deceived by their seeming Sincerity.

All these Words however made but a slight impression upon the King's Mind, till Madame *Cosel*'s Enemies, at the Head of which was the Prince of *Furstemberg*, mentioned the Count of *Lecheremme*, as the Rival he ſhould be in fear of. Hereupon he went to his Miſtreſs, to expoſtulate with her about the matter. He found her in her Cloſet looking conſiderately upon a Picture, wherein was repreſented the Ceremony of his Coronation. ‘ How ! Madame, ‘ (ſaid he in a diſdainful manner) do you ‘ ſtill condeſcend to look upon my Picture ? ‘ or is it ſome other Object, which you ‘ regard ſo ſtedfaſtly upon that Table ? ---- ‘ How can a Perſon, Sir, (ſaid ſhe) ſo ‘ graceful as yourſelf, have any reaſon to ‘ think, that Spectators can fix their Eyes ‘ upon any other Object but yourſelf ; ‘ and if you are even enamoured with the ‘ moſt fickle Woman on Earth, your ſhining Merit ſhould keep you from all jealous Thoughts ---- Hitherto (replied the ‘ King) I thought I had no Grounds for ‘ Suſpicion ; but find myſelf highly miſtaken, and thoſe Perſons who judge only ‘ by outward Appearance, are moſt apt ‘ to be deceived.’ By theſe Words Madame *Coſel* ſoon perceived the King's Jealouſy, at which ſhe felt a ſecret Joy, it proving ſufficiently that he loved her. In the mean while, pretending to be offended at his Diſcourſe ; ‘ I cannot imagine the ‘ meaning of thoſe intricate Terms, Sir, ‘ (ſaid ſhe) and till you expreſs yourſelf in

‘ a

'a more intelligible manner, you cannot
'expect me to ſay anything for my own
'Juſtification --- You will perhaps find it a
'more difficult matter to juſtify yourſelf,
'(replied the King in a ſerious manner,
'which begun to perplex Madame *Coſel*)
'than I ſhall to convince you of Things
'which you wiſhed undoubtedly not to
'reach my knowledge.' She made no further Anſwer to theſe Words, than her former Tokens of Tenderneſs; put into practice whatever a moſt paſſionate Love could inſpire her with, and the Tears, which accompanied all theſe Tranſports, appeaſed the Anger of her incens'd Lover. She no ſooner ſaw him a little pacified, than ſhe begg'd he would tell her what had occaſioned theſe Reproaches which ſhe had juſt before heard; ſhe ſwore to own the plain Truth; and added to this, that if ſhe did even think herſelf criminal, ſhe repos'd ſo great a Confidence in him, and was perſwaded that his Love to her was ſo great, as to pardon any Folly ſhe had been guilty of. The King told her all he had heard to her Prejudice, and ſhe did not deny that the Count of *Lecherenne* had made amorous Addreſſes to her; but would not own that ſhe had ever given ear to them. She told him, that he ſhould have been baniſhed her Preſence, but that

ſhe was exceſſive uneaſy during his Abſence, and therefore thought a little Converſation with the Count would not be criminal; and that ſhe had only admitted him to her Company, after having forbid him ever to mention Love again. The King comforted her, and promis'd for the future not to regard the ſlanderous Reports of envious Perſons; he proteſted that no ridiculous and ill-grounded Fear ſhould ever induce him to loſe the Affection he had ſworn ever to retain for her; and deſired ſhe would be perſwaded of that by his own Word and Promiſe ----- 'O! Sir, (ſaid ſhe) if your 'Majeſty ſuffers Detractions of that kind 'ſo nearly to approach your Throne, I 'have reaſon to fear that your Perſon 'will in a little time be injured by them, 'and they will offend that, which I 'eſteem moſt ſacred --- Be no longer per-'plexed about it (replied the King) I ſhall 'myſelf regulate thoſe matters. She ſtill inſiſted upon being told who was the Perſon that firſt rais'd this Report; but the King refus'd. 'Let it ſuffice (ſaid he) that 'I look upon them as evil Reports, which 'I ſhall never believe.' He then left her fully convinced of her Innocence, and greatly prejudiced againſt thoſe who injured her by aſſerting theſe Falſities, and more eſpecially againſt *Lecherenne*, for oc-

caſion-

casioning them to speak evil of his Mistress, whom he ordered instantly to quit his Service, and directly afterwards to leave Dresden.

This unfortunate Gentleman was desirous before his Departure to see Madame *Cosel*, and in order thereto attended at her Door, but she sent him Word, she could not admit those whom the King banished from his Presence. To let him know however, that she saw him depart with much Regret, she sent him a Ring, which the King had some time before presented her with, with this Ring the Count left Dresden. Few days after this the King seeing her dress herself, observed that she had not the Ring and demanded the reason of it. She seemed surprized at the Loss, and asked her Servants, whether they had seen the Ring, who unfortunately, or for want of better Instructions answered, that they had not seen it within the four or five last days. This being exactly the time of Count *Lecherenne*'s Departure, the King doubted not of her having given him the Ring at their last Farewel. This Thought revived his Jealousy, and enraged him in an uncommon manner; he reproached her severely, and the Countess heard him with Patience, which had she been innocent, she would have resented.

Whilst

Whilſt theſe trifling Affairs were tranſacting at Court, *Charles* XII. who had caus'd *Staniſlaus Leczinski*, Palatine of Poſnania to be crowned at Warſaw, advanced towards Saxony with the new King, the ſhining Trophy of all his Victories. The King having no Army to oppoſe him, was forced to ſign the Treaty of Peace, ſuch as that implacable Prince was pleas'd to preſcribe. This did not however prevent the King of *Sweden*'s March further into Saxony, where he rais'd immenſe Contributions. Whoever is converſant in the Hiſtory of thoſe Times, cannot be ignonorant, that That Prince left Saxony with the Deſign of dethroning the then Czar ; and that he was himſelf the moſt remarkable Inſtance of the Inconſtancy of Fortune, and Inſtability of humane Grandeur.

Frederick-Auguſtus retain'd his uſual Magnanimity during the whole Courſe of his Adverſities. He was never heard to bemoan his unhappy Fate, nor to complain of the Ingratitude of the Polanders. Madame *Coſel*, daily apprehenſive of his being troubled with ſome private Uneaſineſſes, did her utmoſt Endeavour to remove all the Troubles of his Mind ; ſhe prepared every day ſome new Entertainment for his Diverſion. The King loved Pleaſure, but

was

was not wholly given over to them. War and Hopes of Glory were his chief Delight; and as the ſtate of his Affairs would not ſupply him with a ſufficient Number of Forces to carry on a War againſt the Uſurper of his Crown, he went into Flanders in ſearch after Renown in the Army of the Allies. He made his Appearance there *incognito*, and made uſe of the Equipage belonging to Prince *Eugene* of *Savoy*. All the Men of various Nations of which this Army was compos'd admired his great Experience in the Art of War, and undaunted Courage. He expos'd his Life ſeveral times with ſo little Precaution, that Prince *Eugene* and the Duke of *Marlborough* took the liberty of remonſtrating the Danger to him. He anſwered them laughing, *That Warriors ought to be* Calviniſts, *and ſincerely believe Predeſtination.*

This Great Monarch, after having acquired an entire knowledge of the Nature of an Attack, and foreſeeing that the Siege of Liſle would perhaps be extended to a great length of Time, even after the French would have ceas'd making freſh Attempts to raiſe the Siege, reſolved to return into Saxony. He paſſed through Bruſſels, and to avoid all tedious Ceremonies aſſumed the Name of Count of *Torgau*, and arrived at that Town juſt before

fore the Gates were ſhut. He went the ſame Evening to the Opera; there he ſaw a Dancer named *Duparc*, who was poſſeſſed of great Beauty and extraordinary Graces, and deſerved inconteſtably the Preference to any Dancer out of France at that time. The King was pleaſed with her, and deſired her Company at the Houſe of *Vernus* a celebrated Cook, who kept a very great Ordinary. She readily accepted of the Invitation, and *Duparc* appeared with three other Comedians at the Entertainment. The King was by the Name of Count of *Torgau* accompanied by Mrs. *Fitztuhm*, *Bauditz*, and the Count of *W*---- who had joined in their Converſation. When they were at Table *Duparc*, who was extreamly beautiful, but more particularly with a Glaſs in her hand, wholly captivated the King's Heart. He entertained her with pleaſant Diſcourſes, and charmed the Coquet, whoſe Diſcernment was certainly great. But as her Prejudice in Favour of the French Nation was ſo great, ſhe could not imagine any but a Frenchman to be given ſo much to Gallantry, ſhe could not be perſwaded the Count of *Torgau* was a German. 'You are a Native 'of France (ſaid ſhe) your Gallantry, Air 'and Politeneſs witneſs it ---- No, really, '(anſwered the King) I am an honeſt

Saxon,

'Saxon, whose Words correspond with his
'Thoughts, and give every thing its true
'Appellation ------ Are you a Saxon? (re-
'plied *Duparc*) then I beg you would de-
'scribe your King to me; I have heard
'that he is really an incomparable Prince.'
She added, that within the two last Years she had teazed an old Aunt of her's who belong'd to a Company of French Comedians at Dresden, to procure her a Place in the King's Service; but that all the Answer she could receive, was, that no Place was vacant for her. The King replied, that her Aunt surely did not take much Pains, or was not very desirous of seeing her there, else it would be no difficult matter to get her the Place of chief Dancer: That if she did still intend to go to Dresden, he would procure her Admission and some advantageous Post. *Duparc* accepted the Offer, and the King told her, if she pleas'd she might go the next day, and offered her a Place in his Coach: but she thank'd him under pretence that some Affairs detained her at Brussels, promis'd however to follow him thither in a Month's time. The King, to engage her to the performance of her Promise, gave her a Purse of a Thousand Ducats to defray the Expence of her Journey. He desired to exact some pleasant Acknowledgment of her;

her; but ſhe, quite contrary to the Cuſtom of Perſons of that kind, told him in a merry Air, that he poſſeſſed not only the gallant Diſpoſition, but alſo the Vivacity of a Frenchman; but that, though her Virginity was loſt, yet did ſhe not love to be wholly taken up with Amours; that her Heart muſt firſt be captivated before ſhe gave any eſſential Tokens of her Love: but before ſhe entred into any amorous Engagement ſhe would firſt be acquainted with the Character of the Perſon to whom ſhe diſcover'd her Heart. The King oppos'd her Sentiments, but in vain; and his Paſſion for her became more violent. He conjured her not to delay her Journey to Dreſden, which ſhe promis'd, and at his Departure he adorned her Finger with a Ring of great Value.

The King quitted Bruſſels the next Morning, and arrived in few days at Dreſden. He there found Madame *Coſel* a ſecond time in Child-bed, and his Family increas'd by another Daughter. His Miſtreſs made grievous Complaints of the Prince of *Furſtemberg*, Stadtholder, and the Field-Marſhal Count *Flemming*, whom ſhe accus'd of having behaved very diſreſpectfully to her; theſe Noblemen, having received Inſtructions from the King, had indeed refus'd to obey Madame *Coſel*'s Orders, ſuch as ſhe thought

thought herself entitled to give them. The King, who was never fond of private Broils, occasioned by Envy or Malice, and always desirous of a happy Union between his Mistress and Ministers, reconciled them; but this Reconciliation did not remove their great Desire to injure each other as much as possible, for which they neglected no Opportunity.

The King enjoyed a happy Peace with Madam *Cosel*, a Peace not interrupted by any Jealousy, till *Duparc* came to disturb their Felicity. She arrived at Dresden whilst the King was at Mauritzburg; and enquired every-where for the Count of *Torgau*, but could no-where be informed how to meet with him. Her Aunt conducted her to Mr. *Murdacho* Chamberlain and Director of the King's Diversions, who gave her a Reception very different from that, which Persons of her Function commonly met with at his hands; he told her, that the King had given him Orders to admit her to the Number of the Dancers belonging to the Court, to provide her handsome Apartments, and to furnish them as would be found necessary and agreeable to her Pleasure, and that his Majesty desired she would begin to dance at the Opera of *Elida*, which the Comedians were to repeat to represent her at the

King's

King's Return. *Duparc* was ſurprized with Wonder and Delight at ſo gracious a Reception; ſhe teſtified her Acknowledgment to Mr. *Murdacho*, and aſked by what ſingular Fortune ſhe was honoured with the King's Acquaintance? He anſwered, that he had good reaſon to think ſhe was obliged to the Count of *Torgau* for the King's unexpected Munificence. She could get no better Information, and retired with her Aunt, who was no leſs aſtoniſhed than her Niece at what had happened. They could not imagine who was this Count of *Torgau*, and dared not to name the King, tho' he was ſuſpected to be the Perſon: The Aunt was in fear leſt ſhe ſhould flatter her Niece too much, was ſhe to ſpeak of it; and the Niece was fearful of being deceived in her Expectation, and having the Aſperſion of a vain Perſon. 'But if it 'was the King (ſaid ſhe to herſelf) why 'ſhould he conceal his Name? why ſhould 'he be unwilling to acquaint me with his 'Dignity? what could be his Intention in 'ſending for, and receiving me in this 'manner.' In this Perplexity did ſhe remain till the Day on which the King made his Appearance at the Theatre, ſaying to herſelf, *It is the King undoubtedly*, and perhaps a Moment afterwards, *It cannot be.*

The

The ſame Morning an extraordinary Preſent was brought her of a Box cover'd with Crimſon-Velvet and Gold-Lace, and was told, that it came from the Count of *Torgau*. The Bearers of this Box would not inform her of any further Particulars, notwithſtanding her diligent Enquiries, they remained as it were ſpeechleſs, and returned her no other Anſwer but by intelligible Signs. When ſhe open'd her Box ſhe found in it two Rich Suits of Cloaths, one for the Stage, and the other to wear in Town: to theſe were added all the Things requiſite to dreſs her from Head to Foot, not even the Slippers were wanting. The Pockets were full of Toys of a great Value, among which was a ſmall Pocket-Book enriched with Gold. She open'd it, and found upon the firſt Leaf the Count's Excuſes for not having paid her any Viſit yet: He begg'd her acceptance of the Cloaths he ſent her, as Fore-runners of the Kindneſſes he ſhould diſtinguiſh her by; and finiſhed the Letter, by telling her, he intended to pay his Reſpects to her at Supper the ſame Evening. *Duparc* was overjoy'd, when informed of the true Condition of her Lover.

She dreſſed herſelf with all the Care of a Perſon, intending to gain a great Conqueſt, and at laſt appeared upon the Stage, more

more like a Queen than a Dancer, ſo bright was her Appearance. All her Companions were in Admiration of her, and could not comprehend from whence ſhe received ſo magnificent a Dreſs.

They waited ſome time for the King, who at laſt appeared with Madame *Coſel*. The young and amiable *Duparc* was extreamly impatient to ſee him, and for that purpoſe plac'd herſelf in a Wing directly oppoſite to the Monarch's Seat. But how can I deſcribe her Joy at finding her Lover was the King himſelf! *Pſyche* could not be more pleas'd, when told, that the God of Love had rais'd her to the fatal Rock. The King ſeeing her ſwoon away, called to *Beltour* a Comedian to run to her Aſſiſtance, and reach'd to her from his Seat a little Flaſk of Carmelite's Water. Madame *Coſel* was highly diſpleas'd at the King's great Civilities to a Stranger; and reproached him for it. ' It ſeems, Sir, ' (ſaid ſhe with a diſdainful Air) that you ' are very profuſe of your Kindneſſes, in ' conferring them on a Creature utterly ' unknown to you, and undoubtedly little ' deſerving your Regard.' The King offended at her Inſolence, anſwered with Indifference, that he might juſtly be blamed for being munificent to a great degree, and to Perſons who abus'd his Liberality; but

but that he hoped for better Tokens of Gratitude from the hands of *Duparc*. Madame *Cosel* exasperated at his Reply, told him, that none but Vagabonds were the Objects of his Love. The King unwilling to let all the Court be Witnesses of their Differences, rose up, and went to the Queen's Apartment, who was discoursing with her Brother the Margrave of *Brandenburg-Bareith*. Madame *Cosel* scarce capable of putting up with the Affront, and unable to conceal her Wrath, feigned an Indisposition, and left the Theatre. The King was not so complaisant as to follow her, nor did he send any Messenger to enquire after her Health; which made her Uneasiness insupportabe. The King having been some time with the Queen, called Mr. *Murdacho*, and whisper'd to him, that he had ordered his Servants to carry the Supper to his House, and had invited *Duparc*, with three other Actresses, whose Names he mentioned.

The Comedy was no sooner finished, than the King went immediately to Mr. *Murdacho*'s. His beloved *Duparc* made her Appearance there in the Apparel, which the pretended Count of *Torgau* had sent for her Use in the Town. The King ran to meet her, when he saw her coming; but she kneel'd down and thank'd him for his

ex-

excessive Goodness. The King rais'd and embraced her, and told her that she was not to lye at his Feet; and that he should not even suffer that Deference, if he had not conceived those tender Sentiments for her, which render all Conditions equal. This Preamble was succeeded by many Demonstrations of Joy and Tenderness. *Duparc* could not yet recover from her Astonishment; she thought herself in a Dream, to see a King her Lover, and moreover a polite, generous, amiable King, a King who testified a Regard for her, due to none but a Princess.

They were not so merry at Supper as could have been expected. The King and his new Mistress spoke in a very low Voice to each other; and after the Dyssart they went together into a Room hard by. The other Ladies were put to a stand, and, tho' well accustomed to act the parts of Queens and Princesses, could not find Expressions suitable to the Presence and Company of a real King. But they were in much better Humour, when *Duparc* returned with the King, and told them, that his Majesty intended to present each of them with a new Suit of Cloaths; to which the King added an hundred Pistoles to each.

Since

Since that time *Duparc* was the King's private Miſtreſs, for Madame *Coſel* remained Reigning-Miſtreſs all this while, the King being unable to ſurmount the great Aſcendant ſhe had gained over him. She was nevertheleſs inform'd of the King's frequent Viſits to *Duparc*, but did not either look upon her as a formidable Rival, or was in fear of offending the King by too outrageous Jealouſies, and only gave him ſlight Reproofs for it. 'You invent 'Chimeras (anſwered the King) for Arms 'to reſiſt me with; for, what reaſon have 'you after all to complain? do you find 'me leſs fond, leſs liberal, and not ſo free-'hearted to you as uſual? How can you 'think that I am enamour'd with *Duparc?* 'Can't I ſee or ſpeak to a Woman without 'being enamour'd with her? I conceal 'nothing from you: Was my former 'Love in the leaſt diminiſh'd I ſhould in-'ſtantly forſake you for miſtruſting me in 'this manner?' Madame *Coſel* was greatly pleas'd with the Trouble the King took to juſtify himſelf; ſhe anſwered jeſting: 'I 'know that I tire you with my Re-'proaches; but I know alſo that I can-'not have too watchful an Eye upon your 'Gallantries, and that you are never in 'want of means whereby to deceive me 'and thirty other Miſtreſſes as ſuſpicious

'as

'as I am.' By these trifling Reproaches and Justifications the King and Madame *Cosel* supported their mutual Love, which would else have been subverted or remain'd in a languishing State.

About this time *Frederick* IV, King of Denmark, whom an earnest Desire to see Italy once more, which had afforded him Abundance of Diversion in his Youth, had induced to quit his Kingdom, returned from his Journey. Before he went to his own Metropolis, he resolved to visit the King of Poland and her Royal Highness, Mother to the latter, and Aunt to the former. The Danish Monarch met with a splendid Reception, and all the other Ceremonies usual on the like Occasion. The King sent the Princes of the Blood, the Prince of *Furstemberg*, the Counts of *Flemming* and *Pflug*, and several Noblemen and others to meet the Royal Guest. He went himself two Miles from Dresden to meet the King of Denmark, with whom he made a grand Entry into that Town. The Queen and Prince-Royal of Poland waited upon and received them at the Bottom of the Stair case, and after they had testified their Pleasure in seeing him, they placed him between them. The King of Poland walk'd by himself. The Guest was conducted into the Hall, where the Queen pre-

presented to him the Ladies of the greatest Quality at Court. Madame *Cosel* was not present there, the King being unwilling so far to mortify the Queen, as to oblige her to present that Lady to the King of Denmark, nor did he think proper to present her publickly to that Prince. The King of Denmark, after having for some time conversed with the Queen and Prince-Royal of Poland, went with his Majesty to the Apartment intended for his Use, and from thence the two Monarchs went to Madame *Cosel*. They remained with her till they were called to Supper, which was certainly very splendid, and where none of those grand Ceremonies commonly used on the like Occasions were omitted. The King of Denmark sate between the King and Queen. When he drank the first time twenty-four Pieces of Cannon were fired, and the Supper was accompanied by a fine Consort of Musick. Among the Ladies, that surrounded the Table, appeared Madame *Cosel* shining with Jewels of all kinds. The King of Denmark was unwilling to see her stand, and desired his Majesty to permit her to sit down: A Chair was directly reach'd her, which displeased all the other Ladies, and kept them in a disagreeable Humour all Night.

The following Days were ſpent in Entertainments and Feaſts, and the forty Days of his Daniſh Majeſty's Stay at Dreſden were all ſignalized by ſome new Diverſion, whoſe wondrous Magnificence both ſurprized and delighted them. Madame *Coſel* was the principal Object of theſe Feaſts; every one, even the two Monarchs, honoured her by wearing her Coat of Arms every-where. No King's Miſtreſs was ever diſtinguiſhed by more ſplendid Honours.

The two Kings went to Lichtenberg to viſit his Royal Highneſs. From thence they departed for Pretſch, where they were magnificently treated by the Queen. They departed from this Palace for Potzdam, to pay a Viſit to *Frederick* I. King of Pruſſia, who by the Reception he gave them, deſervedly maintained the Sir-name of *Magnificent*, which he had before acquired. Both Monarchs were equally gallant in reſpect to the Ladies of the Pruſſian Court; and tho' his Daniſh Majeſty could not boaſt of ſo fine an Aſpect as *Frederick-Auguſtus*, yet was he equally fond of the Fair Sex, and ſeldom without a Miſtreſs. The Pruſſian Court was adorned with a vaſt number of beautiful Ladies, but they had not that gallant Diſpoſition innate to thoſe of Saxony, and appeared very

very diſagreeable to the two Kings. The Counteſs of *Wartenberg*, Wife of the Great Chamberlain, and Prime Miniſter to his Pruſſian Majeſty, thought her Charms ſufficient to enſlave the King of Poland; and for that purpoſe made bold and indecent Addreſſes to him; but as no Beauty could be found in her Perſon, her Complexion excepted, and as her Converſation ſavour'd too much of the meanneſs of her Extraction †, the King could not be pleaſed with her. He knew that Lord *Rabbi* §, the Britiſh Ambaſſador was her Lover; for which Reaſon, when *Fitztuhm* took notice of the Counteſs's inceſſant Endeavours to pleaſe him, he anſwered that Favourite, that whatever Pains ſhe took, ſhe ſhould not be able to ſet him at Variance with the Maritime Powers. The Counteſs was in Deſpair, when anſwered ſo coldly by the King; as ſhe was the moſt vain and moſt prejudiced in her own Favour, of all other Women, ſhe was almoſt certain, that ſhe ſhould not fail of her Conqueſt, and that the King's amorous Heart could not eſcape her victorious Charms. She was in conſtant and careful ſearch after Opportunities

† She was Daughter to a Waterman of Emmerick.
§ At preſent Earl of St——d.

of ſpeaking to him in private, and he a-voided them as carefully. Fortune was at laſt inclined to favour the Counteſs. The King of Poland's chief Deſign in viſiting the Pruſſian Court was to perſwade *Frederick* I. to lend him ſome Aſſiſtance towards his Re-acceſſion to the Throne of Poland: Thoſe Times happen'd luckily to be favourable to his Deſign. *Charles* XII. of Sweden was involved in great Troubles in Muſcovy, and conquered by the Czar, without any extraordinary means. The King of Denmark had promis'd to invade Sweden, and if he could but perſwade the King of Pruſſia to declare himſelf in his Intereſt, the Recovery of his Crown was not impracticable. But the Pruſſian Miniſters ſeem'd little inclined, ar rather averſe to interpoſe in the civil Broils of other Nations; the King knew, that by gaining Count *Wartenberg*'s Intereſt, who was abſolute Regent of his Maſter, he could not fail of that of his Pruſſian Majeſty; and as he was not ignorant of that Miniſter's vaſt Fondneſs for his Wife, he thought it moſt proper to obtain her Favour firſt. In order thereto he was obliged to viſit her, which he could ſcarce prevail upon himſelf to do; but the Neceſſity of his Affairs required it. He ſent Mr. *Fitztuhm* to acquaint her, that he ſhould pay her a Viſit

that

that Afternoon; and as he desired to consult with her about Affairs of Importance, he desired she would be alone. The Countess took particular Care not to displease him by inviting others. He found her on a Couch, lying as tho' she had been indispos'd. All the Light they had in the Room penetrated thro' Silk-Curtains of a Crimson-Colour, which were drawn before the Windows. Her Deshabille was of Green Silk enriched with Silver; and she had under pretence of the Heat of the Weather, laid open her Arms and Breasts, which were really very beautiful. She directly made Excuses to the King, for receiving him upon a Couch; and told him, that the Honour of hearing his Commands was the only Cause of her rising that Day, since she was perplexed with a violent Head-Ach. The King told her, that he was very sorry his Visit should put her to any Inconvenience, that he would not abuse the Regard she testified for him, but tell her in few Words the Occasion of his coming there. He then informed her of his Intentions, and desired she would perswade her Husband to induce the King of Prussia to second his Views. The Countess promis'd to do whatever he desired, and accompanied her Answer with so many Protestations of Tenderness, that, tho' *Fre-*

derick-Augustus was never ſcrupulous in Affairs of this kind, yet was he higly diſpleas'd at them. The Situation of his Affairs obliged him however to have ſome Regard to her amorous Expreſſions, anſwered her in his uſual polite manner, being always reſerved, when ſhe endeavoured to draw him into an Amour. The Counteſs abſolutely reſolved to reap ſome Benefit of that Converſation, fell about his Neck, and preſſing him in her Ams, pull'd him upon the Bed with her. His Majeſty, inſtead of being in the leaſt enamoured with her, deſpiſed her, and was at a loſs how to diſengage himſelf from this Adventure, when Lord *Rabbi* the Britannick Ambaſſador happened fortunately to come and deliver him from his Trouble. Tho' the Counteſs had given ſtrict Orders to her Servants not to admit any-body whilſt his Poliſh Majeſty was with her; yet did they little think that a Perſon of ſuch Diſtinction as that Ambaſſador, who had never been refus'd Admittance before, was excepted from ſuch an Order; wherefore they not only admitted, but forgot to tell him, that the King was in Conference with the Counteſs. The Ambaſſador perceiving the King in Madame *Wartenberg*'s Arms, in Reſpect to his Majeſty, was about to retire, but the King called out to him;

' Come,

'Come, come, my Lord, (cried he) your 'Company will not be disagreeable here.' But no Person could come at a more unfortunate Time, than the Ambassador did then for the Countess. It was certainly a very pleasant Diversion to see the Confusion these Two were in. The King could not forbear diverting himself with Railleries upon the Adventure, and afterwards left them alone, since which time he carefully avoided a private Conversation with Madame *Wartenberg*; at which she was so displeased, that for complete Satisfaction to her Resentment, she induced her Husband to disuade *Frederick* I. from entering into an Alliance with that Prince.

The Danish and Polish Monarchs stayed eighteen Days at Potzdam and Berlin, after which the former returned to Copenhagen, and the latter to Dresden. *Frederick-Augustus* was in few Days after his Return informed of the final and total Defeat of *Charles* XII. near Pultowa, and finding that none of his Enemies were in a Condition to oppose him, he resolved to attempt his Re-accession to the Throne of Poland. The Princess of *Teschen* and Madame *Brebentau* proved of important Service to him on this Occasion, by the number of Polish Lords, whom they gained over to his Interest. Before his Majesty went to Poland, he had a Conference with *Frederick* I. King of Pruſſia at Leipſig, and another with *Peter* the Great Czar of Muſcovy at Marienburg. After having received (a ſecond time) the Homages of the Poliſh Grandees, he returned to Dreſden, where Madame *Coſel* and *Duparc* had remained. He found the Counteſs at a wide Variance with all his Miniſters, but more particularly with the Prince of *Furſtemberg*, and the Field-Marſhal Count *Flemming*. This latter was naturally of ſo haughty a Diſpoſition, that he endeavour'd to make every-body ſubject to him; and tho' he did not exact it of Madame *Coſel*, yet he could not comply with her Commands, tho' that imperious Favourite required him. His Majeſty endeavoured to reconcile them once more; he obliged them to ſpeak to one another in a friendly manner; but all his kind Offices proved entirely ineffectual, the Miſtreſs and Favourite-Miniſters proceeded to bitter Invectives even before his Majeſty; and whatever Arguments he made uſe of to reconcile them, they parted fully reſolved to bear a perpetual Hatred and Malice to one another.

Since that time they have formed continual Plots for each other's Deſtruction. The Prince of *Furſtemberg*, tho' formerly an an Enemy to Count *Flemming*, aſſiſted his Endeavours to effect the Counteſs's Ruin. They were thus diſpoſed when the King went to Warſaw. As Madame *Coſel* was big with Child ſhe remained at Dreſden, and Count *Flemming* departed with the King. This ſhewed little Policy in Madame *Coſel* to conſent to let him follow the King, and was certainly a Fault moſt conducive of any to her own Perdition. This Nobleman conſulted with his Couſin upon the Means whereby they might occaſion in the King an Oblivion of his Miſtreſs. The reſult of their Conference was, that they muſt procure another for him; and after having conſider'd all the Ladies they knew, they made choice of the Counteſs of *Denhoff*, Daughter of the Great Marſhal *Bielinski*. 'She is ſufficiently 'amiable (ſaid Madame *Brebentau*) to be 'capable of pleaſing, but her Mind is 'not ſo exalted as to be able to rule;' but the whole Plot conſiſted in rendering the King amorous, and overcoming the Scruples they feared to meet with in Madame *Denhoff*. This latter Difficulty ſeem'd to be of little Importance, Madame *Brebentau* undertook to remove all her Doubts, and render her as compliable as the Affair would require. 'If ſhe oppoſes me (ſaid 'ſhe) I will perſuade her Mother the Great

'Marſhaleſs, my intimate Friend, to per-
'ſuade her to Reaſon, who foreſeeing the
'deplorable Situation their Affairs will be
'in after the Great-Marſhal's Deceaſe, will
'be extremely pleaſed to find that Oppor-
'tunity of reſtoring the former Proſperity
'of their Family.' But to render the King
amorous ſeemed their utmoſt Difficulty;
for tho' he was naturally fickle and gallant,
yet every Woman would not ſuit his Fancy; a briſk and lively Diſpoſition could
only captivate him, and this was the chief
Quality Madame *Denhoff* was deficient in,
who with a dull heavy Air affected the
Modeſty of a Virgin, which was directly
oppoſite to the Character the King required of his Miſtreſſes. Madame *Brebentau*
and Count *Flemming* were ſenſible that ſhe
would not ſuit their Monarch's Fancy, but
knew no Lady at Court more proper to
propoſe to him, and hoped to ſucceed in
their Deſign, provided they could obtain
the Intereſt of Mr. *Fitztuhm*, whom the
the King had appointed Count of the Empire, whilſt he himſelf was Vicar of it,
ſince the Death of the Emperor *Joſeph*.
They mentioned the Matter to him. Mr.
Fitztuhm anſwered, That he ſhould not
oppoſe their Intention, but could not ſecond it; that he was reſolved to continue
his former Conduct, that is, neither to
pro-

propoſe, nor deprive that Prince of any Miſtreſs, and ſhould always reſpect thoſe, to whom he was pleaſed to give his Heart.

This Refuſal did not diſhearten Madame *Brebentau*; ſhe mentioned Madame *Denhoff* to the King, as the moſt accompliſhed Lady in the Kingdom; this excited in his Majeſty a Deſire of ſeeing her. She was at her Huſband's Seat in the Country, and a Courier was diſpatch'd to call her to Warſaw, where ſhe arriv'd ſoon afterwards. The two Ladies *Bielinski* and *Brebentau* told her the reaſon of her being ſent for ſo ſuddenly, and what ſhe muſt do in order to get the Love of her Sovereign; and after having ſettled all neceſſary Matters, they gave the King the next day an Opportunity of ſeeing her. This was at an Entertainment which Madame *Brebentau* gave the King. The Counteſs made her Appearance at the appointed Time, accompanied by her Mother and the Staroſtine *Cherinska* her Siſter. Madame *Brebentau* preſented her to the King, who received her in that graceful manner which was natural to him, and attracted the moſt inſenſible Hearts; he diſcourſed gallantly with her for ſome time, but his Heart could not yet be affected by her Beauty. A Ball was given after Supper, which the King

King opened with Madame *Denhoff*; he liked not her Dancing; and ſhe did not in general anſwer the advantageous Deſcription Madame *Brebentau* had given of her.

The King, when alone with Mr. *Fitztuhm*, 'I am to be forced to love (ſaid he) 'but till they find a better than Madame '*Denhoff*, I doubt whether I ſhall be un- 'faithful to Madame *Coſel* ------- I fear not '(ſaid he) your Majeſty's forgetting her; 'you may love Madame *Denhoff* at War- 'ſaw, and Madame *Coſel* at Dreſden; 'which is what I take the liberty of advi- 'ſing you to. For, as your Majeſty has 'two Courts, one in Saxony, and the 'other at Warſaw, you ought to be a com- 'pleat Monarch, and in Juſtice, keep a 'Miſtreſs at each Court. This will con- 'duce undoubtedly to the Satisfaction of 'both Nations. At preſent the Polanders 'except againſt your keeping a Saxon 'Miſtreſs. If you forſake her, to be ena- 'moured with a Poliſh Lady, the Saxons 'will find equal Reaſon to complain: 'whereas by being amorous ſix Months in 'Poland, and the other ſix Months in 'Saxony, both Nations will be ſatisfied --- 'You divert yourſelf at my Expence (re- 'plied the King) becauſe your Miſtreſs 'never diſturbs you; but if, like me, you

'was

was to receive by every Poſt a Letter,
' in which you are accuſed of Treachery
' or Inconſtancy ; and on the other hand,
' be here perplexed by Perſons, whoſe
' only Deſign is to render me unfaithful,
' it would certainly cauſe a great Uneaſi-
' neſs in you ------ No indeed (replied Mr.
' *Fitztuhm*) I ſhould follow my own Incli-
' nation, and not regard the Trouble they
' endeavoured to give me.'

In the mean while Madame *Bielinski* perſiſted in her Reſolution of rendering the King amorous of her Daughter, and invited him to Supper. At this Entertainment the Company was more choice and leſs numerous than at Madame *Brebentau*'s; the Ladies ſung after Supper; and the Staroſtine *Cherinska*, and the Counteſs of *Denhoff* exerted their Voices: They ſung the Scene of *Atys* and *Sangaritis*. Madame *Denhoff*, who ſung the Part of *Sangaritis*, look'd inceſſantly upon the King, and addreſſed to him all the languiſhing Looks and tender Expreſſions belonging to her Part. Her Endeavours did not prove ineffectual, for the King was affected, and begun to divert her with his uſual gallant Diſcourſes, which ſhe anſwered only by her tender and languiſhing Looks. Her Mother and Siſter ſpoke for her, and the King might conſequently be ſaid truly to have

' courted

courted three Perſons at once. As he was very much diverted at Madame *Bielinski*'s, he frequented it conſtantly; and at laſt on purpoſe to viſit Madame *Denhoff*, and by the ſlow Addreſſes ſhe made to him, his Heart was enſlaved. Whilſt he was entering into this new Amour, Madame *Coſel* was deliver'd of a Son at Dreſden. She was no ſooner informed of the Change ſhe was threatened with than ſhe was reſolved to depart for Warſaw, intending to retain the King's Affections, either by Tears or Arms. But the Prince of *Furſtemberg*, acquainted with her Departure, diſpatch'd a Meſſenger to the Count *Flemming*, to give him Notice of it, and deſire him to be careful that he was not deceived by his own Intrigue. This Letter ſurprized thoſe of Madame *Denhoff*'s Party extremely. They met at Madame *Brebentau*'s, becauſe ſhe was conſtantly indiſpoſed, and kept her Bed. No Dyet was ever managed with more Unanimity; all the Members of that illuſtrious Aſſembly determined that they muſt endeavour to prevent Madame *Coſel*'s Arrival at Warſaw, and that in order thereto Madame *Denhoff* muſt perſuade the King to give Orders for her Return to Saxony. As their Danger was imminent, Madame *Denhoff* undertook the ſame Evening to prevail upon the King to com-

ply

ply with her Request. At the time when the King was accustomed to come, she laid down upon her Bed, with her Head leaning upon one Hand, and holding a Handkerchief in the other; she look'd stedfastly before her, as a Person greatly perplexed. The King, sorry to find her in this Condition, desired pressingly to be acquainted with the Cause of her Distress. The Countess cover'd her Face with her Handkerchief, and pretended the Tears she shed hindered her from speaking. The King, moved to Pity, squeezed her Hands, kiss'd them, and conjured her to declare the Cause of her Grief. Alas! Sir (replied 'at length Madame *Denhoff*) I am threa-'ten'd to lose my Life. This I should 'esteem as a Trifle, could I carry your 'Affections along with me; but alas! 'the loss of my Life is to be accompanied 'with that of your Heart, which I am 'speedily to be deprived of. Madame '*Cosel* is on her Journey hither; perhaps 'now arrived, and you are only come to 'give me Notice to make Way for that 'happy Rival -------- I! Madam (replied 'the King) can I tell you any such thing! 'do you think me capable of it, and can 'you imagine that I shall ever be induced 'to forsake you? No, Madam, I am tied 'to you by indissoluble Chains; your

'agree-

'agreeable Diſpoſition, that Evenneſs of
'Temper, and thoſe incomparable Charms
'only appropriated and to be met with in
'you, may aſſure you, that Madame *Coſel*
'ſhall never be able to do you any Pre-
'judice -------- O! dear Prince, (anſwered
'the Counteſs) I wiſh your Thoughts cor-
'reſponded with your Words, and your
'Love for me was as ſincere, as I can
'truly ſay mine is for you! For I declare
'before you, that I ſhould be willing and
'ready to die; but to leave ſo great a
'Happineſs, as I enjoy in your Affection,
'is utterly impoſſible to me; and be aſ-
'ſured, that I ſhall ſooner loſe my Life,
'than thoſe pleaſing Hopes you have oc-
'caſioned in me. Love me therefore,
'which if you ceaſe to do, the loſs of
'your Heart will render my Life bur-
'thenſome to me ------What an enormous
'Crime ſhould I be guilty of (replied the
'King) if after what I have heard from
'your dear Mouth, I ſhould be devoted
'to any other beſides you! -------- Alas!
'how pleaſing are theſe Hopes which you
'give me (ſaid ſhe) but I cannot be ſa-
'tisfied; my Rival approaches, you will
'ſee, and ſuffer her to reſume the Domi-
'nion ſhe has ſo long enjoyed over your
'Heart ---- How unjuſt and even induſtri-
'ous are you (replied the King) to tor-

'ment

'ment yourſelf after this manner. Tell
'me, for God's Sake, what you require
'me to do, and what will conduce to
'your preſent and future Eaſe. Suffer
'your Rival to come, that ſhe may ſee
'your Triumph, and openly undergo her
'own Defeat ------ No, Sir (anſwered ſhe)
'Madame *Coſel* is coming, I muſt leave
'Warſaw; I am too fearful of ſome Vio-
'lences ſhe will commit.'

When ſhe had done ſpeaking, Madame *Bielinski*, who had liſtened all the while, came in, as if ſhe had been ignorant of the King's Preſence with her Daughter. 'Come hither, Madame, (ſaid he) come, 'and aſſiſt me in removing from your 'Daughter's Heart thoſe Fears wherewith 'ſhe perplexes me ------What reaſon (an-'ſwered ſhe) has my Daughter to ſuſpect? 'If ſhe doubts of your Fidelity, Sir, your 'Majeſty may look upon that as a Token 'of her exceſſive Fondneſs.' The King related to her the Apprehenſions Madame *Denhoff* ſeemed to be troubled with. 'I 'cannot, Sir, (replied Madame *Bielinski*) 'in the leaſt blame my Daughter for har-'bouring Suſpicions of that kind; and 'even your Majeſty ought to be in fear 'of Madame *Coſel*, after the Threats ſhe 'has dared to pronounce in your Preſence '--With all my Heart (anſwered the King)

'Ma-

'Madame *Denhoff* and you ſhall be ſa-
'tisfied; I am going inſtantly to give Or-
'ders for Madame *Coſel*'s Return to Dreſ-
'den. O! dear Daughter (cried Madame
'*Bielinski*) how happy are you in the Love
'of ſo accompliſhed, ſo amiable a Prince!
'But, Sir, (continued ſhe addreſſing her-
'ſelf to the King) ſince your Majeſty is
'ready to promote my Daughter's Eaſe,
'permit me to ſay, that a Perſon in
'whom you can well confide muſt be ſent
'againſt Madame *Coſel*, who, being natu-
'rally ſo very imperious, will undoubtedly
'refuſe to obey your Orders.' The King gave her Leave to ſend whom ſhe thought moſt proper. Madame *Bielinski* thanked him for his great Kindneſs, and propoſed *Montargon*, a French Gentleman, who came into Poland with the Abbot of Polignac †, and who, by being truly attached to the Great Marſhal's Family, had obtained the Place of Gentleman of his Majeſty's Bed-Chamber. *Montargon* was ſent for, and the King gave him proper Orders. 'But,
'Sir, (ſaid that Gentleman) if Madame
'*Coſel* refuſes to obey, what muſt I do?
The King remained penſive ſome moments, and reſolved upon ſending as an Aſſiſtant with him *La Hay*, Lieutenant-Colonel in the Life-Guards, to whom he gave

† At preſent Cardinal.

gave Orders to take fix Soldiers with him, which he thought would furely fuffice to bring Madame *Cofel* to Reafon. Madame *Bielinski*, and her Daughter the Countefs of *Denhoff* were inexpreffibly joyful at what they heard; they tired the King with Praifes and Thanks. The Lover and his new Miftrefs pleafed themfelves with tender Expreffions, and reciprocal Affurances of an everlafting Affection. The King having fent for *La Haye*, gave him the fame Orders which *Montargon* received before, enjoining both to be very expeditious.

The two Ambaffadors prepared themfelves with all poffible Expedition, in order to fet out on their Embaffy. They met Madame *Cofel* at a fmall Town called Widawa in Poland on the Borders of Silefia. They pretended to be arrived there by Chance, defiring to pay their due Refpects to the Countefs, who received them with great Civility, defiring their Company at Dinner. When Dinner was over, Mr. *Montargon* chief Ambaffador, begun to difcourfe about the matter in hand. He fpoke as by his own Authority, and as a Friend who was willing to give her fome good Advice. But Madame *Cofel*, not then difpos'd to give Ear to his Counfel, anfwered him in a very arrogant manner, threatening to make him repent of his audacious

dacious Deportment. He then ſpoke in the King's Name, but ſhe refuſed to obey, ſaying, the King had hearken'd to the Advice of his Enemies, and would not be angry with her for diſobeying thoſe Orders. *Montargon* being naturally of a mild Diſpoſition, and his Actions all very gentle, told her with a diſdainful Sneer, he begg'd ſhe would not force him to proceed to violent means. 'How! (ſaid ſhe) will you 'be ſo raſh to proceed ſo far?' He replied, the King's Orders required her immediate Return to Dreſden, and if ſhe could not be perſwaded to comply with fair means, ſhe muſt be forced by rough uſage. At theſe Words Madame *Coſel* was enraged, calling *Montargon* a petty Notary's Clerk †, and taking up a Piſtol (for ſhe never travelled without Arms) threatned to kill him. *Montargon* ſeeing her Sex muſt be indulged, for the little Regard ſhe had to the Law of Nations in abuſing his Perſon, retired, and left his Aſſiſtant *La Haye* to manage the Affair, who ſpoke in the King's Name, and by his ſoft Expreſſions inſinuated himſelf into the Counteſs's Favour, whoſe Diſgrace he pretended to bemoan; perſuading her the Situation of

† He was Son to a Notary of the Village call'd Chaillot near Paris.

her

her Affairs then required her Return to Drefden; that the King would fhortly be there, that there was no probability of the Countefs following him thither, and then fhe would perhaps find it an eafy matter to regain his Love, and triumph over her Enemies. Madame *Cofel* found fhe could follow no better Advice, agreed to return to Drefden. *Montargon* difpatch'd a Courier with this agreeable Account to Madame *Bielinski*. He afterwards followed Madame *Cofel* with *La Haye* and the other Guards, and arrived always at the Inns as foon as fhe left them. They accompanied her in this manner within one Day's Journey from Breflau, and then returned to Warfaw to receive the Thanks of the new Favourite.

The Countefs of *Denhoff* had one more Trouble, the Removal of which would complete her Happinefs; this was her Hufband, who being informed of her Conduct, defired by Letter, fhe would come to his Country-Seat without Delay. This was directly contrary to the Countefs's Intention, as well as to that of Madame *Bielinski*. They fuffer'd the Count to complain for fome time, till they were tired with his Reproaches, then Madame *Bielinski* undertook to bring him to Reafon. She went to his Country-Seat, owning without any

Eva-

Evaſions the Reaſon of Madame *Denhoff*'s Detention at Warſaw. 'If you are diſ-'pleaſed, Sir, (ſaid ſhe) at your Wife be-'ing the King's Miſtreſs, you muſt con-'ſent to a Divorce. The Nuncio *Grima-'ni* † is ſo intimately acquainted with me, 'that I don't doubt of obtaining his Ho-'lineſs's Conſent.' The Count of *Denhoff* accepted of the Offer willingly without Heſitation. Madame *Bielinski* returned to Warſaw, ſpoke to the Nuncio, the Divorce was ſolicited at Rome, and *Clement* XI. granted it.

The new Favourite loſt her Father at the Beginning of her Proſperity. This Nobleman, the moſt magnificent and moſt amiable Perſon Poland ever produced, left the Affairs of his Family in great Diſorder; but the Counteſs of *Denhoff* reſtored their former Wealth in a little time. She induced the King to confer the Effects of his Munificence on her Mother, Brother, and Siſter; theſe Preſents might juſtly be called a Shower of Gold, and *Bielinski*'s Family became ſoon afterwards poſſeſſed of more Wealth, than it could ever boaſt of before. Madame *Denhoff* was perhaps of all the King's other Miſtreſſes, ſhe, whom

† He died in this preſent Year 1734, a Cardinal-Legate of Poland.

he loved beſt; but may be manifeſtly proved to have been the moſt expenſive, and who found herſelf richeſt of any, when in Diſgrace. It was chiefly owing to the Induſtry of her prudent Mother, who knowing very well no Regard would ever be had to Lovers Oaths, provided for herſelf and Family againſt the Sunſhine of Proſperity forſook her; ſhe demanded inceſſantly what ſhe pleaſed with ſo much Confidence, that ſhe never met with a Refuſal, or was ever thought exorbitant in her Requeſts.

The Grief of *Bielinski*'s Family was ſoon allay'd; the Great Marſhal's Funeral-Obſequies were ſcarce yet ſolemnized, when his Widow, Daughters and Sons viſited Balls, Races, and other Diverſions, which the King prepared to comfort his Miſtreſs. But theſe Entertainments ſeemed too trifling to *Frederick-Auguſtus* at the Beginning of a paſſionate Love; he could procure more grand and magnificent Feaſts at Dreſden, and invited Madame *Denhoff* to go thither, and be Witneſs of the Truth of what he ſaid. She did not refuſe her Conſent to this Journey, but was in fear of Madame *Coſel*'s Preſence. She inform'd the King with her Apprehenſions, and begg'd Madame *Coſel* might be forced to depart from Dreſden. The King ſent Orders

ders to the Prince of *Furstemberg* for that purpose; but she refused to obey them, saying, If his Majesty thought her guilty of any Misdemeanour, he could summon her before the Judges, and proceed to the Rigour of the Law with her; but as she deserved no Blame for any thing else, than having been too firmly attach'd to the King, she hoped he would grant her the Favour of enjoying an easy Tranquility in her own House. The Prince of *Furstemberg*, satisfied in seeing her humbled, would not insult her in Disgrace, but left her at home. The King, thro' his new Mistress's Intreaties, sent Mr. *Tienen*, Aid de Camp, to Madame *Cosel*, ordering her instantly to leave Dresden. She was perplexed and in great Despair, telling Mr. *Tienen* whatever she thought would affect him, and her mournful Expressions mov'd the young Officer to Pity, who proceeded to more Rigour with her. She gave him as a Token of her Acknowledgment a fine Diamond-Ring to the Value of four Thousand Dollars, and sent him back to the King with a very submissive Letter, which she wrote to persuade him to suffer her to remain in her House. Mr. *Tienen* met the King at the Distance of a day's Journey from Dresden. His Majesty was highly enraged with his Aid de Camp, send-ending him back to the Prince of *Furſtemberg*, and the Great-Marſhal Baron of *Lowendahl* to enjoin them to ſend Madame *Coſel* from Dreſden either by fair or violent means. The Great-Marſhal having acquainted her with the King's Reſolution, ſhe at length complied, and retired to Pilnitz the day before the King's Arrival.

Madame *Denhoff* was informed of this Retreat by a Courier ſent to her on purpoſe. She then proceeded on her Journey, accompanied by Madame *Bielinski* her Mother, the Staroſtina *Cherinska* her Siſter, Madame *Brebentau*, and ſeveral other Ladies, the Choice of which the King had left to her Diſcretion. She arrived at Dreſden in Triumph, convoyed by Mr. *Chatira*, Lieutenant-Colonel, and ſix Cadets of the Life-Guard. She was lodg'd in the Houſe of the Prince of *Furſtemberg*; the King's Officers attended her whilſt ſhe ſtaid in Saxony, and Mr. *Chatira* directed her domeſtick Affairs. The King commanded him to guard the Counteſs all Night for her better Safety, ſhe being ſtill in fear of Madame *Coſel*. Her Fear would indeed have vaniſh'd, had not the Field-Marſhal Count *Flemming* endeavoured to revive it in her, intending to enrage her more vehemently againſt the Counteſs of

Cosel, whose Disgrace had not yet satisfied his revengeful Mind. ' Pilnitz (said he to ' Madame *Denhoff*) is only three Leagues ' distant from hence. Your Rival may be ' here in two or three Hours; the King ' may happen to see and be again ena- ' moured with her. Believe me, let her ' be imprison'd, then you may be secure ' from any fatal Event which may happen. Madame *Denhoff*, more generous than the implacable Count *Flemming*, answered, she could not prevail upon herself thus to abuse a Lady of Quality, who had never injur'd her.

Count *Flemming*, who had gone too far to desist at once, was resolved that Madame *Cosel*'s Ruin should be for ever, persuaded the King to send a Messenger to her and demand the Promise of Marriage he had formerly given her. He foresaw in her present Rage she would refuse to return it; not doubting but so great a Provocation would induce the King to arrest her. The Event did luckily answer his Expectations. The Countess of *Cosel* refused to return the Billet, and as she did not doubt but her Refusal would give her Enemies a good Pretence for arresting her, she left Pilnitz secretly, and went to Berlin. But this Place was not so safe a Refuge for her as she expected. The

King

King of Pruſſia having acquainted her by an Officer her Stay in that Town highly diſpleaſed him, ſhe retired to Halle. Her Enemies would not ſuffer her there neither, they intended to deprive her of her Liberty, and perhaps of her Riches likewiſe: they accuſed her before her former Lover of ſpeaking diſreſpectfully of him, and fomenting a Conſpiracy againſt his Majeſty's Perſon. The King, who was continually more exaſperated, wrote to the King of Pruſſia, deſiring him to deliver her up. The King of Pruſſia gave Orders inſtantly to *Ducharmoi*, Lieutenant in the Prince of *Anhalt-Deſſau's* Regiment, to ſecure her, and conduct her with a Detachment of Soldiers to the Frontiers of Saxony, and there to deliver her up to an Officer who would come from the King of Poland to fetch her. O barbarous Injuſtice! (cried the Counteſs of *Coſel*, when they told her ſhe was a Priſoner. She fell preſently afterwards into a raving Fit, and when ſhe ſaw the Detachment of Saxon Soldiers come to receive her, ſhe begg'd of *Ducharmoi* to accept of her fine Snuff-Box and Gold Watch, which ſhe conſtantly wore; but when he modeſtly refuſed them, ſhe preſſed them more upon him, ſaying, 'Take them, Sir, I beſeech you to take 'them; I would chooſe rather to ſee you 'reap ſome Advantage from theſe Trifles, 'than thoſe unworthy Saxons, whoſe Slave 'I'm now going to be.' She gave ſome Money to the Pruſſian Soldiers under whoſe Guard ſhe had been; but ſpoke not one Word to the Saxons, who received and conducted her to Leipzig, from whence ſhe was carried to Pilnitz, and from thence to ——— ——— a Seat belonging to the Count of *Frieſe* †, her Son-in-law. Here the Counteſs enjoy'd her Liberty again, but in great Retirement. Her Enemies, not able to find any real Pretences for aſperſing her Character in a publick manner, inſinuated, ſhe was going privately into Holland there to change her Religion, and turn Jew. The Artifice was not very cunning, but the Vulgar eaſily gave Credit to it; and the common People, more ſuperſtitious in Saxony than any other part of the World, prayed for a Bleſſing upon thoſe, who had prevented ſo ſhameful an Action. Madame *Coſel* lived however to ſee the Death of all her Perſecutors, and ſurvived her Rival's Favour.

A Deſcription of the Entertainments the King gave to Madame *Denhoff*, and the Ladies her Attendants, would require a

† This Nobleman was married to Madam *Coſel*'s Daughter.

par-

particular Volume. That Prince was certainly fruitful in ingenious Inventions conducive to the Splendor of his Court. Madame *Denhoff* was however only present at these Feasts *incognito*; she was commonly masqued, and never appear'd openly, or with her Face uncover'd before the Queen. This Singularity raised her a great many Enemies, and the more because she obliged the King to shut himself up with her; so that he was scarce ever seen in publick. This induced Mr. *Kiau* to say, they ought to pray in all Churches for the Deliverance of their King imprison'd by the Polanders.

The King however was soon tired with that sort of Life. All the Courtiers were surprized he could be pleased with it so long. To be a little free from Slavery he went to Leipzig-Fair. Here he was enamoured with Mademoiselle *Dieskau*, a young Lady of Quality, who was, her mind excepted, the most accomplished Creature Nature ever formed. Her Shape and Actions were majestick, her Features incomparably regular, nothing could equal her white and lovely Complexion; her blue Eyes were beautifully large, and expressed her natural Inclinations to Love, neither could she govern that Passion; her Hair was of the finest light-colour that was ever beheld; her Neck was of a dazzling Whitenefs, and the fight of her Hands completed the Idea of a Compofition of all that was moft perfect under the Sun. But, how beautiful foever Mademoifelle *Dieskau* really was, fhe could be called no better than a Lump of Snow, no Vivacity could be found in her, fhe made no other Anfwers than Yes and No. The King was charmed with the great Beauty of her Perfon, he fpoke to her at the Redoubt, but was in Defpair when he found fo little Life in her. 'If Made-'moifelle *Dieskau*'s Mind was equal in 'Charms to her Body, (faid he to Mr. '*Fitztuhm*) I fancy fhe would fettle my 'Heart for all my Life-time ------ God 'forbid that! Sir, (anfwered Mr. *Fitz-*'*tuhm*) we fhould then be foon threatened 'with the Lofs of your Majefty ------ 'Thefe are your ufual Railleries (replied 'the King) but my Comfort is, you are 'as inconftant as I ------ If I might 'be excufed the Liberty (replied the 'Count) of calling your Majefty to an 'Account, I fhould find it a very eafy 'matter to prove you have had ten Mif-'treffes, whereas I have only my fixth 'now. This is certainly conformable to 'the right Rules of Amours, for we find 'in all Romances, Gentlemen diftanced

'their

'their Servants by far. But faithfully to
'discharge my Trust, I ought to take care
'of Mademoiselle *Dieskau*, and cultivate
'her Mind, that she may be capable of
'making worthy Returns for all your Ma-
'jesty's Kindnesses ------ No (replied the
'King) I shall ease you of that Trouble.
'You may become amorous of her, and
'Madame *Lowendahl*, whom I esteem,
'will be displeased with me for having con-
'tributed to her the Loss of your Heart.
In the mean while the King did not profess open Love to Mademoiselle *Dieskau*, her Hour was not yet come; but her beautiful Person made a speedy Impression upon his Heart, and removed Madame *Denhoff* from thence by slow degrees, who, nevertheless, supported herself in his Favour for some longer time, more by the Artifices of Madame *Bielinski*, than her own Charms.

The King returned with Madame *Denhoff* to Warsaw, but staid a very litle time in Poland. After having held the Diet, which broke up without coming to any Determination, he returned into Saxony, pretending, that Affairs of great Importance recalled him to that Electorate. His last moments with Madame *Denhoff* were employed in tender Expressions, he promising soon to return to her with a faithful Heart. I cannot determine whether ſhe gave Credit to his Words, but ſhe pretended at leaſt to believe them. She told him, if he gave any Rival the Preference to her, ſhe ſhould undoubtedly die of Grief, but that, if ſhe ſurvived ſo great a Misfortune, ſhe ſhould paſs the Remainer of her ſorrowful Life in a Convent. The King accuſtomed to Propoſals of this kind, took theſe for Flams, and was not at all concerned about them. He ſwore however, that Death only ſhould ſeparate him from her. They ſupped at Madame *Bielinski*'s, and after Supper the King intended to depart, when Tears were ſhed, and Cries heard. Madame *Denhoff* fell down upon a Couch as if ſhe had been dead; her Mother ſigh'd and groan'd; the Staroſtine *Cherinska*, whoſe Voice was naturally very harſh, cried in a manner very offenſive to all Ears; the Count *Bielinski*, who had been lately made Staroſt, ſeemed highly afflicted; and all the other Ladies, particular Friends and Relations to the Family, with a truly cordial Affection. The King, and the Counts of *Fitztuhm* and *Frieſe* ſeemed only inſenſible of Grief, and were employed in comforting the Afflicted. The King was near the dying Fair, he ſprinkled Water in her Face, gave her ſome Elixirs to drink, kiſſed her Hands, called

called her his Heart, his Angel, and conjured her to live. She opened her Eyes at laſt, fixing them tenderly upon him, and in a manner which expreſſed the Trouble his Departure gave her. The King conjured her to reſume her former Vigour. 'If I am dear to you, (ſaid he) think of 'living, for your Death will be ſoon fol'lowed by mine.' She at length recover'd her Senſes. Our two Lovers repeated the Sentiments of their Hearts ſeveral times, aſſuring each other of their mutual Affection, and an endleſs Duration of it. When the King gave Orders for his Departure, Madame *Denhoff* cried out telling him, that her Death would be inevitable, and by theſe Cries and feigned Tears detain'd him very late. He at length appeas'd her, and having recommended her to the Care of her Mother, and all the Ladies, he ſtepp'd into his Chariot, and departed; afterwards conſulting Reaſon, the Company left off immoderate Sorrow, wiped their Eyes, were comforted, and went to Bed to take their Reſt.

The King arrived at Dreſden, where all the Court was in Expectation of him, and after having repoſed himſelf ſome days, he left that Place to be preſent at the opening of the Fair of Leipſig, where the Queen waited for him. At this Princeſs's

Apartment he had once more an Opportunity of ſeeing Mademoiſelle *Dieskau*. She appeared more beautiful than even *Venus* herſelf. The King could not defend his Heart from the powerful Attacks of her bright Charms; he declared his Paſſion to her, but could receive no other Return than a Bluſh and her Eyes fixed wiſhfully upon him. The King was ſufficiently mortified in finding ſo little Vivacity in ſo beautiful a Perſon; but to comfort himſelf, he ſaid, 'Her tender Years 'occaſion it, which, together with a pri'vate and retired Education, renders her 'thus timerous; ſhe will undoubtedly im'prove herſelf, by learning to ſpeak, and 'behave with more Livelineſs, when ſhe 'has ſeen more of the World.' Some days paſſed after this, in which the King could not yet tell whether his Sentiments were agreeable to his Beloved. His Impatience would not permit him to ſtay, wherefore he applied to the Mother of the young Lady, acquainting her with his paſſionate Love for her Daughter, and deſiring her to be favourable in employing her good Offices for him. Madame *Dieskau* thought herſelf greatly honoured by the Confidence the King placed in her, and her Daughter very happy in being beloved

loved by so great a Monarch. She promis'd to persuade her to be as obliging as his Majesty could wish. But, as she was an Enemy to tedious Ceremonies, and naturally very bold, she demanded a considerable Sum for her Daughter's Virginity, which was readily granted, and paid soon afterwards.

Mademoiselle *Dieskau*'s Simplicity and Obedience to her Mother induced her to give Consent to perform the Engagements she had enter'd into for her. On the day appointed for the Feast she was dress'd in a Deshabille of Silver, and crowned with Flowers like a married Woman, when conducted to the Altar. The King was charmed with her beautiful Appearance, and could not help looking stedfastly; but as she did not in Opposition to his constant Looks hide her Charms, he had Time and Opportunity to contemplate all the Perfections of Nature.

In the mean while however strong this Passion was, Mademoiselle *Dieskau* was soon obliged to give Way to Mademoiselle *Osterhausen*, who was not in the least inferior to her, either in Beauty or Birth, and vastly superior to her in the Knowledge of the World. She had no Parents, was at her own liberty of acting, and possessed

ſeſſed vaſt Wealth; ſhe appear'd frequently at Court, and it may be ſaid ſhe always made a bright Appearance there. Her fine Shape was incomparable, and her Mind ſo refined, that her Converſation was both pleaſant and improving. She enjoy'd, beſides theſe excellent Qualities, a Sweetneſs of Temper, an Air of Modeſty, and a Deportment extremely engaging; ſhe was ready to ſerve, benevolent and generous; a Lover of Grandeur and expenſive Pleaſure; ſhe deliver'd her Expreſſions in ſuch a manner, that occaſioned thoſe to whom ſhe ſpoke, to believe ſhe deſired their Heart. The King ſaw her at the Queen's Apartment at firſt, and was directly enamoured with her.

The firſt Account ſhe received of her approaching Felicity was brought to her by Madame *Watzdorff*, who perceived the Monarch's Paſſion by his Enquiry after her in an Aſſembly of Ladies of the firſt Rank, of Mademoiſelle *Oſterhauſen*'s particular Merit, by the Delight he took in hearing Commendations of her, and by his proteſting ſo beautiful and divine a Perſon was worthy of the moſt tender Affection; and that he was not ſurprized that every-body ſigh'd for her.

No

No Perſon was ever ſenſible of greater Tranſports of Joy than Mademoiſelle *Oſterhauſen* felt when ſhe heard of the King's Paſſion for her. She remained ſilent near a quarter of an Hour, not being able to return any Anſwer to Madame *Watzdorff*, who brought her this joyful Information; ſhe was greatly ſurprized at her Silence, which ſhe took as a Token of Indifference or Inſenſibility. 'How (cried ſhe) Made-'moiſelle, does the King love you, and are you inſenſible of his Affection? ——— 'Oh! (replied Mademoiſelle *Oſterhauſen* 'fetching a deep Sigh from the bottom 'of her Heart) I am inſenſible, and more 'than you can imagine. But I fear you 'flatter me with vain Hopes; I fear my 'Merit is not ſufficient to preſerve the 'good Fortune I am going to enjoy.' She then begg'd of Madame *Watzdorff* to tell her every Word the King ſpoke, and adviſe her what would be moſt requiſite for her to do at this critical Juncture of entering into Happineſs. She did not refuſe her Advice, and Mademoiſelle *Oſterhauſen* practis'd it ſo well, that in few days ſhe was aſſured of the Poſſeſſion of the King's Heart; who to convince her the better, that no other Perſon could juſtly boaſt of being an Object of his

Love

Love besides herself, he married Mademoiselle *Dieskau* to Mr. *Loos*, Marshal to the Count, and since chief Master of the Horse. I shall not here relate the passionate Dialogues between the King and Mademoiselle *Osterhausen* in the beginning of their Amour; it would be a very difficult matter to find Terms whereby to express their mutual ravishing Enjoyments: they were never better but when alone, every day producing some fresh proof of a tender Love.

The King acted at first with great Caution in regard to Mademoiselle *Osterhausen*'s Reputation; but it proved at length difficult to the Mistress's Ambition and the Lover's great Passion for a long time to conceal a Secret of this nature. The Courtiers easily perceived it, and her sole Aim was being respected like a Favourite. She reaped all the Benefits of it, but her uncommon Generosity kept her from pecuniary Advantages. Satisfied with being beloved by her Sovereign, she was contented with moderate Presents, never demanding any for herself; and the King, by Age, being more frugal, gave her but little, in comparison to the immense Sums he enriched others with.

Whilst

Whilst the Flames of the King's Love were sparkling in his Heart at the Saxon Court, the Count *Flemming* concluded the Treaty of Marriage at Vienna between the Prince-Royal, only Son of *Frederick-Augustus*, and the Archdutchess *Maria-Josephina*, eldest Daughter of the late Emperor *Joseph*. The Electoral Prince of *Bavaria*, at present Elector, was his Rival, but the Emperor gave the Preference to the Prince of Saxony, by Virtue of a Contract the deceased Emperor his Brother had formerly made with the King of Poland. The Electoral Princess was received with such extraordinary Grandeur at Dresden, I may truly say, all the Ceremonies were wonderful, no King however magnificent could boast of Inventions equal to those of *Frederick-Augustus*; for he was himself the sole Contriver of all the Feasts, which were innumerable, and so diversified, not in the least resembling each other; the Expences amounting to four thousand Dollars. Mademoiselle *Osterhausen* made a bright Appearance, and partook of all the Diversions at Court; these Feasts however abated the King's Love by degrees. He found himself employed several months in ordering these extraordinary Rejoicings, which deprived him of the Company of his Mistress.

treſs. She reproached him for his Coldneſs, but he anſwered, he could not entruſt any Perſon beſides himſelf with the management of theſe publick Solemnities; his only Deſign was to procure Amuſements worthy herſelf, that ſhe was the chief Cauſe, and ſhould be the chief Ornament of them. Mademoiſelle *Oſterhauſen* was ſatisfied with his Reaſons: ſhe was afraid the King would engage in ſome other Amour, but did not believe he could ceaſe loving her, and renounce all others.

This was nevertheleſs the Event: the King's mind wholly employed upon the direction of the intended publick Grandeur, the Arrival of the Archdutcheſs, and ſenſible of the Obligation he was under to promote the Honour of his Court, then viſited by Numbers of foreign Nobility, accuſtomed himſelf by degrees to live without a Miſtreſs. He paid no more Viſits to Madame *Oſterhauſen*, except when he diſcharged her; at which ſhe was in great Deſpair, and applied to him for Redreſs by writing ſeveral Billets; but the King excuſed himſelf, and promis'd to ſee her the next day, and to acquaint her with the Obſtacles that hindered him from viſiting her. He aſſured her ſhe was always dear to him, and intreated her not to be uneaſy

at

at his Abſence. He continued to act in this manner, whilſt the whole Town was taken up with Rejoicings occaſioned by the Princeſs-Royal's Arrival. He afterwards left Dreſden without taking Leave of Mademoiſelle *Oſterhauſen*, at which ſhe was inconſolable, but Time, the Remedy of all Evil, at laſt allay'd her Grief.

She went as uſual to viſit the Princeſs-Royal; but met with ſuch a cold Reception, that it ſenſibly mortified her: but her Vanity would not ſuffer her yet to leave the Court; perhaps ſhe flattered herſelf with the pleaſing Hopes of regaining the Heart of her Sovereign at his Return thither. Her next Endeavour was to inſinuate herſelf into the Princeſs-Royal's Favour; and as ſhe hoped to obtain her End by turning Roman-Catholick, ſhe abjured Lutheraniſm in the Chapel belonging to the Palace. The Princeſs-Royal congratulated her on her Converſion, but told her, that to be diſtinguiſhed by the Name of a Roman-Catholick was not ſufficient, but it was likewiſe requiſite that both her Faith and Actions ſhould demonſtrate her to be ſuch; and if ſhe would convince her of her real Converſion, ſhe muſt retire to ſome Convent for a Year or two, and there be wholly employed in

fol-

following the Precepts of the Religion ſhe had ſo lately embraced. Mademoiſelle *Oſterhauſen* not expecting the Princeſs to make ſuch a Propoſal to her was put to a Stand; but Neceſſity obliged her to be virtuous. She anſwered the Princeſs, that it was her Intention, and ſhe hoped her Royal Highneſs would condeſcend to name a convenient Place for her Retirement. The Princeſs propoſed Prague to her, and ſhe faithfully promiſed her to go thither.

She did, in purſuance of her Promiſe, ſet out for that Place in few days afterwards, and was particularly recommended to the Counteſs of *Collobradt*, Daughter of the Counteſs of *Hireſau*, Lady of Honour to the Princeſs-Royal. All the Nobility of Prague received her with particular Tokens of Reſpect. She was look'd upon as another *Magdalen*; all the Corporations came in ſeveral Bodies to pay their Compliments, and congratulate her upon her Converſion. She reſided there for ſeveral months before ſhe could prevail upon herſelf to go into a Convent, and at length took an Apartment amongſt the *Urſeline*-Nuns in the new Part of the Town; but ſhe only lay there, and ſpent the Days in publick Pleaſures.

She

She had led this penitent Life for the ſpace of three months, when a Poliſh Gentleman demanded her in Marriage. This was Mr. *Staniſlafski*, Chamberlain of the King of Poland, who not being poſſeſſed of very great Wealth, propoſed to gain immenſe Riches by marrying Mademoiſelle *Oſterhauſen.* She ſuffer'd him not to ſigh for her long; the Pleaſure of returning to Dreſden, and appearing again at Court, hindered her from enquiring whether or no Mr. *Stanilafski*'s Rank was ſuitable to hers. The Marriage-Ceremony was celebrated at the Houſe of Madame *Collobradt*, and the new-married Couple departed in few days afterwards for Dreſden; where I muſt leave them, and return to the King in Poland.

This Monarch lived there free from all Paſſion; paternal Fondneſs ſucceeded his amorous Inclinations. He gave a particular Token of that to the Daughter of *Henrietta*, whom *Fatima*'s Son had diſcovered to him to be his Daughter. This young Lord, whom the King created Count of *Rotofski*, when he acknowledg'd him to be his Son, was moved to Compaſſion at the obſcure Condition of *Henrietta*'s Daughter. He had taken her into his Houſe, expecting an Opportunity of ſhew-

ſhewing her to the King, which happened ſoon after. His Majeſty, after he had reviewed his Regiment, walked up and down in the Palace-Garden, and ſaid, he was extremely well ſatisfied with the Behaviour of his Soldiers at the Review. The Count of *Rotofski* informed him, that he had a young Lady at his Houſe, more expert at the military Evolutions than the moſt experienced Soldier. The King deſired to ſee her, and ſhe came in a Man's Dreſs, the Livery of one of the Grenadiers of the Life-Guard. The King was at the Sight of her moved to Compaſſion; her Features aſſured him that ſhe was his Daughter. He embraced her, called her his Child, and created her Counteſs of *Orzelska*. Some days after this he promiſed her large Penſions, and preſented her with a fine Palace, whoſe Furniture was very ſplendid. When ſhe was thus provided for, the King paſſed his Evenings at her Palace; the whole Court reſorted thither, and ſhe enjoyed the Honours due to a lawful Daughter. The King conducted her into Saxony, where the ſhining Grandeur of his Court dazzled before her Eyes. Several Ladies ſtrove to gain the Royal Heart, but their Endeavours proved ineffectual; paternal Love had ſmother'd

in